CRITICAL ISSUES IN CLINICAL AND HEALTH PSYCHOLOGY

POUL ROHLEDER

Los Angeles | London | New Delhi
Singapore | Washington DC

First published 2012

Apart from any fair dealing for the purposes of research or private study, or criticism or review, as permitted under the Copyright, Designs and Patents Act, 1988, this publication may be reproduced, stored or transmitted in any form, or by any means, only with the prior permission in writing of the publishers, or in the case of reprographic reproduction, in accordance with the terms of licences issued by the Copyright Licensing Agency. Enquiries concerning reproduction outside those terms should be sent to the publishers.

SAGE Publications Ltd
1 Oliver's Yard
55 City Road
London EC1Y 1SP

SAGE Publications Inc.
2455 Teller Road
Thousand Oaks, California 91320

SAGE Publications India Pvt Ltd
B 1/I 1 Mohan Cooperative Industrial Area
Mathura Road
New Delhi 110 044

SAGE Publications Asia-Pacific Pte Ltd
3 Church Street
#10-04 Samsung Hub
Singapore 049483

Library of Congress Control Number: 2011937033

British Library Cataloguing in Publication data

A catalogue record for this book is available from the British Library

ISBN 978-1-84920-761-4
ISBN 978-1-84920-762-1 (pbk)

Typeset by C&M Digitals Pvt Ltd, Chennai, India
Printed in India at Replika Press Pvt Ltd
Printed on paper from sustainable resources

CONTENTS

ACKNOWLEDGEMENTS

This book was an initial rough idea about two years ago. Its completion would not have been possible without the encouragement and support of colleagues, friends and family. There are some specific people that I would like to thank. I am very grateful to Michael Carmichael and Sophie Hine and the rest of the team at Sage Publications for all their encouragement, advice and help throughout the production of this book. Thank you also to the two anonymous peer reviewers for their very helpful comments and suggestions of early draft chapters. This book was in large part made possible from the support of a sabbatical from Anglia Ruskin University. I'd also like to thank Sue Rathe for her assistance in researching some of the literature. Particular thanks to Ronelle Carolissen, Leslie Swartz and Rachel Cook for their insight and helpful comments on earlier drafts of some of the chapters. A personal thanks to Mark for his continuous support, and putting up with lost weekends.

ABOUT THE AUTHOR

Dr Poul Rohleder is acting programme leader and principal lecturer in psychology at Anglia Ruskin University, UK. He is a Chartered Clinical Psychologist and works as an honorary clinical psychologist at the sexual health clinic at Addenbrooke's Hospital, Cambridge. He is also an honorary senior lecturer at the department of psychology, Stellenbosch University, South Africa. He completed his clinical training in South Africa, which is where he became interested in the public health aspects and psychosocial consequences of HIV/AIDS. His doctorate explored the provision of HIV prevention for people with disabilities in South Africa, and he has continued to work on projects in this area. He is lead editor of the book *HIV/AIDS in South Africa 25 Years On: Psychosocial Perspectives* (published by Springer in 2009, co-edited with Leslie Swartz, Seth Kalichman and Leickness Simbayi).

INTRODUCTION: CRITICAL ISSUES IN CLINICAL AND HEALTH PSYCHOLOGY

1

Why do women live longer than men? Why are ethnic minority groups in the UK and USA more often diagnosed with schizophrenia? Why is HIV concentrated in sub-Saharan Africa? Why is it that the poorer you are the more ill-health you experience? Epidemiological studies have observed such disparities and more in the prevalence and experience of health, illness and disease. We also have different beliefs about what causes health, illness and disability. Consider HIV/AIDS for example. Medical scientific research has established that the conditions collectively known as AIDS is caused by the Human Immunodeficiency Virus (HIV). Yet so many people understand HIV/AIDS as a divine punishment for deviancy and sin. Some illnesses, diseases and disorders are responded to with relative neutrality, while others (such as cancer or schizophrenia) are responded to with fear. We may hold different assumptions about a man diagnosed with depression than we might do about a woman diagnosed with depression. Such differences and disparities challenge our assumptions that ill-health can be explained only in terms of things like viruses, bacteria and brain abnormalities.

This book provides an introductory exploration to some of these issues, by looking at various social aspects that are associated with differences in physical and mental health and disability. Although primarily a book for psychology, it draws on a variety of related disciplines, such as sociology, public health and medical anthropology, to explore how social processes impact on individual health. In focusing on both mental and physical health as well as disability, this book covers the sub-disciplines of clinical psychology and health psychology. Books generally deal with one sub-discipline or the other, so let's first consider the differences and overlaps of these different disciplines.

1.1 LOCATING THE FIELD

1.1.1 WHAT IS CLINICAL PSYCHOLOGY?

Clinical psychology is a scientific and clinical profession that is concerned with the understanding, treatment and prevention of psychological distress, the relieving of symptoms of distress and promotion of well-being. In most countries, clinical psychology is a regulated health profession. Clinical psychologists typically work as part of a mental health care team, which includes psychiatrists, nurses, social workers, and occupational therapists. Such a team is usually led by a psychiatrist, who would take on the medical responsibility for service users, diagnosing mental health problems and prescribing medication for its treatment. Clinical psychologists take responsibility for providing therapy for service users, and may take part in the process of assessment and diagnosis of mental health problems. This system of care is organized around the assessment and diagnosis of mental health *disorders*, and its treatment, and is rooted in a medical model of mental health, which assumes that mental health problems are understood as being the result of underlying physiological abnormalities, particularly abnormalities in brain functioning. Treatment typically involves drug therapy, which modifies the underlying physical abnormality, in combination with psychological therapy. Psychiatry, and as a consequence clinical psychology, draws on the classification system of mental disorders of the World Health Organization's (WHO) *International Classification of Diseases* (WHO, 1992), now in it's tenth edition, and perhaps more so from the American Psychiatric Association's (APA) *Diagnostic and Statistical Manual of Mental Disorders*, now in its fourth (revised) edition, the DSM-IV-TR (APA, 2000). A fifth edition of the DSM is currently being developed, with a much anticipated release date for 2013 (see www.dsm5.org).

The DSM is a multi-axial system, which allows for an individual's state of mental health to be evaluated along five different axes:

Axis 1 includes the presence of most acute (and chronic) mental health syndromes, usually as the primary diagnosis. This would include, for example, mood disorders, anxiety disorders, eating disorders and psychotic disorders.

Axis 2 includes the presence of long-term stable conditions, which include learning disabilities and the various personality disorders. A learning disability on its own is not considered a mental health problem requiring treatment. Only if a dual diagnosis of an axis 1 disorder is present, is this then a matter for a mental health care team. In some cases a diagnosis of a personality disorder may be the primary diagnosis.

Axis 3 includes any relevant information about the physical health of the individual.

Axis 4 includes any psychosocial and environmental problems that may exacerbate the mental heath problem (for example, inadequate housing, unemployment and relationship difficulties).

Axis 5 includes a rating on a scale of 1–100 of an individual's global level of functioning, with 1 being most problematic to 100 being symptom free.

Although psychosocial and environmental problems are included in axis 4, the primary focus of treatment is usually an axis 1 diagnosis.

1.1.2 WHAT IS HEALTH PSYCHOLOGY?

Health psychology is a broad field that is concerned with applying psychological theory and practice to issues of health, illness and health care (Marks, Murray, Evans, & Estacio, 2011). It is concerned primarily with physical health, focusing on key topics such as pain, health behaviours such as smoking, drinking and exercise, stress and coping, as well as issues related to health care such as the doctor–patient interaction, health literacy and health promotion. Health psychology emerged as a sub-discipline of psychology in the 1970s (Marks, 2002a), when increased attention was given to the role of individual psychological factors in health, and how individual lifestyle and behaviour affect health (see Chapter 2).

Marks (2002a) outlines four different approaches in health psychology, which focus on different values and beliefs regarding important considerations for health. These are:

1 Clinical health psychology, which is the dominant approach in health psychology. Clinical health psychology is highly research based, and is located within the clinical health care system. Clinical health psychology has many overlaps with clinical psychology, and is concerned with applying psychological theories to promoting health and well-being, preventing illness, and identifying causal factors to the development and maintenance of illness. It is also concerned with treatment of illness and with improving health care systems. Clinical health psychology draws predominantly on the biopsychosocial model of health (see Chapter 2), investigating the biological, psychological and social causal factors of illness. This is the approach of health psychology which is represented in most textbooks of health psychology. As a sub-discipline, clinical health psychology has aligned itself with the medical profession, and much of the work of health psychologists take place in clinical health settings, with clinical populations.

2   Public health psychology, like clinical health psychology, is focused on the clinical health care system, but is more concerned with the improvement of the health of the population. Its focus is on health promotion, rather than treatment of illness. This is a multi-disciplinary approach, concerned with not only health promotion, but also health policy, health communication, and epidemiological studies of illness prevalence.

3   Community health psychology is based on community-level research and action. Community health psychology is concerned with working in partnership with members of vulnerable communities with the aim of empowering the community and facilitating social change to address the social and structural obstacles to health (such as poverty). Community health psychology is concerned with promoting both physical and mental well-being. This approach shall be discussed further in Chapter 3.

4   Critical health psychology is concerned with structural factors, analysing how issues of power, politics, economics, and social processes influence or shape health. The context of this approach is the broader social and political system, and is concerned with "the political nature of all human existence" (Marks, 2002a: 15). We shall return to this in more detail in Chapter 2 with reference to critical psychology more broadly.

The more dominant approaches in health psychology are clinical health psychology and public health psychology, which, as the above definitions suggest, are aligned quite closely to the medical sector.

1.1.3 THE OVERLAPS BETWEEN PHYSICAL AND MENTAL HEALTH

Clinical psychology and health psychology are two separate and distinct sub-disciplines within psychology, each with its own specialization of training. The body of knowledge is contained in different volumes of work, with separate textbooks devoted to clinical psychology and to health psychology. Typically, textbooks do not consider both, understandably given the different areas of specialism. However, there are many overlaps between clinical and health psychology.

First, many conditions that are considered mental health problems are also concerns of health psychology. Most notable here are substance use disorders and eating disorders. While health psychology is more concerned with the health risk aspects of drinking alcohol and drug use, clinical psychology is more concerned with problems of dependence and regular abuse as behavioural mental health problems. The issues here exist on a continuum from little or no use to regular abuse and dependence. The consequences for physical health are well established. Similarly, with eating practices, health psychology is concerned with the health consequences of unhealthy eating, while clinical psychology is concerned with disordered eating considered as a behavioural mental health problem. As with substance use disorders, eating disorders are associated with significant physical health consequences.

Secondly, some conditions which are diagnosed as mental health problems, involve physical symptoms. Obvious examples here include the somatoform disorders, which are disorders characterized by physical symptoms and complaints for which there are no medically diagnosable physical cause. Perhaps the most commonly known of these is hypochondriasis, which is characterized by a fear of getting or having a serious disease, as a result of misinterpretations of physical symptoms (APA, 2000). Thus, a headache will be interpreted as a possible sign of a brain tumour. People suffering from hypochondriasis are frequent visitors to the health care system as they seek confirmation or reassurance of their symptoms. Many people experience somatic complaints as part of the expression of emotional distress, most notably depression. This shall be looked at more closely in Chapter 4 with regards cultural variations in how emotional distress is expressed.

Thirdly, research evidence suggests a strong association between mental health and physical health outcomes. For example, Moussavi and colleagues (2007) analysed data from the WHO World Health Survey, which collected data from a total of 60 countries across the world. Moussavi and colleagues investigated the role of depression in overall health status, and found that a co-morbid depression with any of four chronic illnesses (angina, asthma, arthritis or diabetes) made the biggest contribution to worsening health status than having a chronic illness without depression or having a combination of chronic illnesses. The data also shows that people with chronic illnesses are more likely to suffer with depression than people without a chronic illness. Physical illness may also affect mental health. Research has indicated that having a chronic illness or surviving a critical illness is associated with the development of psychological disorders, such as depression and anxiety (Cooke, Newman, Sacker, DeVellis, Bebbington, & Meltzer, 2007; Sukantarat, Greer, Brett, & Williamson, 2007).

Finally, a number of physical illnesses can induce symptoms of mental disorders. For example, Malaria can cause cognitive impairments; Lupus may cause fatigue, mood and anxiety symptoms, as well as cognitive impairments; and hypoglycaemia may cause low mood (see Williams & Shepherd, 2000).

1.1.4 INCLUDING DISABILITY STUDIES

Many chronic diseases and mental health problems have serious disabling effects, and are classified as a disability. When considering the term 'disability' most of us would think of persons who have physical impairments and require the use of wheelchairs, or people who may be blind or deaf. However, mental health problems, particularly those that can be severe and chronic (for example, schizophrenia) are classified as a disability. Cognitive and neurological problems such as dementia and epilepsy are disabilities. Likewise many physical illnesses, such as AIDS, osteoarthritis and diabetes, are classified as disabilities. It seems pertinent then to consider disability issues in a book referring to health and clinical psychology. However, disability issues are often neglected in textbooks of health and clinical psychology. Disability studies is a growing, interdisciplinary academic field concerned with the experience of disability and the role of persons with disabilities in all aspects of society. Much of the discussion in this book is about disability, particularly discussions about mental health problems, but at times the book also takes a look at disability as a general concept in relation to the specific topics discussed.

UNDERSTANDING HEALTH, ILLNESS AND DISABILITY

1.2 This book takes a critical approach to our understanding of physical and mental health and ill-health, and disability. The field of health is dominated by the science of medicine and the medical model, which understands illness, diseases and health conditions in terms of biological factors, requiring biological treatment and interventions. It is of course important to pay attention to such biological factors. However, the medical model neglects the roles that psychological, social and structural factors may play in who becomes ill, or how such ill-health is experienced and understood. The medical model has not always been the way that we have understood health and ill-health. It is actually a relatively recent approach to understanding health. At this point it is worth taking a more detailed look at the medical model, within a historical context.

1.2.1 EARLY CONCEPTUALIZATION OF THE BODY AND DISEASE

How we, in the western world, have sought to explain and understand health and illness has changed over the centuries. I use the term the 'western world' to refer to countries in Europe and North America (see Chapter 4 for further discussion about the concept of the 'western world'). Alternative understandings exist in other parts of the world, although there has been an influence of dominant 'western' views. There is also a diversity of understandings within societies, influenced by religious and cultural beliefs.

In early cultures in Europe and in other regions of the world, people believed that the spiritual world was responsible for health and illness. Diseases or illnesses were understood to be caused by evil spirits, while health and good fortune were caused by positive spirits. In ancient Greece, such spiritual explanations for health and illness were less prominent, as the early Greek philosophers advocated the process of rationalism and naturalism (Lawson, Graham, & Baker, 2007).

Rationalism refers to the view that phenomena can be explained and understood by means of systematic observation. Naturalism refers to the idea that the physical world and our experience of it can be explained and understood by physical principles and laws, rather than through supernatural causes. Hippocrates, who is often referred to as the 'father of medicine', proposed a theory that linked disease with physiology. He argued that the body contained four liquids called *humors*, which are: blood, phlegm, black bile, and yellow bile. When the body's humors were out of balance, disease occurred. Hippocrates thought that an excess of black bile was the cause of mental health problems (Cockerham, 2011). When the humors were in balance, the body was in a state of health. Similar notions of balance of energies in the body and health are found in other cultures, such as in Ayurvedic medicine traditional to India. Hippocrates argued that diseases were located in the body, and had nothing to do with the mind, and furthermore had nothing to do with supernatural or spiritual forces. This was a radical new idea for the time. Among such ancient Greek philosophers, the mind was considered as a separate entity to the body (a position referred to as dualism). This remained the dominant view in Greece and in the Roman Empire, and debates about the mind/body split still remains today. The ideas of Hippocrates were developed further by Galen, a physician who, from dissecting the bodies of animals, was able to discover that diseases can be localized in specific parts of the body, and that different diseases had different physical effects.

During the Middle Ages (the fifth to the fifteenth centuries) in Europe, after the fall of the Roman Empire, advancement in medical and scientific knowledge slowed down with the influence of the Catholic Church. A spiritual influence to understanding health and illness re-emerged with people's understanding about the cause of illness having a strong Christian influence. Illness was understood to be God's punishment for sins, or possession by demonic spirits. Priests became involved in treating illnesses, with practices such as exorcising the evil spirits from a sick individual's body. Beliefs about the soul rendered the body sacrosanct, and dissection of bodies was forbidden. The soul was understood as inhabiting all parts of the body and thus there was a return to viewing the mind (in the form of the soul) and the body as a single entity (a position referred to as monism).

The Middle Ages came to an end with a period of growth in scientific and intellectual enquiry, a period known as the Renaissance. The French philosopher and mathematician, René Descartes, was an important figure in the development of scientific and medical knowledge. He had a renewed interest in the mind and body, which he continued to conceptualize as separate entities. However, he proposed that the mind and the body could communicate via the pineal gland, and thus they were linked. Furthermore, he conceptualized the body as a machine, the mechanics of which can be observed and studied. He proposed that an individual's soul left the body once the person died, and thus it was acceptable to dissect and investigate the body after death. The church conceded to this, and as a result of dissection and investigation, there was a rapid growth in scientific and medical knowledge about the body. With these investigations, scientists were able to establish that diseases were caused by micro-organisms, rather than humors or spirits. Physicians were the holders of medical knowledge, replacing the role of priests. With these advances, a new model for understanding health and illness began to emerge – the biomedical model, which proposes that all physical disease and illness "can be explained by disturbances in physiological processes, which result from injury, biochemical imbalances, bacterial or viral infection, and the like" (Sarafino, 2006: 7). The explanation of disease and its treatment was based solely on physical explanations.

1.2.2 THE BIOMEDICAL MODEL

The biomedical model became the dominant, accepted model for understanding health and illness during the nineteenth and twentieth centuries, and remains dominant in medicine today, including psychiatry. The biomedical model proposes that illness and disease are afflictions of the body, caused by biological factors. Psychological and social factors are separate and have little direct bearing on the understanding and treatment of illness. Thus the biomedical model has a dualistic view of the body and mind as separate entities. All diseases can be explained by abnormalities in the physiological processes, caused by infections, injuries, biochemical imbalances and other types of biological factors. Health is seen as the natural state, and the body is healthy when there is an absence of biological disease. Thus health is restored when the pathogen is removed. Treatments act upon the disease or pathogen and not on the person. The person's subjective experience is not generally considered by the biomedical model.

The biomedical model can be well illustrated with reference to understanding and explaining disability. Disability has traditionally been understood in terms of the biomedical model, or what has been referred to as the medical model of disability, which emphasizes physical impairment as the cause of disability.

The medical model of disability

The medical model of disability views disability as resulting from physical or psychological impairments caused by an underlying physical disease or disorder (Johnston, 1996). In earlier years the World Health Organization (WHO) used this medical model to conceptualize disability as: "any restriction or inability (resulting from an impairment) to perform an activity in the manner or within the range considered normal for a human being" (WHO, 1980: 1). The WHO differentiated between 'disability' and 'handicap', which they conceptualized as the disadvantage experienced by the individual as a result of their impairment or disability that limits the extent to which the individual can lead a 'normal' life. Figure 1.1 provides a conceptual diagram of the WHO medical model.

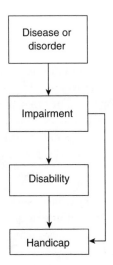

FIGURE 1.1 The WHO model of disability (WHO, 1980)

In this model, a person's disability may cause them to be socially handi-capped. However, a person may be handicapped because of an impairment, but not necessarily be disabled. For example, a person who has a facial disfigure-ment, such as a birthmark or scar, may be socially handicapped as a result, but not necessarily disabled by it. The impairment is seen as central to the person's experience of disability or handicap. The social handicap or social struggles faced by the person is attributed to the person's physical impairment, rather than to any social barriers that the individual may face (see discussion of the social model of disability in Chapter 2). Edwards (1997) highlights three char-acteristics of 'disability' within this medical model. That is:

1 that 'disability' result from an individual's impairment;
2 that 'disability' is "context-neutral" (p. 591) and not determined by the individual's particular social context; and
3 that 'disability' is intrinsic to the individual.

Disability in this model is a form of medical anomaly (Arney & Bergen, 1983), and solutions to such defects are found through medical interventions. The assumption is made that it is the individual who is alterable, while the individual's physical environment is fixed and unalterable (Barnes & Oliver, 1993). This model has been critiqued by social scientists, who emphasize the social, political and environ-mental barriers as central to the experience of disability (see Chapter 2).

Some critiques of the biomedical model in health

The biomedical model has influenced considerable advances in health and the prevention and treatment of illness. Research within the biomedical approach has resulted in the development of vaccines to prevent many infectious diseases (for example, polio and measles). It has allowed for the development of antibiotics to treat bacterial infections. Surgical procedures have been advanced, and there has been a rapid development in medical technology for use in testing, diagnosis and treatment. In more recent years biomedical research has sought to identify the genes that may cause various physical and mental disorders. Although the biomedical model has been important in the advancement of medicine, it has received considerable criticisms. Hardey (1998) summarizes key elements of the medical model against which criticisms are raised:

- The biomedical model is reductionist, seeking only biological explanations for disease. In so doing, it ignores the complexity of factors involved in health and illness, which may include psychological and social factors.
- The model has a dualistic view of the body and mind as separate, thus ignoring psychological influences on the body.
- The model is mechanistic, assuming that every disease and illness has a biological cause; a view that something has gone wrong biologically and can be fixed.
- The model assumes that the biological causes of diseases can always be objectively observed, and that the objects of observation are "only subject to natural forces" (p. 9).
- The model advocates interventionist treatment, which may be overly intrusive on the body.

The problem with this model is that it is also clear that individual behaviour, lifestyle and personality have an important role in affecting health and illness. With its emphasis on the physical body, the person as a unique entity is not included (Engel, 1977). The criticisms against the biomedical model were influenced by two important changes that took place during the twentieth century in western societies: the changing pattern of the types of disease and illness affecting the majority of the population, and the increased prominence of considering *health* over illness (Lyons & Chamberlain, 2006). First, during the twentieth century, we have witnessed a dramatic decline in the prevalence of acute illnesses (such as tuberculosis and pneumonia) and an increase in chronic illnesses (such as cancer and heart disease). While the decrease in acute diseases were thought to be as a result of the development of vaccines and medical treatment, it is evident that this change began to occur prior to the availability of vaccines as a result of improvements in hygiene, reduction in poverty and improved nutrition (McKeown, 1979). McKeown concludes that "the contribution of clinical medicine to the prevention of death and increase in expectation of life in the past three centuries was smaller than that of other influences" (p. 91). Chronic diseases are related to issues of lifestyle, with behaviours like smoking, diet, alcohol consumption, and exercise associated with incidence of disease such as cancer and heart disease (Mokdad, Marks, Stroup, & Gerberding, 2004). These changes in disease prevalence point to the importance of social and lifestyle factors in disease, for which the biomedical model does not account (we shall return to discuss the role of lifestyle and behaviour in Chapter 2).

Secondly, there has been an increased emphasis on health, which in 1948 the World Health Organization defined as "a state of complete physical, mental and social well-being and not merely the absence of disease or infirmity" (WHO, 2006a: 1). With this definition, health was not understood as only the absence of disease (which the biomedical model would suggest), but also includes the social and the personal (mind).

These observations of the importance of psychological and social factors in health and ill-health influenced the development of the biopsychosocial model, which considers psychological and social factors as well as biological factors in health and ill-health. These developments in understanding health and ill-health also influenced the development of health psychology as a sub-discipline of psychology, concerned with the psychological aspects of physical health. These developments will be discussed further in Chapter 2.

The biomedical model, psychiatry and clinical psychology

Psychiatry has tended to be influenced by a biomedical model to mental ill-health, which, as we have seen above, is based on a positivist, scientific epistemology. The main assumptions of such an approach is that mental health problems are a result of underlying biological factors which can be measured, observed, and treated biologically. The emphasis is on biological, physical factors, such as genetic abnormalities, the role of neurotransmitters and brain abnormalities. Such an approach assumes that mental health problems (or 'mental disorders') are diseases which are found universally. In this approach, mental disorders, like physical diseases, should be treated medically, typically with the use of drug therapy. Other more controversial treatments include electroconvulsive therapy (ECT) and psychosurgery (brain surgery). However, it became clear that it was difficult to attribute most mental health problems to biological causes. Spitzer and Wilson (1975, cited in Cockerham, 2011) point out how most mental disorders do not meet the four criteria for a physiological disease: (1) having a definite etiology, such as a virus; (2) that there is an observable physical change; (3) the mental disorder is qualitatively distinct from normal functioning; (4) and that there is an internal process that once initiated, proceeds independently of the external environment. Yet the biomedical model in psychiatry still dominates. As discussed above, psychiatry has a system of classification of mental disorders in the DSM-IV-TR (APA, 2000), and the ICD-10 (WHO, 1992). Both systems of classification are primarily medical diagnostic tools, and assume that abnormal mental states are distinguishable from normal mental states, and that mental disorders can be identified through presentation of discrete symptoms.

Cockerham (2011) argues that the persistence of the biomedical model in psychiatry may be explained by the medical training of psychiatrists, where psychiatrists are trained as medical doctors, and thus trained within the biomedical model. Furthermore, mental health problems are not regarded as 'diseases', but rather as 'disorders', which are treatable through medical intervention. This extends the definition to include human suffering and functional impairment that cannot be considered a 'disease', but that nevertheless can be treated medically, and responds to medical treatment. Cockerham also points out how psychiatrists may wish to align themselves fully with a prestigious medical profession, and eagerly promote the treatment efficacy of psychoactive drugs.

Clinical psychology in the UK (and in the USA) emerged in an era of mental health care, concerned with post-war treatment of war trauma, which was dominated by the biomedical model (Cheshire & Pilgrim, 2004). Hans Eysenck, one of the profession's leaders at the time, advocated for clinical psychology to be a scientific discipline concerned primarily with psychometric testing and diagnosis and research. Eysenck did not consider therapy to be the domain of clinical psychology, and distanced the profession from psychoanalysis in particular, which he felt was unscientific and ineffective (Cheshire & Pilgrim, 2004). Only later did he include behavioural therapy as part of the work of clinical psychologists. The aim was to establish clinical psychology within the medical profession.

Clinical psychology is now less concerned with diagnosis, but rather on the assessment and formulation of mental health problems. It has as its influence psychoanalysis, and more predominantly, behavioural and cognitive models of abnormal behaviour. These will be discussed in Chapter 2. Mental health problems are assessed and formulated according to the different factors that contribute to its development: predisposing factors (that may include biological factors or biological vulnerability), precipitating factors and maintaining factors. In this way, mental health problems are understood in terms of the biological, psychological and social factors that contribute to their development (this follows the ideas of the biopsychosocial model, discussed in Chapter 2). However, clinical psychology still relies on the DSM as its diagnostic tool, and is increasingly influenced by cognitive neuroscience, which perpetuates the influence of the biomedical model.

Cockerham (2011) outlines a number of criticisms of the biomedical model of mental disorders. First, Cockerham points out how the defining condition of mental health problems as biological is that they can be treated by medication, rather than on whether they necessarily have a medical cause. In this way, the symptoms are treated, without always understanding their cause. This relates to a second criticism that the biomedical model of mental health problems "focuses almost exclusively on controlling symptoms rather than on cures" (Cockerham, 2011: 57). Thirdly, Cockerham argues that the biomedical model has formulated medical treatments for mental health problems, but has not been able to provide explanations for the exact cause of them. A large number of research studies find support for genetic, neurological and other biological causes for mental disorders, but equally a large number of research studies find support for environmental and social causal factors. The result is that we do not have a clear, definitive understanding of what causes mental disorders, in the same way that we know that malaria is caused by Plasmodium parasites, for example.

CRITICAL ISSUES IN CLINICAL AND HEALTH PSYCHOLOGY

1.3

I have briefly introduced some of the key criticisms made of the biomedical model in relation to physical health, mental health and disability. The remainder of the book will proceed from this starting point to explore aspects of health, illness and disability that provides a critique of the assumptions of a biomedical understanding. The book is partly structured around four key 'issues': socio-economic status (SES), culture, gender and sexuality. These are by no means all, but are four of the primary social aspects that shape the development, understanding and experience of health and ill-health. These are areas that are typically only given brief mention in mainstream health psychology and clinical psychology textbooks, and thus are areas that often remain neglected in the health and clinical psychology curriculum. There are books that focus specifically on each of these various issues, for example books on culture and health or gender and health. The relationships between SES, culture, gender, sexuality and health are complex, and these are vast subjects. This book can only provide an introduction to these issues for students of health psychology and clinical psychology and related disciplines.

The remainder of the book is divided into seven chapters:

Chapter 2 explores the various critiques made of the biomedical model and alternative models that have been developed that take into account the psychological, social and structural factors associated with physical and mental health and disability. The chapter first explores some of the dominant models used in health psychology, namely the biopsychosocial model, and in clinical psychology, the cognitive-behavioural model and the psychoanalytic model. These models still have as their primary focus factors within the individual as the most important areas of consideration with regards understanding health and ill-health. More recent critiques have focused more centrally on social and broader structural factors in relation to our understanding of health, illness and disability, and these are explored in the second half of the chapter.

Chapter 3 explores models developed to understand health behaviour, which has been influential in considering how to change people's health behaviours. This chapter is primarily focusing on models used in health psychology, although also used sometimes in mental health research. The chapter introduces a few of the most influential models of understanding health behaviour used in mainstream health psychology. These models have been critiqued for focusing almost exclusively on factors within the individual that influence health behaviours, such as attitudes, perceptions and motivation. These models fit within a biopsychosocial paradigm, which although they take into account psychological and social factors as well as biological, they have been critiqued for their remaining focus on the individual, and for remaining, to a certain extent, aligned to a biomedical model for understanding health. Critical approaches emphasize the importance of social and structural factors for facilitating and even shaping individual health behaviours, which are explored in the later parts of the chapter.

These two chapters (and this introduction) provide a conceptual basis for the next four chapters. In Chapter 4, the universalist assumptions of the biomedical model is challenged with an exploration of cultural differences in the understanding and experience of physical and mental health. This chapter explores cultural relativism in relation to understanding health and ill-health, highlighting how many of our assumptions, which do not exist universally, are influenced by a 'western' culture. The chapter explores cultural differences in the understanding and experience of cancer and pain (relevant for the discipline of health psychology), and explores cultural differences in understanding mental health problems, particularly depression. The chapter also looks at disordered eating, which overlaps both health psychology and clinical psychology, and highlights the influence that western notions of the ideal body have on the development of eating disorders. Such cultural differences in understanding and experiencing health and illness are important for working in multicultural contexts, where cultural clashes may occur between professionals and their clients who have different perspectives on the issues involved. The chapter ends by exploring different systems of health care that people may draw on, and also looks at cultural competence in health care.

Chapter 5 explores the important influence of socio-economic status on health. There is a well-observed health gradient that shows how health improves as one moves up the SES hierarchy. Globally, differences exist between poorer countries and wealthier countries with regards the prevalence of different diseases and mortality rates, which can be attributed to issues of poverty and inadequate resources that facilitate good health. But differences are also found *within* countries, with health disparities existing alongside income inequality. A consistent pattern found is that the poor live shorter lives than the rich, and experience more illness during that shorter life. This is explored in relation to physical and mental health and disability. The chapter presents some theoretical models for understanding these SES health inequalities.

Chapter 6 explores the issue of gender differences in health. As with other topics, this is a vast subject area, and the chapter can only introduce some areas for consideration. The chapter explores both issues of femininities and masculinities in relation to health, illness and disability. Epidemiological studies have shown clear gender differences in health between men and women, with women living longer than men, but experiencing more illness during their lives than men. Gender differences also exist with regard to different mental health diagnoses, with more women that men being diagnosed with mental health problems such as depression and borderline personality disorder. Gendered aspects of diagnosis are also explored in relation to sexual disorders, and the medicalization of sexual problems for both women and men. The chapter includes a focus on notions of masculinities in particular, and how this influences men's health behaviours, such as smoking and drinking. Masculinities and health has been generally neglected until recently, with more attention given to women's social roles and health. Masculinity will also be explored in relation to body image and eating disorders, again an area of overlap for health psychology and clinical psychology.

Chapter 7 explores issues of sexuality and health, and focuses predominantly on three issues of sexuality. First, the concept of a mental disorder is critiqued with reference to the history of the pathologizing of homosexuality in psychiatry. Up until 1973, homosexuality was included in the DSM as a mental disorder, which could be treated by psychiatric means. The historical account of the removal of homosexuality as a diagnosis in the DSM provides an interesting account of how 'medical' concepts can rest on biased, subjective assumptions. The chapter progresses from this to the continuing demonizing of sexuality in relation to HIV/AIDS, at first with regards homosexuality and HIV and, in more recent years, Africa and 'African sexuality' in relation to HIV. This discussion also provides an example of how a disease is not just about biological factors, with HIV providing a good example of how illnesses carry specific meanings and representations that have more to do with social identity than with biology. The chapter then explores sexuality in relation to people with disabilities, which has been an area of oppression for many years, and continues to be in some cases. People with disabilities, particularly learning disabilities, are often wrongly assumed to be asexual, and are thus excluded from leading full sexual lives. The chapter explores the issues in relation to HIV, and how people with disabilities have been generally excluded from HIV prevention work, despite evidence suggesting that they may be at equal risk for HIV infection.

Finally, Chapter 8 describes some of the different research methods that are used for a more critical approach in clinical and health psychology. Qualitative methods in particular have been argued as being valuable in exploring the different subjective meanings and experiences of health, illness and disability. Different qualitative methods lend themselves to exploring different kinds of questions, and are useful for different types of research project. Although many of the studies drawn on in the chapters of this book come from epidemiological studies that reveal disparities in health and illness prevalence and incidence (see Box 8.1), the chapters also draw on qualitative research that has been useful in providing some understanding of the complexity of different issues. Interspersed across the chapters are text boxes containing examples of qualitative studies exploring different aspects on the issues covered, providing examples of some of the methods described in the last chapter.

As stated earlier, each of these topics is a vast field, and not all aspects of each topic can be covered in a book of this scope. This book thus provides an introduction to the issues for students. The issues explored are complex, and require a multi-disciplinary lens. Thus the book draws on literature from a variety of disciplines, including sociology, anthropology, public health, disability studies, and psychiatry as well as psychology. At the end of each chapter I have listed some recommended further reading (not all of them from psychology) for a more detailed exploration of some of these issues and more.

PSYCHOSOCIAL AND CRITICAL MODELS OF HEALTH, ILLNESS AND DISABILITY

2

INTRODUCTION

2.1 How do you understand health? When you fall ill, to what do you attribute its cause? The medical model understands disease as caused by purely biological factors. However, when we fall ill with a cold or flu, many of us think we have fallen ill because we are stressed or 'run down' rather than because we have contracted a virus. Many others may have a spiritual understanding of their health or ill-health, attributing it to an act of God or other spiritual forces. It is common to hear of praying for the improved health of a loved one. We have different beliefs and ideas about health and ill-health. Likewise there are different academic, theoretical models for understanding health, illness and disability.

In the previous chapter we briefly discussed the biomedical model, which is the dominant approach in understanding physical and mental ill-health. Theoretical developments from the disciplines of psychology and social science disciplines, such as sociology, have challenged the biomedical model to understanding health, illness and disability for not taking due account of how psychological and social factors influence health. These challenges and criticisms of the biomedical model, and some of the alternative models, shall be explored in this chapter.

Psychology has had an important influence in our understanding of health and illness, as it has highlighted how psychological factors, such as lifestyle, behaviour and personality have an important influence on health and illness. This has led to the development of the biopsychosocial model, which has become very influential in both clinical psychology and health psychology. This chapter will first look at the development and outline of the biopsychosocial model. Following this, the chapter will explore two prominent psychological (rather than biomedical) models of mental health: the psychoanalytic model and the cognitive-behavioural model. The biopsychosocial model and the psychological models of mental health are dominant approaches in 'mainstream' health psychology and clinical psychology. However, the discipline of sociology has provided important and interesting critiques of biomedical approaches to health, illness and disability, and the chapter will explore some of these. Finally, the chapter will consider critical psychology as a sub-discipline of psychology and its relation to clinical and health psychology. This is a marginal approach in 'mainstream' psychology, but has developed important arguments regarding social and structural influences on understanding health and illness. This chapter, together with Chapter 3, provides a theoretical starting point for the remaining chapters, which explore social processes that influence and even shape health.

HEALTH, ILLNESS AND PSYCHOLOGY

2.2

We have so far discussed the dominance of the biomedical model in understanding disease, including mental health problems and disabilities. This model emphasizes biological causes for diseases, mental health problems and disabilities. However, the importance of individual behaviour and lifestyle and of personality has been increasingly recognized as important in understanding health and illness. These two groups of factors – lifestyle and personality – have been established as having a key role in the maintenance of health and development of illness, highlighting the importance of needing to consider psychological and social factors as well as biological factors.

Lifestyle refers to an individual's "everyday patterns of behaviour" (Sarafino, 2006: 9). The focus here is on people's individual behaviours that increase the risk for the development of a disease or illness. The disease or illness is caused by biological factors, to which a person's behaviour might make them more susceptible. Evidence suggests that there is an association between particular behaviours or lifestyles and particular diseases. For example, heart disease is one of the leading causes of death in the world. Although the disease is caused by the condition of the heart, people's individual behaviours may make a person more at risk for developing heart disease. It is well known that behaviours such as smoking, or doing very little or no exercise, or eating foods with high fat content, increases the risk for heart disease. Similarly, many types of cancer may be associated with lifestyle behaviours, such as smoking and drinking alcohol in excess. An individual can lower that risk by reducing these risk behaviours and maintaining a 'healthy' lifestyle. The importance of healthy behaviours to health outcomes is established by a study of 7,000 adults in the Alameda County in California, USA (Belloc & Breslow, 1972). The participants, aged from 20 to over 75, were followed over a period of 15 years. All participants were considered to be in good health at the start of the study. Differences were compared between participants who had developed disease and those who remained healthy along key behavioural factors. These healthy behavioural factors have come to be known as the 'Alameda seven' and include:

- not smoking
- getting 7 to 8 hours of sleep a night
- being within 10% of one's ideal weight
- drinking moderate amounts of alcohol (no more than one or two drinks a day)
- engaging in regular exercise
- eating breakfast
- eating regular meals, with no snacking between meals.

The researchers found that at different age groups, there was an association between the key behavioural factors and the participant's health, for both men and women. In a follow-up study (Breslow & Enstrom, 1980), it was found that the participants who reported partaking in more of these seven health behaviours had lower rates of mortality than those participants who had engaged in less of these healthy behaviours. Behavioural factors are well established in relation to HIV, where behaviours such as promiscuity, sex without a condom, and substance use increase the risk for HIV infection.

While research has established that many lifestyle behaviours are associated with different diseases, it has become evident that it is difficult to change people's behaviours and lifestyle choices. Some attention has been given to personality factors that may influence people's lifestyle choices. Personality factors and their association to other types of disease have also been investigated. For example, it is commonly believed that people who tend to worry or are anxious may get ulcers or headaches or upset stomachs. Thus the person's personality may be associated with particular illnesses. Personality here refers to an individual's behavioural, cognitive and affective tendencies or traits that remain fairly stable over time, and in different situations.

Early theories of personality and its relation to ill-health gave rise to the field of psychosomatic medicine. This was influenced by the psychoanalytic theory of Sigmund Freud (see below for a brief discussion of elements of psychoanalytic theory). In psychosomatic medicine, the mind and body are not seen as separate entities, but rather as linked, where matters of the 'mind' (personality, behaviours and cognitions) have an influence on the body. Freud made this link explicit in his psychoanalytic theory of conversion hysteria (see Freud, 2005, for an introduction to his work). Freud argued that unconscious emotional conflicts in the individual may manifest as physical complaints. In this case, physical illness may be present where there is no underlying organic cause. Freud, with his colleague Josef Breuer, presented the case of 'Anna O' (Freud & Breuer, 1895), a woman suffering from various physical complaints, including paralysis and numbness along the right side of her body, and disturbances and occasional impairments in vision and hearing. Under hypnosis, 'Anna O' recalled distressing memories of past childhood traumatic incidences. After this talking treatment some of her symptoms reportedly disappeared. Thus the physical symptoms were understood to be a physical communication for under-lying emotional problems that were otherwise not expressed. The case of Anna O has received some criticism as to accuracy and success of treatment. However, it was an important initial study that helped conceptualize how unexplained physical symptoms may have psychological causes. Psychosomatic conditions are included in the DSM-IV-TR, for example conversion disorder, which is characterized by physical symptoms affecting sensory or motor functioning, for which there is no underlying organic cause, and are associated with preceding stress or conflict (APA, 2000).

Later studies have investigated the relationship between various personality traits and particular diseases. For example, studies have observed how people with 'type A' personality, characterized by competitiveness, hostility, an ambitious drive and time urgency, are found to be at increased risk for coronary heart disease (Smith & Anderson, 1986). Such people may experience greater degrees of frustration and stress, and may choose environments that are more demanding. This may result in greater physiological activity. However, in recent years, the type A personality theory has become less popular, with later studies not supporting the relationship between type A personality and heart disease. A meta-analysis of published studies show that the effect sizes of these studies are small and largely insignificant, and thus no significant correlation between type A personality and coronary heart disease is evident (Myrtek, 1995).

There has been considerable interest in the role of various positive and negative moods and health, with negative moods or characteristics (e.g. depression, pessimism and negativity) being associated with poor health, and positive moods or characteristics (e.g. happiness, optimism, and high self-esteem) being associated with good health (Marks, Murray, Evans, & Estacio, 2011). Here the emphasis is on affective or mood states, rather than characteristics of a particular personality type (as in type A personality). For example, reviews of research studies have shown a strong relationship between depression and anxiety and coronary heart disease (Hemingway & Marmot, 1999). Other psychological and social factors found to be related to chronic heart disease include stress, depression, hostility, social support and socio-economic status (Krantz & McCeney, 2002). Friedman and Booth-Kewley (1987) conducted a meta-analysis review of studies investigating the links between personality and diseases considered to have psychosomatic components – coronary heart disease, arthritis, asthma, headaches and ulcers. They argue that there may be a "generic 'disease-prone personality'" (p. 551), which includes emotions of depression, anxiety, anger and hostility, which may have some association with the development of disease, particularly coronary heart disease. This is echoed by Suls and Bunde (2005), who argued that the difficulty with studies measuring the relationship between psychological factors such as depression, anxiety and hostility is the degree of overlap between the three, and suggest that a "general disposition to experience chronic and intense negative emotions" (p. 292) is a more important causal factor in cardiovascular disease. Research has also been conducted on the link between depression and cancer. Findings are inconsistent, but suggest that there is not a strong link between depression and cancer (Adler & Matthews, 1994; Knekt et al., 1996; Penninx et al., 1998). However, depression may act as a factor influencing lifestyle behaviours that may cause disease. For example, Knekt and colleagues (1996) suggest that depression may modify risk for lung cancer, through its affect on smoking behaviour. What some of this work has indicated is the importance of psychological and social factors in the cause and development of illness and disease. This work has challenged the medical model, and highlighted the importance of psychology for medicine.

THE BIOPSYCHOSOCIAL MODEL

2.3

Engel (1977, 1980) proposed the need for a new model to replace the biomedical model that would take into consideration the psychological and social factors in health and illness. This model is referred to as the biopsychosocial model, which proposes that all three factors – the biological, the psychological and the social – interact and have an influence on a person's health; both affecting health as well as being affected by a person's health. Within the biopsychosocial model, biological factors include genetic factors that we inherit from our parents, as well as the structure and function of the physical body. This would also include biological entities that affect the functioning of the body (such as viruses and bacteria). Psychological factors include personality, behaviour and lifestyle. Key psychological processes that are focused on here are the role of cognition, emotion and motivation. Social factors include the social systems that influence the individual. These social systems include society, our community and our family. For example, our behaviours may be affected by the influence of our peers, such as peer pressure to drink alcohol or smoke cigarettes. Societal norms about health and appropriate behaviours may also influence our behaviour. The media has a particularly important role in communicating societal norms and values. These three systems – the biological, psychological and the social – are in constant interaction with one another.

The biopsychosocial model has been strongly supported by psychologists concerned with the individual and health, both physical and mental. In health psychology, the biopsychosocial model has become a standard model for conceptualizing the factors involved in health and illness. Similarly in clinical psychology, the biopsychosocial model has been a reference point for considering how personal and social factors affect mental ill-health. Engel, the proponent of the biopsychosocial model, was a psychiatrist who was dissatisfied with the reductionist approach of the biomedical model, which took little account of the patient and their social context. However, the biopsychosocial model has had its criticisms. Stam (2004) argues that the biopsychosocial model has become embedded in health psychology as a standard, but highlights how many textbooks go no further than merely describing the model without critical discussion of it. Stam suggests that the biopsychosocial model is "neither a theory nor a model" (p. 19), as Engel fails to define and develop the model, other than just providing examples of how psychological and social factors may influence physical health. Similarly, Marks (2002b) argues that the biopsychosocial model is not really a model, but rather a "way of thinking about health and illness which has a useful heuristic function" (p. 13). A model is a representation of a system of relationships between factors that are believed to influence each other. A model allows for the investigation of the different components and relationships of that system. However, Engel (1977) does not properly define the model, and Marks (2002b) considers the biopsychosocial model as more like an "attitude", rather than a model.

Armstrong (1987) argued that the biopsychosocial model remains essentially biomedical with the theoretical underpinnings of the social and psychological factors not being properly worked out. The model places the biological system at the top of the hierarchy, and thus the model is a "new medical model" (to use Engels' description) that attempts to think about the role that social and psychological factors may place in medical illness, but that gives a secondary, inadequately conceptualized consideration of these factors. Armstrong thus argues that the biopsychosocial model is not "new" at all, but "simply the old one with a gloss" (p. 1217). The biopsychosocial model remains marginal in the medical professions, where the biomedical model remains dominant (Suls & Rothman, 2004).

Stam (2004) points out how although mainstream health psychology places importance on the biopsychosocial model, the discipline fails to fully engage with the political and social issues that impact on health and health care. In health psychology (and clinical psychology) individual behaviours that influence health and illness are typically explored, with broader political, social and cultural issues receiving less consideration. Where the biopsychosocial model is adopted, social factors are typically measured by means of self-report measures of things like social support or relationship satisfaction, and broader socio-cultural factors are included as demographic variables, such as age, gender and ethnicity (Suls & Rothman, 2004). Thus the model does not do enough to include a proper consideration of broader social issues.

PSYCHOLOGICAL MODELS OF MENTAL HEALTH

2.4

Earlier we considered the biomedical model of mental disorders. Psychiatry is largely a biomedical discipline. However, clinical psychology has drawn on different psychological models for understanding mental disorders, most influential of which has been the psychoanalytic (or psychodynamic) model and the cognitive-behavioural model, which shall now be briefly discussed.

2.4.1 PSYCHOANALYTIC MODEL

In the psychoanalytic model, psychopathology or mental disorders are understood to arise from unconscious psychic conflicts. The focus is on internal psychological, rather than physiological, processes. Freud, the founder of psychoanalysis, originally attempted to ground his theory to biological factors, with his theory of instincts. Freud (see Freud (2005), *The essentials of psycho-analysis*) argued that our personalities and our behaviour are affected by the aggressive and the sexual instinctual forces. Freud conceptualized the mind (and personality) as having three structures: the id, which is concerned with gratifying innate instinctual needs and is located mainly in the unconscious mind; the ego, which refers to the rational part of the psyche and is the structure of the mind (and personality) that acts as a mediator between the subjective inner world and the external world; and the superego, which is the part of the mind (and personality) that internalizes the social norms, morals and values. Conflicts, often unconscious, between the id, the ego and the superego, result in anxiety as generally instinctual energies threaten to break into consciousness. This anxiety is managed by means of defence mechanisms (for example, denial, repression and projection). The unsuccessful resolution of these conflicts results in symptoms of distress, which may develop as mental health problems.

Various conflicts arise at different stages of the individual's development. Freud referred to five stages in an individual's psychosexual development: the oral stage, the anal stage, the phallic stage, the latency stage, and the genital stage. Freud's theory was of psycho*sexual* development as he focused on the role of the sex instinct and bodily pleasure. The *oral stage* occurs during the first year of life. This is a period where the baby moves from a total subject state that is 'objectless' (or primary narcissism) to gradual recognition of the primary caregiver (usually the mother) as a separate object. During this stage the area in which the libidinal (sexual instinct) energy is focused, is on the mouth, where pleasure is derived through activities such as sucking and feeding. The *anal stage* occurs during the second and third years of life. During this stage, as the name suggests, the anal zone becomes the focus of libidinal energy. Babies experience pleasure through the sensations of their bowel movements. During this stage the child has to renounce some of his or her instinctual pleasures during toilet training. During the *phallic stage* of psycho-sexual development (occurring during years 3 to 6), the sex organs become the zones of libidinal energy. According to Freud, during this stage the libidinal energy has as its object the opposite-sex parent. During this stage, male children experience the *Oedipus complex*, where the boy is unconsciously attracted to the mother and has feelings of hostility towards his father, whom he perceives as his rival for his mother's affections. However, the boy, fearing punishment from his father (in the form of castration) renounces his desires for his mother and identifies with the father. Girls experience the *Electra complex* where the girl, aware that she does not have a penis, renounces her affection for the mother (who the girl holds responsible for her being born without a penis), and turns her affection towards the father, who does have a penis. Freud referred to the girl experiencing *penis envy* during this stage. The girl eventually either renounces her affection for her father as she is frustrated by him, or she identifies with her mother as the object of her father's affection. The superego develops out of the resolution of the Oedipus complex and Electra complex, as the child internalizes the moral laws governing sex roles and sexual desires. The *latency stage* is a relatively quiet period of psychosexual development. With the development of the superego, sexual and aggressive energies are now latent (unconscious) and with the maturing ego the child develops greater control over the instinctual desires. During this stage (ages 6 to 11 years) the child directs his or her energies to social pursuits. The final stage is the *genital stage*, starting at puberty. At this stage, the sexual energy re-emerges in full force, and threatens the established ego defences. The feelings related to the Oedipus and Electra complex re-emerges as the child enters into competition with the same-sex peers for the affections of opposite sex peers. This establishment of romantic relationships allows the child to free him- or herself from the parents, gaining independence and maturity. Conflicts from earlier stages re-emerge and there is opportunity to resolve these. Psychopathology or mental health problems may also be caused by a fixation to any of these stages of development. Fixation may develop as a result of excessive frustration or excessive gratification. Adults may also regress to a fixation at an earlier stage during times of stress. When fixated to a particular stage, we maintain a preoccupation with the libidinal pleasures of that stage. For example, a fixation at the oral stage results in preoccupation with oral pleasure, such as food or other substances (e.g. smoking and drinking). A fixation at the anal stage results in preoccupation with issues of cleanliness and control. This may be present in obsessive-compulsive disorders.

The theories of Freud have received considerable criticisms, and have been argued to be unscientific, individualistic and reductionist, as well as regressive in its focus on the past at the expense of considerations of people's futures (see Davies & Bhugra, 2004, for a brief discussion of these). However, as Frosh (2006) points out, many critics of psychoanalysis begin and end with Freud, and do not always consider developments in psychoanalytic theory over the past 100 years. Later psychoanalytic theory (for example, object relations theory and intersubjective psychoanalysis), moved away from an emphasis on instincts, and focuses more on the quality of early child–parent relationships as significant for the development of the self, the development of emotional regulation and quality of relationships to others. This has been integrated with psychological theories of human development, such as attachment theory, for which considerable research evidence has been collected (see, for example, the work of Fonagy, Gergely, Jurist, & Target, 2004). There has also recently been much work exploring psychoanalytic concepts in neuroscience (see, for example, Solms & Turnbull, 2002).

2.4.2 COGNITIVE-BEHAVIOURAL MODEL

Although behavioural models and cognitive models have different explanations for mental health problems, it is discussed together here, as clinical psychology typically draws on both and the two are combined in cognitive-behavioural therapy approaches to treatment.

A behavioural model of mental health problems, views psychopathology as caused by learnt maladaptive behaviours. In this model, maladaptive behaviours are learnt just as other behaviours are. Learning theory posits that behaviours are produced by stimulus–response relationships (Davies & Bhugra, 2004). Two particular forms of such learning are classical conditioning and operant conditioning. Classical conditioning refers to the learnt association between two stimuli. In classical conditioning, the individual learns that the presence of a first stimulus (or the conditioned stimulus) may predict the occurrence of a second stimulus (or the unconditioned stimulus). Thus the presence of the first stimulus will provoke a response on the basis that a second stimulus is expected. For example, some phobias are understood to be caused by classical conditioning. A fear of dogs, might be explained when a person has previously experienced being mauled by a dog; the presence of a dog may elicit a fear response due to this association. In operant conditioning, a behaviour is learnt because that behaviour is associated with specific rewarding or reinforcing consequences. For example, substance abuse may be a learnt behaviour because of the initial stress-reducing or pleasurable rewards of taking that substance. Maladaptive behaviours may also be learnt socially through modelling our behaviours on those observed in significant others.

Maladaptive behaviours may also be caused by misinterpretations of events. Thus we may have maladaptive behaviours due to dysfunctional cognitive processes. Dysfunctional cognitive processes might include irrational beliefs about ourselves or about the world, information processing biases, or dysfunctional thinking. For example, Beck (1989) considered depression in terms of what has been referred to as the negative cognitive triad – depression results from the person developing negative views about themselves, negative views about the world, and negative view about their future. These negative views and beliefs maintain a depressed mood.

The aims of cognitive-behavioural treatments of mental health problems thus involve changing behaviours that are maladaptive, and elucidating the learning processes which have led to maladaptive behaviour. The aim is also to identify and challenge dysfunctional cognitive processes that maintain emotional and behavioural problems. Cognitive and behavioural models have been highly influential in both clinical and health psychology, and have become the dominant forms of psychological understandings of unhealthy and maladaptive behaviours. As we shall see in the next chapter, the models used in health psychology for understanding and changing health behaviours are informed by cognitive-behavioural principles.

The above models have in common the focus on internal factors (whether biological or psychological) in understanding the cause of illness and diseases. Although the social world might be taken into consideration in some aspects of these models, the focus remains on how internal processes may be affected by social factors. For example, how we may learn to behave in certain ways by our interpretation of what we view others doing. Family therapists have also emphasized the importance of considering mental health problems within the context of a family system, where psychopathology may be understood as an outcome of possible dysfunctional family relationships. This may extend to a broader social environment, such as the school environment (in the case of children and adolescents).

The biomedical model, and the psychoanalytic and the cognitive-behavioural models, have been critiqued for not taking enough consideration of environmental, social and cultural aspects. Much of these critiques have come from the social science disciplines, particularly sociology.

SOCIOLOGICAL CRITIQUES OF THE MEDICAL MODEL

2.5

The discipline of sociology has made an important contribution to our understanding of health and ill-health, and various sociological models have made important critiques of the prevailing biomedical model. Some of this work shall be explored here with reference to the anti-psychiatry critiques of mental health, the social model of disability, and examples of diagnostic categories as socially constructed.

2.5.1 THE 'ANTI-PSYCHIATRY' MODEL OF MENTAL ILL-HEALTH

The 'anti-psychiatry' movement is a term used to refer to a group of writers who published radical critiques of psychiatric theory and practice in the 1960s and 1970s. Two of the main proponents of 'anti-psychiatry' were Szasz (1972) and Laing (1990). The 'anti-psychiatry' model is usually viewed as a sociological model, and I have included it as such here. However, this is not entirely accurate as both Szasz and Laing are psychiatrists, not sociologists. Their critique of psychiatry arose out of their dissatisfaction with the profession, and they made a social critique of psychiatry and diagnosis of mental health problems. They critiqued the medical model of psychiatry that viewed mental health problems as illnesses with biological causes, arguing instead that mental 'illnesses' represent a moral and social category. Those persons who are diagnosed as having mental 'illnesses' represent people who have deviated away from social and cultural norms and rules. Behaviour or emotional states that are considered 'abnormal' are associated with value judgements, rather than on objective measurement. For example, psychotic illnesses are distinguished in part by problems of 'reality testing', such as delusions, which are defined in relation to social norms.

Szasz (1972) considered mental 'illness' as a 'myth'. He differentiated between physical and mental illnesses, with physical illnesses having clear, observable organic causes, whereas mental illnesses, having no clear organic causes, cannot be considered illnesses at all. Szasz argued that mental health problems are actually communications of 'problems of living', arising out of conflicts between different socio-cultural norms and values. He argued that psychiatry formulates social, moral and political 'problems of living' as internal problems of the individual. In the biomedical model, the search for causes tends to be within the individual, rather than looking for causes in society or the family. Mental health problems, he argued, become defined by what psychiatrists label as mental 'illness':

> in psychiatric circles it is almost indelicate to ask: What is mental illness? In non-psychiatric circles mental illness all too often is considered to be whatever psychiatrists say it is. The answer to the question, Who is mentally ill? thus becomes: Those who are confined in mental hospitals or who consult psychiatrists in their private offices. (Szasz, 1972: 13)

In the 1960s, Laing (1990) argued that what is considered as 'sane' and 'insane' is dependent on consensus rather than on objective truth. Laing argued that schizophrenia is a "sane response to an insane world" (Cockerham, 2011: 79). He questioned psychiatry's assumption of mental illness as 'irrational' behaviour, arguing that conditions of 'insanity' may make sense when considered from the perspective of the patient. For example, the 'irrational' thought and behaviours of patients diagnosed with schizophrenia can be considered as having a logic, or make sense, if we consider them from the patients' perspective and in relation to their experience of living in a social and relational context that may be intolerable.

Many sociologists have explored the notion of 'medicalization', which focuses on the medical system of diagnosing and treating illness as a form of social control (Iley & Nazroo, 2007). Anti-psychiatrists considered psychiatric services and treatment as a form of social control, arguing that many treatments for mental health problems were coercive (at that time treatments like electro-shock therapy were quite common). They emphasized psychiatric treatment as subjective and based on value judgements, with the views of the patient being disregarded. Some of the work at that time aimed to highlight the problems with psychiatric diagnosis and treatment, such as the well-known study by Rosenhan (1973) described in Box 2.1.

BOX 2.1

A Spotlight on Research: How shall we know the difference between 'sanity' and 'insanity'?

Rosenhan, D.L. (1973). On being sane in insane places. *Science, 179*, 250–258.

Aims: This paper reports on an experiment which aimed to highlight questions regarding the reliability and validity of mental health diagnosis. It aimed to highlight the subjective nature of differentiating 'abnormality' from 'normality' and 'insanity' from 'sanity'. The experiment involved getting 'normal' pseudo-patients admitted into a psychiatric hospital, where they would then act 'sane'. The study aimed to observe how they would be treated by the mental health professions, and whether their 'sanity' would be detected, and thus be distinguishable from the 'insane' patients.

Methods: The experiment involved eight participants who acted as pseudo-patients. The eight 'patients' included three psychologists, one psychiatrist, one pae-diatrician, a housewife, a student and a painter. All used a pseudonym, and those involved in a health profession claimed to be in a different occupation. The author was one of the eight 'patients', whose real presence in the hospital was known by only the chief psychologist and the hospital administrator. The eight pseudo-patients telephoned the admissions offices of 12 psychiatric hospitals in the USA, complain-ing of hearing voices. At a first consultation, each patient gave the same description of hearing an unknown voice of the same sex, and that what the voice said was often unclear, but included words such as 'empty' and 'hollow'. Other than lying about their name, their occupation and hearing voices, each patient gave a truthful account of their life history. Once admitted, the pseudo-patients "ceased simulating any symptoms of abnormality" (p. 251). Some displayed some nervousness about having been admitted into the hospital and fearing that they would be immediately found out as a fraud. The pseudo-patients engaged normally with fellow patients and staff, and when asked how they were they would respond that they were feeling fine and reported no symptoms. They kept notes of their experiences and observation of oth-ers' behaviours.

Results: All but one pseudo-patient were admitted with a diagnosis of schizophre-nia, and none was detected as a fraud while in hospital. All were discharged with the diagnosis 'schizophrenia in remission', thus not technically 'sane'. The pseudo-patients' length of stay in the hospital ranged from seven to 52 days, with an average length of stay of 19 days. Other patients tended to suspect the pseudo-patients 'nor-mality', but not the staff.

Conclusion: The findings that fellow patients, but not staff, detected the 'normality' of the pseudo-patients raise many questions about the validity and reliability of psychiatric diagnosis. It also highlights the strength that diagnostic labels have in the perception of people. In all cases the label of schizophrenia stuck, even if officially 'in remission' upon discharge. In no case was a diagnostic label dropped. Rosenhan highlighted how patients in psychiatric hospitals may be misunderstood, with significant depersonalizing consequences for their identity. As Rosenhan concludes:

A psychiatric label has a life and an influence of its own. Once the impression has been formed that the patient is schizophrenic, the expectation is that he will continue to be schizophrenic. When a sufficient amount of time has passed, during which the patient has done nothing bizarre, he is considered to be in remission and available for discharge. But the label endures beyond discharge, with the unconfirmed expectation that he will behave as a schizophrenic again. (p. 253)

This study is controversial and has been critiqued as pseudoscience. The study purports to challenge the reliability and validity of diagnosis, but rather only demonstrates that psychiatrists in the study did not detect the simulated signs of mental 'illness' by the pseudo-patients (Spitzer, 1975), and so it is about lying not being detected, rather than about the validity of diagnosis. This focuses on symptoms as reported by the pseudo-patients. However, the reports that fellow patients were able to detect the pseudo-patients observed behaviour as normal, whereas staff did not, does raise questions about the notion that mental health problems can be accurately observed and diagnosed.

The 'anti-psychiatry' model has been influential in bringing about changes in psychiatric care and the deinstitutionalization of treatment, but, as with all models, they have also been critiqued. 'Anti-psychiatry' arguments are criticized as being rhetorical and philosophically interesting rather than based on empirical evidence or clinical reality (Cockerham, 2011). It also makes a generalized criticism of psychiatry and its treatment, failing to consider that patients may be genuinely distressed and struggling to cope and that psychiatrists and other mental health professionals may be genuinely motivated by a desire to help, rather than a desire to control. Critics have also argued that mental health problems do not have to be identifiable from observable physiological pathologies in order to be defined as being a disease, as disease can also be identifiable from impaired behaviour or personality (Cockerham, 2011).

In the field of disability, which includes psychiatric disability, a highly influential model that has presented a considerable critique of the medical model, has been the so-called social model of disability.

2.5.2 THE SOCIAL MODEL OF DISABILITY

In the 1970s, disability activists in the United Kingdom began to challenge the prevailing medical model of disability. The medical model's focus on the body as the site of disability was challenged by disability activists who argued that social and environmental barriers contributed centrally to the experience of disability. One of the most influential groups, the Union of the Physically Impaired Against Segregation (UPIAS), an early disability rights group in the UK, was instrumental in reformulating an understanding of disability that moved away from the medical model adopted by the World Health Organization at the time. In defining disability, UPIAS stated that:

> it is society which disables physically impaired people. Disability is something that is imposed on top of our impairments, by the way we are unnecessarily isolated and excluded from the full participation in society. (UPIAS, quoted in Barton, 1998: 56)

Oliver (1986), a disabled academic in the UK, pointed out how people with disabilities have increasingly argued that their personal limitations or impairments in themselves are not what prevent full participation, but rather the restrictions which society imposes upon people with impairments is what disables them (see Box 2.2). He expanded on the UPIAS ideas on physical disability to develop 'the social model of disability' (Oliver, 1986, 1990), which could be extended to all types of disability. Disability studies theorists make a distinction between 'impairment' and 'disability', which Finkelstein and French (1993) define as follows:

> *Impairment* is the lack of part of or all of a limb, or having a defective limb, organ or mechanism of the body.

> *Disability* is the loss or limitation of opportunities that prevents people who have impairments from taking part in the normal life of the community on an equal level with others due to physical and social barriers. (p. 28)

Contrary to the medical model, the social model of disability has the concept of oppression as a focus of the experience of disability, where disability is understood as representing the "social, financial, environmental and psychological disadvantages inflicted on impaired people" (Abberley, 1987: 17). In this model, disability is viewed as "a particular form of social oppression" (UPIAS, quoted in Barton, 1998: 56), in the same way that race or gender can be a basis for exclusion to full participation. This arises from a social environment that is constructed by non-impaired people, and constructed in their interests (Abberley, 1998). As Oliver (2004) states:

> the social model of disability is about nothing more complicated than a clear focus on the economic, environmental and cultural barriers encountered by people who are viewed by others as having some form of impairment – whether physical, sensory or intellectual. The barriers disabled people encounter include inaccessible education systems, working environments, inadequate disability benefits, discriminatory health and social support services, inaccessible transport, houses and public buildings and amenities, and the devaluing of disabled people through negative images in the media. (p. 21)

Thus a person who has a physical impairment may experience limitations in relation to their impairment, which may result in them needing to use a wheelchair. However, their exclusion from buildings with no appropriate access, their possible exclusion from employment opportunities, from educational opportunities, relationships and so on, is what disables them. According to the social model of disability, in order to reduce the experience of disability, an adjustment to the physical and social environment is required that meets the needs of persons with disabilities (French, 1993). This is in contrast to the medical model that focuses solely on physical, medical interventions.

BOX 2.2

Video Clip: The Social Model of Disability

The Disability Rights Commission (UK) created a video illustrating the concept of the social model of disability. The video depicts an able-bodied man trying to make his way to a job interview. The video depicts him as a minority able-bodied man in a society comprising a majority of disabled citizens (all types of disability). The video highlights the barriers he faces in achieving his goal, and in so doing demonstrates in a manner which many of us can identify with, how our attitudes and our environment may create a multitude of barriers that exclude people with disabilities.

The video is available to view at:

http://videos.disabled-world.com/video/80/disability-rights-commission-video-clip.

It is also available on *YouTube*.

The social model of disability has been very influential in changing our understanding of disability and has highlighted the importance of creating environments that are accessible and meet the needs of disabled people. With the emergence of the social model approach to disability and its increasing support, the World Health Organization replaced its *International Classification of Impairments, Disabilities and Handicaps* with the *International Classification of Functioning* (ICF) (WHO, 1998). The ICF attempts to integrate the social model with the medical approach and replaces the use of 'impairment', 'disability' and 'handicap', with:

- *Impairment*: "problems in body function or structure such as a significant deviation or loss";
- *Activity*: "activity limitations are difficulties an individual may have in executing activities"; and
- *Participation*: "Participation restrictions are problems an individual may experience in involvement in life situations". (WHO, 1998: 10)

With these revised definitions, the ICF has barriers to full participation as a central aspect of disability.

Although highly influential, the social model of disability has not been without its critics. Some theorists (Hughes & Paterson, 1997; Oliver, 1996; Shakespeare & Watson, 1997) have pointed out that the social model of disability excludes consideration of the lived experience of impairment. With this criticism, there have been calls to integrate understandings of impairment with the social model of disability (Hughes & Paterson, 1997; Johnston, 1997). Marks (1999) critiques the social model for excluding people's subjective lived experience from its understanding of disability. In an attempt to bridge understanding of impairment with disability, she argues that 'disability' involves a relationship between the body and the environment as well as the psyche, and is thus an embodied relationship. Marks draws on psychoanalytic theory to argue that the stereotypes and stigma that society has for disabled people creates a form of social oppression which is internalized by the person with disability to become an embodied experience. Experiences of exclusion, stigma and "denigration" (Marks, 1999: 25), are internalized by the individual, which impacts on their self-esteem and interaction with others. Oliver (1996) states, however, that the social model is an attempt to understand and deal with the social barriers of disability, and not the restrictions caused by impairment. The social model of disability thus offers a starting point for understanding the social barriers that create disability.

The social model of disability argues that disability is not located in the individual, but rather in society's constructions of the environment and what is considered to be 'normal' and what is 'abnormal'. This may also vary from one context to the other. For example, Marks (1999) illustrates how a person who is deaf may be considered to be severely disabled and excluded in one social context, while in another social context a person who is deaf is more integrated in society. What was considered as normal, in terms of able-bodies and disabled-bodies, became an increased concern during the industrialization of societies (Marks 1999; Oliver, 1993), as a mechanized, uniform workforce was required. With industrialization, also came the creation of unproductive and therefore economically dependent (disabled) people who were contained in specialized institutions and workhouses. Thus Oliver (1993) sees the 'dependency' of disabled people as being socially constructed.

2.5.3 SOCIAL CONSTRUCTIONIST CRITIQUES

Social constructionism is a sociological theory which regards a social phenomenon, not as a 'reality' waiting to be discovered, but rather as a social product formed by human activity. Social constructionism has been influential in psychological approaches which have critiqued the positivist, scientific, experimental dominance of psychological knowledge. In social construction theory, the social world, or what we know as reality and 'true' about the world, is created or constructed through shared discourse and language (Burr, 1995; Gergen, 1985). Social constructionist theorists argue that understanding of self and identity are also constructed socially through shared discourses. Burr (1995) explains:

> All the 'objects' of our consciousness, including our 'self', our notion of what it means to be a person, and our own identity, are all constructed through language, and that it is discourses as coherent systems of representation that produce these things for us. (p. 56)

Thus shared understandings of what we regard as 'normal' and 'abnormal' shape and determine what and who we understand as being 'normal' and 'abnormal'; 'abled' and 'disabled'. In constructing these binaries, it also creates a barrier at which some identities are included and some are excluded. History has disturbing examples where these binaries are taken to the extreme and become the basis for eugenics and euthanasia, as in the case of the systematic murder of disabled people in Nazi Germany.

Utilizing a social constructionist perspective on disease classification is useful in helping us understand how some of our ideas about diseases or abnormalities are in a sense created, rather than resting on facts. In Chapter 7 this is explored in relation to homosexuality as well as to HIV/AIDS. Some social constructionist critiques of two diagnoses – learning disability and post-traumatic stress disorder (PTSD) – shall be discussed here, as an illustration.

The social construction of learning disability

The specific definitions of learning disability provided by the classification systems of the DSM-IV (APA, 2000) and the ICD-10 (WHO, 1992) define learning disability as deficits in intellectual functioning indicated by an intelligence quotient (IQ) score below 70, and deficits in adaptive behaviour. Epidemiological studies estimate the prevalence of learning disabilities as being between 1% and 3% of the general population, with approximately 85% falling within the mild range, 10% within the moderate range, 3–4% within the severe range, and about 1–2% within the profound range (Carr & O'Reilly, 2007). Such classification systems and epidemiological studies rest on the assumption that learning disability is a 'fact' that exists out there in the world, which can be accurately observed and measured in a manner that reflects reality. A social constructionist understanding of learning disability, however, critiques many of the assumptions that are made about learning disability, primarily arguing that learning disability is not an absolute reality, but rather that the meanings and understanding of learning disability are created through social process, in particular the use of language. Social constructionism in psychology takes a critical stance towards taken-for-granted knowledge, arguing that knowledge is situated with particular social, cultural and historical contexts (Gergen, 1985).

Nunkoosing (2000) explores aspects of learning disability from a social constructionist framework. Using this social constructionist approach, he challenges our 'taken-for-granted' understanding of learning disability. A social constructionist approach critiques the notion of knowledge being generated from objective observations of the world, in a manner that make knowledge reflect reality. Science is critiqued for being too positivistic; that is that one can objectively observe factual events in the world and measure it in a manner that reflects reality. Social constructionism takes a stance against this taken-for-granted knowledge, arguing against a positive approach, to state that all observation is subjective, and that knowledge generated from such observation is thus relative. As Gergen (1985) states about social constructionism: "it invites one to challenge the objective basis of knowledge" (p. 267).

With regards to learning disability, the 'taken-for-granted' knowledge is that it is defined by deficits in intellectual functioning, indicated by an IQ score below 70. This relies on the assumption that 'intelligence' exists as a fact that can be accurately observed and measured. However, as Richards (2010) observes, the meaning of what constitutes intelligence and how to measure it has constantly been debated and revised over the years, ever since the first intelligence test developed by Binet and Simon in 1905. Their test involved a series of increasingly complex tasks, which were administered to children, with the aim of identifying "subnormal and backward children" (Richards, 2010: 281). This test generated an average score of 100, which has remained as the average score of intelligence to this day. Debate and controversy has been ongoing as to whether there is a single, general factor of intelligence or whether 'intelligence' comprises various different abilities. As Richards argues, the problem with measurement in psychology is the assumption that a psychometric test can be developed which accurately measures and represents reality, particularly when considerable debate and controversy exists as to what that reality means and how it is understood. Furthermore, Richards points out the problem of circularity when it comes to psychometric measurement, where psychometric tests are devised not only to measure, but also to discover what it is that it is measuring. Thus, in the case of intelligence, psychometric tests were devised not only to 'measure' intelligence, but also to develop an understanding of what intelligence is (the somewhat arbitrary creation of a score of 100 on a series of tasks representing the average score of intelligence being a case in point).

Furthermore, the different categories and classifications of learning disabilities have not remained fixed and stable over time. This is contrary to a positivist approach, which would argue that measurement reflects reality. Edgerton, Lloyd, and Cole (1979, cited in Rapley, 2004) point out how the diagnostic label for learning disability has changed. They show how in previous years someone with an IQ of between 50 and 70 would be referred to as a 'moron'; someone with an IQ of 30 to 50 an 'imbecile' and someone with an IQ of less than 30 an 'idiot'. Today we refer to the following diagnostic categories:

IQ < 25: Profound mental retardation
IQ 25–39: Severe mental retardation
IQ 40–59: Moderate mental retardation
IQ 55–60: Mild mental retardation.

Although these categories are still the diagnostic labels used in the DSM-IV, we more recently refer to mild, moderate, severe and profound 'learning disability', as 'mental retardation' is now regarded as being an offensive term. The differences here are not only with the terms used, but if we compare previous IQ ranges for different categories from the ones we use today, we can see that the range of IQ scores for the different sub-categories have changed. Rapley (2004), though, does point out that there is some historical continuity in the diagnosing of learning disabilities (although the labels have changed), and that many diagnostic definitions of learning disability do not only regard learning disability as a cognitive matter, but also take into account adaptive functioning.

Where diagnosis and understanding of learning disability is perhaps most problematic is with the category of 'mild learning disability' (Jacobson, 2001). Rapley (2004) states how the identification of mild learning disability can be "simply a condemnation of unwanted conduct dressed up as objective behavioural science" (p. 37), where children are identified as having a mild learning disability because they display behavioural 'symptoms' or 'subtle' learning difficulties which are difficult to classify. However, Jacobsen (2001) argues that mild learning disabilities do indeed exist and that children with mild learning disabilities experience real difficulties with learning and real behavioural difficulties; the problem is not with the validity of the assessment and diagnosis, but rather that assessments are misused and interpreted by workers who are overly influenced by social constructionist views and do not recognize the actual problems.

Social constructionism observes the temporal nature of knowledge generation. As mentioned earlier, the social constructionist approach does not regard knowledge as a factual representation of the world as it exists, but rather as created within a particular social, cultural and political context, and thus is an artefact of that time. Our understandings of psychological issues differ also from culture to culture. Our understanding of and the meanings associated with learning disability are likewise socially and historically situated. Above, we have seen how the categorization of learning disability has changed over time, with particular diagnostic categories being used in different historical contexts. Some of our ideas about ability and normality and abnormality are also socially and historically situated. For example, persons with disabilities (including learning disabilities) are often regarded as being passive and dependent on others and thus needing to be protected (Marks, 1999). As we have seen above, the notion of persons with disabilities as dependent arose during industrialization and the need for an 'able-bodied' workforce (Marks, 1999; Oliver, 1993). Disabled people have become excluded from the economic sector as the nature of work and the economy changed as a result of industrialization.

Writing from a psychoanalytic perspective, Sinason (1992) feels strongly about how the vocabulary and terms used to refer to intellectual disability have changed over time. She argues that terms are changed and adapted in an attempt to disguise difference. She provides an extensive historical list of the vocabulary and terms used to describe and refer to intellectual disability – vocabulary such as 'backward', 'deficient', 'feeble', 'idiot', 'moron', 'retard' and 'stupid', among many others. She argues that vocabulary is changed and used as euphemisms for things that begin to feel too emotionally evoking and disturbing. What is being pointed out here is that the diagnostic labels that we use have changed over time and are sustained, or are changed, through social processes. Sinason (1992) focuses on the change of labels used as resulting from the anxieties of non-disabled people. However, some of the changes in terminology over the years have been advocated by disabled people themselves, for example the call to replace 'handicapped' with 'people with disabilities'.

In social constructionism, it is argued that one or some particular under-standings are accepted as the prevailing knowledge at a time, while other understandings are suppressed or marginalized. In this way, certain actions are invited while others are excluded. Thus, for example, the change to the term 'people with learning disabilities' encourages the placing of the notion of the person first, before the disability, although many still resist this term (Nunkoosing, 2000). Furthermore, labelling of disability and its associations of capabilities and abilities often result in people with learning disabilities being excluded from being involved in creating a shared understanding of learning disability. Rapley (2004) and Pilnick and colleagues (2010) have shown how interaction with people with learning disabilities has an effect on eventual out-comes. For example, Rapley (2004) points out how people with learning disa-bilities are often understood as being acquiescent, and thus incompetent to report on their own subjective experience. He demonstrates, by means of con-versation analysis (see Chapter 8) of assessment interviews between a profes-sional and a person with disability, how an acquiescent response may be the product of the interview process, where the professional might ignore certain responses as 'incorrect' replies to questions that the professional assumes a cer-tain answer for. Questions are repeated and rephrased until the interviewee eventually says "yes". Similarly, Pilnick and colleagues (2010) analyse review meetings between professionals and service users and their parents in which transitions from child to adult services are discussed. They show how attempts to invite the participation of service users can be quickly blocked, thus under-mining the service user's choice and control over the agenda of the review meeting. Klotz (2004) argues that people with learning disabilities were gener-ally only ever known professionally in terms of their disability and 'abnormal-ity', denying people with learning disabilities their status as fully human beings. Individuals are treated in terms of the primary perception of abnormality and the full lived experience and needs of the person's life are not always taken fully into account. This can be illustrated with the issue of sexuality and per-sons with learning disabilities (see Chapter 7).

Social constructionist critiques of PTSD

Post-traumatic stress disorder (PTSD) provides an interesting example of how mental disorders might be socially constructed. The DSM-IV (APA, 2000) describes PTSD in terms of a set of symptoms and criteria that include:

- Exposure to a traumatic event in which the person "experienced, witnessed, or was confronted" by "actual or threatened death or serious injury, or a threat to the physical integrity of self or others" (p. 467).
- The person responded with "intense fear, helplessness, or horror" (p. 467).
- The presence of symptoms belong to three symptom clusters: re-experiencing symptoms (for example, recurrent thoughts or dreams of the event); avoidance or numbing symptoms (for example, emotional numbness, avoidance of reminders of the events); and symptoms of hyper arousal (for example, hypervigilance and irritability).

Trauma has been an important construct in mental health and has long been recognized as contributing to mental health problems. The diagnosis of 'hysteria' during the time of Freud was used for conditions which would often now be termed trauma. During the First and Second World War, the mental health profession was faced with trauma in the form of 'shell shock'. However, PTSD was included in the DSM-III in 1980 as a product of a particular time in history (Herman, 2001; Young 1995). Following the Vietnam war, returning war veterans in USA were experiencing mental and behavioural problems akin to 'shell shock'. Veterans argued for a diagnosis that would legitimize their suffering and would make them eligible for disability compensation (Summerfield, 2001). The ensuing political and moral debate about the care and treatment of Vietnam War veterans preceded the inclusion of PTSD in the DSM-III. Thus PTSD was a diagnosis that was created by society and politics, rather than a new diagnosis that was discovered. This is not to say that PTSD does not exist – although there is considerable debate about the validity and universality of PTSD (Kienzler, 2008) – but it is a diagnostic category that was 'created' within a particular socio-political context. Feminists would argue that trauma existed before, but that trauma experienced by abused women prior to PTSD was constituted as 'hysteria', as something to do with personality, rather than acknowledging the seriousness of trauma in the way that PTSD does. Furthermore, some social constructionist critics argue that symptoms relating to remembering and forgetting the traumatic event are socio-culturally embedded, and depend on socio-cultural norms for how recollections are communicated, which runs counter to PSTD as a universal disorder (see Kienzler, 2008).

The diagnostic criteria for PTSD also suggest that the experience of trauma follows a single, discrete event. This is even suggested by the name *post*-traumatic stress disorder. This fits with the experience of Vietnam War veterans at the time, where their diagnosable distress was observed *after* their experiences of war. However, many people experience traumatic lives on a continuous basis, dealing with considerable problems of poverty, oppression, persecution and violence on a day-to-day basis. A diagnosis of PTSD is unhelpful for someone who is trying to survive in a context of continuous trauma. Other diagnoses, such as Complex PTSD or Continuous Traumatic Stress Syndrome, have been suggested (Herman, 2001). The diagnosis furthermore places the 'problem' within the individual in terms of symptoms suggesting 'problem' *responses* to trauma, rather than focusing on the 'problem' of traumatic experiences to which the individual responds with appropriate distress, thus pathologizing the individual. Consider, for example, PTSD in the context of rape, where the survivor of rape would be treated for her or his 'problem', their mental disorder, rather than rape itself being the 'problem' that needs to be treated.

Social constructionism has been critiqued for locating a phenomenon entirely in the social context and denying the existence of a 'reality'. In an extreme approach to social constructionism, there is no such thing as 'reality', only interpretation. More recent theorists have attempted to incorporate positivist notions of an observable reality with interpretive approaches, an approach referred to as critical realism (Archer, Bhaskar, Collier, Lawson & Norrie, 1998). Critical realism accepts the existence of a reality which mediates the interpretations made. Critical realism argues that a social and material reality exists which "constrains action but does not simply determine it" (Rogers & Pilgrim, 2005: 17). In other words, it shapes and constrains our interpretive actions, but does not just simply cause them. This is a useful approach in that it allows a critical theorist to accept the reality of a physical impairment, such as a learning disability, but also allows us to critically analyse power dynamics and whose interests are being promoted by describing and conceptualizing physical and mental health problems in particular ways (Rogers & Pilgrim, 2005).

CRITICAL PSYCHOLOGY

2.6 Critical psychology is an approach to psychology which challenges mainstream psychology as being focused on the individual, and is reliant on a positivist and reductionist scientific method. Fox, Prilleltensky, and Austin (2009) argue that mainstream psychology does not scrutinize or pay adequate attention to social and political aspects, nor the "social, moral, and political implications of research, theory and practice" (p. 4). Critical psychology is concerned with the analysis of power and social control, and rather than being agents of social control (which critical psychologists claim of mainstream psychology) critical psychologists aim to be "agents of social change" (Fox, Prilleltensky, & Austin, 2009: 4). Thus critical psychologists are interested in scrutinizing the role of institutions in society as agents of social control, creating power differentials where some sectors of the population are marginalized, oppressed and excluded and made powerless, while others are privileged. Also scrutinized is power in relation to knowledge, where particular values and assumptions are privileged and are dominant, while others are silenced. Psychology, as with all academic disciplines, forms part of that social structure, privileging particular forms of knowledge (typically science and numbers) over others. Thus critical psychology is more concerned with analysis at the social and structural level, rather than at the individual level.

Clinical psychology remains very dominated by biomedical and cognitive understanding of mental health, focusing on the individual, while neglecting the social and structural. Critical approaches to clinical psychology are concerned with critically examining the validity of diagnosis, which is focused on the individual and often imposes the values and worldviews of people from a middle-class, white, western perspective (Marecek & Hare-Mustin, 2009). A critical approach is rather interested in scrutinizing conceptions of 'normality' and 'abnormality' and attends to social, political and cultural influences on mental health. When discussing 'critical' aspects in clinical psychology, generally the 'anti-psychiatry' movement is referred to. Critical psychology is clearly influenced by sociological critiques of health and mental health, and the 'anti-psychiatry' movement (as we have seen above). However, few contemporary critical approaches within clinical psychology exist (for example, Bentall, 2003; or Parker, Georgaca, Harper, McLaughlin, & Stowell-Smith, 1995), while there are plenty more sociological critiques of mental ill-health. There is also a growing interest in critical psychiatry (Thomas & Bracken, 2004).

Critical health psychology, on the other hand, is more established, although still marginal to clinical health psychology (see Chapter 1). Mainstream health psychology adopts the biopsychosocial model for understanding health and relies on the scientific method for uncovering knowledge about individual behaviour, seeking 'truths' about how individual behaviours and other psychological factors affect health and ill-health. Critical health psychology, in contrast, assumes that the individual cannot be understood outside their social, cultural, political and historical context (Chamberlain & Murray, 2009). Critical health psychology is primarily concerned with interrogating assumptions held, including those by health psychologists, and how different forms of practice and knowledge oppress or empower people. Murray and Campbell (2003) argue that critical health psychology should side "with the interests of the oppressed and disenfranchised masses" (p. 233). Critical health psychology is reliant on theorizing that is reflexive and critical of assumptions held, research methods that are critical and most often qualitative, and practice that is action-orientated, enabling and empowering for participants (Murray, 2004).

Thus critical approaches in clinical and health psychology are concerned primarily with issues of power and social justice. It is an action-orientated approach, where not only is the intention to understand and gain insight into people's experience, but also to empower the disenfranchised and bring about social change. MacLachlan (2006a),writing about critical health psychology, cautions that much of critical health psychology is about criticizing disciplines – being critical *of* instead of *for* others. In this sense, MacLachlan argues that critical health psychology can be critical simply by means of condemnation of others, rather than by means of persuasion. MacLachlan (2006a) goes on to argue that if critical health psychology (and so also critical clinical psychology) wishes to make a valued, critical contribution to global health, addressing issues of inequality and justice, then critical health psychology needs to work with some of the disciplines that it so often critiques.

SUMMARY

2.7

This chapter has outlined various different models for understanding ill-health and disability, including mental health problems. This may present a confusing picture and provides us with no clear answers. But, given the complexity of health and suffering, it may be right that we have such differing perspectives and views. What has been highlighted, though, is that simply understanding ill-health as being caused by biological, physical factors does not encapsulate the complex psychological, social and political influences on health and ill-health. We cannot look at issues of health by focusing on the individual alone, in isolation from the social, cultural, political and historical context. This cannot be explored in one chapter alone, and most of the remaining chapters explore some of these issues further.

FURTHER READINGS

Cockerham, W.C. (2011). *The sociology of mental disorders* (8th edition). Boston, MA: Pearson Education. This book provides a valuable introduction to sociological perspectives on mental disorders. As well as outlining some of the relevant models discussed in this chapter, it also explores various social determinants of mental health problems.

Fox, D., Prilleltensky, I., & Austin, S. (Eds.) (2009). *Critical psychology: An introduction*. London: Sage. This edited book is the most influential textbook on critical psychology. It provides an introduction to the field, and its relevance for many of the sub-disciplines of psychology, including clinical psychology and health psychology.

Marks, D. (1999). *Disability: Controversial debates and psychosocial issues*. London: Routledge. This book presents the various perspectives of understanding disability, discussing both the medical model and the social model. It also draws on psychoanalytic theory to explore and understand our emotional responses to disability.

Sarafino, E.P. (2006). *Health psychology: Biopsychosocial interactions* (5th edition). Hoboken, NJ: John Wiley & Sons. This textbook on health psychology adopts the biopsychosocial model to explore the relationship between biological, psychological and social factors in health and illness.

UNDERSTANDING AND CHANGING HEALTH BEHAVIOURS

3

INTRODUCTION

3.1 This chapter is more concerned with health psychology, rather than clinical psychology. The chapter reviews some of the most cited models of health behaviour, which are used in health psychology as models for predicting and changing health behaviours. As we shall see, these models have as their emphasis the individual and factors within or close to the individual that influence behaviours. These models, although well researched and supported, have received considerable criticisms. The chapter outlines a number of these, and details the lack of consideration of broader social and environmental factors as a key limitation of these models. The chapter goes on to explore community health psychology as a sub-discipline concerned with understanding and addressing health problems at the community level. Community mental health will also be briefly explored.

COGNITIVE-BEHAVIORAL MODELS OF HEALTH BEHAVIOURS

3.2 A number of theoretical models have been developed to conceptualize why it is that people engage in particular behaviours that may improve or may damage their health. The models have been used as a theoretical framework for understanding how damaging health behaviours may be changed. Three of the most often cited models in health psychology are the health belief model (Rosenstock, 1974), the theory of reasoned action (Ajzen & Fishbein, 1980), and its revision, the theory of planned behaviour (Ajzen, 1991).

3.2.1 HEALTH BELIEF MODEL

The health belief model is the oldest and perhaps the most frequently used model for understanding and predicting health behaviour. The health belief model was developed by psychologists in the US Public Health Service, with the aim of trying to explain why it was that people did not make use of preventative or screening tests for early detection of disease which do not have clearly identifiable early signs and symptoms (Stroebe, 2000). The model was also used to understand how patients may respond to symptoms and medical regimens. Rosenstock (1974) points out how various demographic variables, such as socio-economic status, were observed to be associated with utilization of preventive health services and preventive health behaviours, with more affluent people making more use of preventive health services. These differences could not be modified through education alone, or even when preventive heath services were government-financed. The health belief model sought to define personal characteristics which predicted behaviour.

According to the health belief model, whether or not a person engages in a particular health behaviour is based on the extent to which that person believes himself or herself to be at risk for or susceptible to a particular disease or illness, and the degree of perceived severity of the consequences of getting that disease (Rosenstock, 1974). A person would perceive himself or herself to be under a health threat, if he or she perceives that they are susceptible to getting the disease and that this will have serious consequences. This can be aided by continuing reminders, or cues, of the health problem (Rosenstock, 1974). These cues can include physical symptoms, media or medical information or knowledge of someone who has the disease. Furthermore, a person will engage in the health behaviour if the perceived benefits of changing their behaviour outweigh the costs or barriers (i.e. if the 'pros' outweigh the 'cons'). Becker and Maiman (1975) later highlighted the importance of motivation in whether an individual engages in preventative health behaviour or not, and thus general health motivation was added as an additional variable (see Figure 3.1).

Interventions using this model aim to convey to people that they are at risk for developing the particular disease or illness, and that the disease or illness has serious consequences. Furthermore, interventions aim to persuade that the benefits of engaging in the healthy behaviour outweigh the costs. Many public health campaigns are informed by this model, for example anti-smoking campaigns, where images on the tobacco packaging aim to persuade smokers of their susceptibility to and the severity of throat and lung cancer. Further, campaigns stress the benefits of stopping smoking (such as improved general health and money saved), which outweigh the costs (for example, financial costs of tobacco and poor general health).

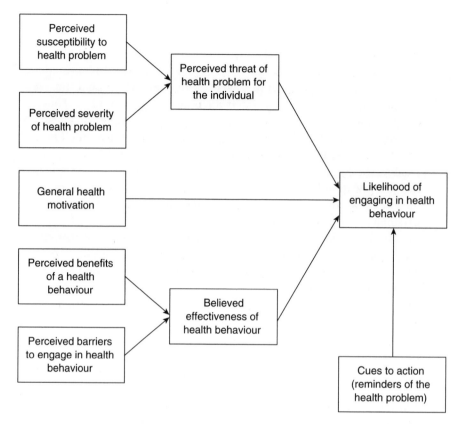

FIGURE 3.1   The health belief model

A review of studies using the health belief model (Janz & Becker, 1984) provides support for the health belief model, although the strengths of the relationship between the various variables may be relatively weak (Harrison, Mullen, & Green, 1992). The health belief model has been utilized in various studies to investigate the association between the different variables in the model to predicting preventive health behaviours. Example studies include: explaining screening behaviour for colorectal cancer among older women (Hay et al., 2003), predicting coronary heart disease preventive behaviours among women (Ali, 2002), predicting non-compliance with anti-psychotic medication among patients with schizophrenia (Perkins, 2002) and predicting condom use among teenagers in Scotland (Abraham, Sheeran, Spears, & Adams, 1992).

Although the health belief model has been widely used and supported, there are a number of weaknesses (Morrison & Bennet, 2009; Stroebe, 2000), which include:

- Different versions of the health belief model have been utilized in studies, with varying questionnaires used. The variables of motivation and cues to action have not always been included in studies using the health belief model.

- The relationships between the variables in the model have not been explicitly specified. Most research has assumed that the relationship is additive, and thus the belief in a personal threat can be high if the one component variable is high, even if the other variables are low. Thus, for example, in the case of a severe disease like Ebola, the perceived severity for this disease is very high, but the perceived susceptibility is very low (unless you live in countries such as Sudan or the Democratic Republic of Congo which have seen outbreaks of Ebola in the past few decades). The reality is that there is a low personal threat for Ebola, but the health belief model suggests that the perceived personal threat will be high.
- The model is a static model that suggests that the various beliefs occur simultaneously and an assessment is made on that basis at one time. Thus the model does not take into account the potential for gradual or dynamic changes in beliefs.
- The model fails to include a number of other important determinants of health behaviour. The model does not take into consideration that there may be perceived positive aspects of 'unhealthy' behaviours, such as the enjoyment of taking drugs or smoking. Other health behaviours may be related to factors unrelated to health, for example working out at the gym in order to have a toned body that is considered attractive, thus the motivation may be to look good.
- The model fails to consider potential barriers to health behaviours, such as self-efficacy and perceived control of one's behaviour, and social influences and norms. The variable related to perceived barriers in the health belief model refers more to the costs of engaging in a health behaviour. For example, the use of condoms is beneficial in that it protects against sexually transmitted diseases, but the barrier to condom use is that it reduces enjoyment during sex.
- The model does not consider that one's behaviour may be influenced by one's intentions, and not only one's health beliefs.

3.2.2 THE THEORY OF REASONED ACTION AND THE THEORY OF PLANNED BEHAVIOUR

The theory of reasoned action was first developed by Ajzen and Fishbein (1980). The model makes the assumption that people's behaviours are goal-directed and involve rational decisions to behave. According to this model, behaviour is linked to the intention to behave, which in turn is linked to attitudes towards the behaviour and subjective norms. The individual's attitudes are a result of beliefs about participating in specific behaviours and their evaluation of the possible outcomes of the behaviour. Subjective norms are a function of the individual's beliefs about how significant others expect them to behave, and their motivation to comply with these expectations. Thus the model links behaviour with attitude and wider social influences (see Figure 3.2 for these components within the theory of planned behaviour model). Eagly and Chaiken (1993) point out how the theory of reasoned action (as the term suggests) assumes that people will "behave as they intend to behave" (p. 173) in a manner that allows them to obtain positive outcomes and meet the expectation of significant others.

The model highlights the need to focus on changing people's intentions to behave; intentions which are influenced by individual attitudes and subjective norms. Therefore interventions need also to target these areas. For example, campaigns to promote the use of condoms as a protection against sexually-transmitted diseases would involve focusing on changing people's attitudes about condoms, and social norms about condoms, so that this in turn influences an individual's intention to change their behaviour. Making condoms 'sexy' and acceptable and not a cause for embarrassment has been an important aspect of HIV prevention. The importance of individual attitude or subjective norms will vary between the behaviours in question. Stroebe (2000) uses the examples from research on breast-feeding and on abortion, where decisions about breast-feeding or bottle-feeding is more influenced by individual attitudes rather than subjective norms (Manstead, Proffitt, & Smart, 1983) and decisions about whether or not to have an abortion are more influenced by social norms (Smetana & Adler, 1979). Thus whether to target individual attitudes or whether to target subjective norms will depend on the behaviour change in focus.

Numerous studies have supported the model of reasoned action for predicting health-related behaviours (see Eagly & Chaiken, 1993). However, a review of the model of planned behaviour (Armitage & Connor, 2001), which is a later development of the theory of reasoned action (see below), suggests that subjective norms are a weak predictor of behaviour, in part due to the difficulty in defining and measuring subjective norms. The theory of reasoned action has been criticized for not taking into consideration the individual's sense of control over their actions. Intention to behave depends on whether or not the individual feels that they are able to act. Thus behaviour depends on whether or not behaviours are under the volitional control of the individual (Eagly & Chaiken, 1993). For example, a woman may hold the motivation and intention to use condoms during sex, but the use of condoms for safe sex is often not under the control of the woman, but rather the man. An individual's control over their actions may also be dependent on the level of skill such actions require and the resources available to them. Eagly and Chaiken observe how studies that support the model involve behaviours that typically do not require much skill or resources.

These criticisms led Ajzen (1991) to modify the theory of reasoned action, and consequently developed the theory of planned behaviour. The theory of planned behaviour is the same as the theory of reasoned action, but includes the component of perceived control as a factor influencing an individual's intention to change behaviour (see Figure 3.2). Perceived control has an

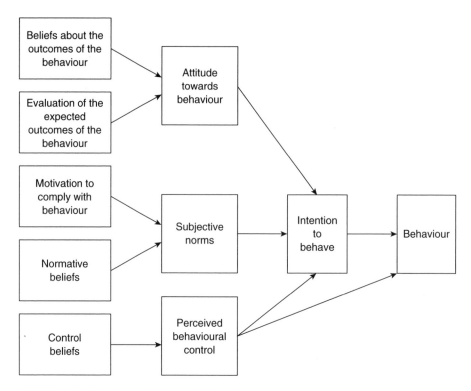

FIGURE 3.2　The theory of planned behaviour

indirect affect on behaviour through its affect on intentions, but can also at times have a direct affect on behaviour. According to Ajzen (1991), perceived behavioural control can be influenced by both internal and external factors. Internal factors are factors within the individual, such as skills, abilities and will-power. These factors can also be influenced by past experiences, for example a person may know from past experiences that he or she has little will-power to keep exercising. Internal factors thus include self-efficacy, the confidence one has in one's own ability to perform a task. External factors include dependence on others and opportunities to perform a behaviour. So, for example, a person may have the intention to go to a class at gym straight after work, but this would be dependent on whether the boss allows them to leave work a little early or not in order to make the class.

A review of studies utilizing the theory of planned behaviour (Armitage & Conner, 2001) lends support to the model and the importance of perceived behavioural control as a mediating factor on intentions to behave. Later critics have suggested the addition of other important factors, such as moral norms and anticipated affect (Conner & Armitage, 1998). The theory of planned behaviour has been frequently used in studies on health-related issues. For example, the theory of planned behaviour has been utilized in studies predicting healthy eating (Conner, Norman, & Bell, 2002), binge-drinking (Johnston & White, 2003), condom use (Albarracín, Johnson, Fishbein, & Muellerleile, 2001) and exercise behaviour (Armitage, 2005). The theory of planned behaviour has also been used in studies on mental health topics. For example, O'Connor and Armitage (2003) used an extended theory of planned behaviour (including moral norms and anticipated affect as additional factors) to understanding parasuicide behaviour. They found that the theory of planned behaviour was useful in predicting parasuicide behaviours when comparing a sample of participants with a history of parasuicide behaviours with a sample without a history of parasuicide behaviour.

The theory of reasoned action and theory of planned behaviour have been criticized for not taking into consideration other important factors that contribute to an individual's intention and motivation to change their behaviours. Some of these criticisms have been discussed above in relation to the theory of reasoned action, which is also relevant to the theory of planned behaviour. Other criticisms that have been made include the importance of past behaviours in determining an individual's intention to change behaviour (e.g. Ouellette & Wood, 1998). For example, Bentler and Speckart (1979) found that previous history of taking alcohol or drugs predicted the likelihood of intention to perform these behaviours again in future. Sarafino (2006) further argues that attitudes and intentions to act and actual behaviour are "only moderately related" (p. 152), citing a study by Stacy and colleagues (1994) that show that attitudes predict some behaviours (marijuana use and alcohol use), but not others (smoking, binge-eating and drunk driving). Eagly and Chaiken (1993) also observe how the theory of reasoned action (and thus the theory of planned behaviour) assumes the *reasonableness* of action, which does not capture behaviours that may be considered unreasonable, such as criminal behaviour, that may be influenced by other factors, such as personality and poverty. In this sense, the two models do not account for an individual's sense of moral obligation.

3.2.3 CRITIQUING THE COGNITIVE-BEHAVIOURAL MODELS OF HEALTH

The above models (health belief model, theory of reasoned action and theory of planned behaviour) are social cognition models that focus on behaviours as governed and mediated by cognitive processes. They assume that attitudes and beliefs are major determinants of behaviour. Attitudes can be defined as a tendency to negatively or positively evaluate an object towards which the attitude is directed (Eagly & Chaiken, 1993). Positive or negative evaluations can be directed at any object (e.g. medication or condoms), behaviour (e.g. exercise or smoking), person (e.g. nurses or doctors), or even abstract ideas and concepts (e.g. religion). Attitudes involve a cognitive (thought) component, an affective (feeling) component, and a behavioural component. For example, a person with a negative attitude about dentists, will have negative thoughts about going to the dentist ("It is going to hurt") as well as negative affect (e.g. fear). He or she may have avoidant behaviour about going to the dentist, which completes his or her negative attitude. Attitudes are related to beliefs that we have about the attitude object. Furthermore, the models assume a process of rationale reasoning that individuals engage in making decisions regarding health-related behaviours. According to these models, people make evaluations about the consequences of their behaviours and whether or not then to engage in the behaviour. This evaluation and subsequent action can be made through conscious reflection or by means of more automatic procedural choices. Thus, the emphasis in the models of health behaviour is on factors within the individual, most notably cognitive and behavioural. Although some of the models of health behaviours do include 'social' factors, these are generally considered from a social cognitive approach, which refers to how external information is processed by the *individual*. The emphasis is thus on individual cognitive processes (thoughts, attitudes, beliefs and perceptions) as learned or influenced by the social environment (usually significant others). Thus the 'social' in these models refers to such things as *perceived* social norms, *perceived* control of one's own behaviour, or knowledge gained from others. This greater focus on factors within the individual has been criticized for not taking due account of the broader social, economic, political and cultural context in which the individual is placed.

The cognitive-behavioural models of health behaviour have been extensively researched, and considerable evidence has been found to support these models. These models have proved useful and important in considering how individual behaviours may be understood and influenced to change. However, these models have received considerable criticism. We have reviewed some of the specific criticisms of particular models earlier. But criticisms have been made of the cognitive-behavioural models collectively. Some of these shall be explored further now in terms of methodological weaknesses, their assumptions of the individual rational decision maker, the emphasis on the individual level over factors at the social level, and the laying of responsibility on the individual. The challenges faced in addressing the HIV epidemic, more than any other public health problem, offers a significant critique of the cognitive-behavioural models, and so I will draw predominantly on this literature.

Methodological weaknesses

The various variables in the models and ways of measuring the different variables have not always been clearly defined. These criticisms have been made in relation to the various variables and the relationships between them in the health belief model, as well as for the variables in the theory of reasoned action and theory of planned behaviour (particularly the variable of subjective norms). Ogden (2003) argues how many studies purporting to support the cognitive-behavioural models of health do not always have an adequate construct of all the variables in the model, and leave a large portion of the variance in the outcome behaviour unaccounted for. Ogden further argues that the use of questionnaire instruments to measure the different variables (e.g. attitude) in the studies may lead to a change in cognitions and behaviour rather than accurately measure the way the participant thinks. Darker and French (2009) asked research participants to reflect out-loud their thoughts while completing a theory of planned behaviour questionnaire, and found that participants had numerous problems in interpreting questions related to normative aspects in particular, for instance questions about subjective norms, normative beliefs and motivation to comply. For example, participants found it difficult to respond to questions about subjective norms because of the variability in the perceived subjective norms of others. Furthermore, they found that participants made answers that were inferred or based on plausibility rather than based on actual knowledge, and in some cases chose answers in the middle of a series of options in an effort to provide *an* answer.

While research has found support for these models in that the variables measured in studies have been found to predict behaviours, the models have not been very successful in changing behaviours, as seen by how difficult it is to get people to adhere to healthy lifestyles. Campbell (2003) argues that these models offer insight into which individual cognitive factors are related to health behaviours but do not adequately provide guidance on how to change these cognitive factors. Considerable effort has been made in promoting condom use as an HIV prevention strategy, yet many people continue to not use condoms, as evident by remaining high prevalence of HIV globally and other sexually-transmitted diseases. While individual cognitive factors may predict individual condom use within an experimental situation, it has remained difficult to change behaviours at a population level.

Assumption of the individual as rational decision maker

The models make the assumption that behaviour change involves a process of rational decision making on the part of the individual. The models assume that if the individual is equipped with the necessary knowledge, that they will compute that knowledge, weigh up the options, and make the decision to change behaviour in a rational way. And 'incorrect' decision would be regarded as irrational. Some people may make a 'rational' decision for engaging in a health-risk behaviour, for example smoking as a method of relaxation during a stressful time. For example, Flowers and colleagues (1997) explored gay men's understandings and decisions around unsafe sex in the context of relationships, and found how many gay men participating in their study made calculated choices to have sex without a condom with their partners as indicative of a deepening romantic relationship. Sex with a condom was more readily practised with casual sex partners, but when a relationship was developing to a higher level of commitment, having sex without a condom was a carefully considered act that demonstrated love and commitment (see Box 7.1 for a description of this study).

The models also do not take into account the emotional components of decision making. Individuals may engage in risk behaviours, but may create rationales for considering themselves not at risk in a manner that is defensive against risk to the self. Joffe (1999) draws on psychoanalytic theory and social representations theory to argue how individuals may position themselves in relation to constructions of risk in an attempt to defend against threats to the self. Joffe uses the HIV epidemic and social representations of HIV and AIDS to illustrate her argument. Social representations refer to the shared explanations that people have for a phenomenon. Since the emergence of HIV in the early 1980s, a number of representations have been made of HIV and AIDS that draw on metaphors of sin, deviancy and punishment (Sontag, 1991). Joffe argues that with serious diseases such as HIV, individuals fear their body becoming invaded and polluted by viruses. With such intense fears and threat to personal health and safety, individuals need to "draw a distinction between 'us' and 'them'" (Joffe, 1999: 23). With HIV this distinction was made from the start, with HIV being associated with what Treichler (1999) refers to as the "4-H list": homosexuals, Haitians, heroin addicts and haemophiliacs. HIV was seen to affect certain risks groups, rather than the general population. We still refer to risk groups in relation to HIV, with risk groups now being expanded to include African migrants, for example (see Chapter 7 for further discussion of this). Treichler (1999) argues that the construction of risk-groups, "contributed to the view that the major risk factor in acquiring AIDS is being a particular kind of person rather than doing particular things" (p. 20). She goes on to argue that such representations of HIV and AIDS are fuelled by existing divisions in society:

> The reproduction in AIDS discourse of existing social divisions appears to be virtually universal, whether it is white or black AIDS, gay or straight AIDS, European or African AIDS, wet or hot AIDS, East or West German AIDS, central or west African AIDS, foreign or native AIDS, or guilty or innocent AIDS. (p. 116)

Joffe (1999) uses psychoanalytic theory to argue that people draw on these social representations to distinguish between 'us' and 'them' as a defensive mechanism. In relation to perception of HIV risk, we tend to split off 'bad' aspects of ourselves (deviant, sexual, dirty) onto others, who then come to represent those affected by HIV/AIDS. Joffe (1999) shows how representations of AIDS are constructed as being a disease originating from the 'Other'; it is represented as being foreign and affecting outsiders. It is also associated with deviant and perverse practices. Representing AIDS as a disease that affects 'others', functions as a defence against the anxiety and fear of being at risk for infection. Thus HIV/AIDS is seen as affecting 'others' and 'not me'.

This can be illustrated by taking the study by Woodcock and colleagues (1992) as an example. They explored perceptions of HIV risk in a qualitative study of 16–25 year-olds. The study is useful in demonstrating how the variable of risk perception used in cognitive-behavioural models of health is a lot more complex than what a questionnaire is able to measure. Woodcock and colleagues found how many of the participants denied that their behaviour had placed themselves at risk, by minimizing the severity of HIV or their susceptibility to it. Participants gave reasons for why they felt their behaviour did not place them at risk for HIV, which included the perception that HIV was not something that would happen to them, that they were not in a high-risk group or high-prevalence area, and that their partners (and themselves) were faithful and not promiscuous. Reasons given thus related to perceived invulnerability to HIV. This perception of risk may be underlined by unconscious emotional aspects.

Emphasis on the individual level over factors at the social level

The greatest criticism made against cognitive-behavioural models of health is the emphasis on the individual as the focus of analysis. Campbell (2003) has argued that because of this emphasis on the individual, the cognitive-behavioural models are limited in explaining complex behaviours. She argues that the models' emphasis is on proximal determinants of individual behaviours, such as cognitions, knowledge, motivation and intentions, but that the models fail to show how these proximal determinants are influenced or even shaped by contextual realities. Mann and colleagues (1992) have similarly argued that the focus on the individual, although necessary for considering individual behavioural risk, is not sufficient as it does not account for how such individual behaviours may be "both mutable and societally connected" (p. 578). Individual behaviours are influenced and shaped by societal factors at the community, national and international level. Tomlinson and colleagues (2010) have argued that behaviours that reduce risk for HIV are "only partly volitional and are often governed by larger structural issues that may, to various degrees, be resistant to change" (p. 973). What is highlighted is the importance of the social and structural factors that shape individual behaviour. Social factors may include neighbourhood conditions, social support, social relationships, gender relationships, family systems and so forth. Structural issues refer to broader forms of social structures, such as economic, legal and political systems. These structural factors may act as facilitators or barriers to individual behaviour and activity (Shriver, Everett, & Morin, 2000). Some structural factors may *influence* behaviour which can be changed relatively easily, for example laws and policies around smoking and drinking, and the availability of tobacco and alcohol products. Cohen and colleagues (2000) refer to many such structural factors, identifying four categories of structural factors: (1) the accessibility of consumer products that can be either beneficial or harmful to health; (2) physical (including product) structures that either increase or decrease opportunities for health protective behaviours and outcomes; (3) social structures in the form of laws or policies that facilitate or prohibit behaviours that influence health; and (4) media that influences cultural norms. Other structural factors may *shape* behaviours, and require extensive and multi-level change.

Farmer (2004), a medical anthropologist, refers to the notion of 'structural violence' when considering structural factors that facilitate or act as barriers to health. He argues that disease in certain parts of the world, for example AIDS in Haiti, needs to be understood in relation to the historical, political and economic structures in which the disease is embedded. 'Structural violence' is a term coined by Galtung (1969) to refer to large-scale social injustice which can be considered violent, but which does not have an identifiable actor. Galtung (1969) differentiates between direct or personal violence, where there is an actor committing a violent act on a subject, and indirect or structural violence, where there is no such identifiable actor. Structural violence are thus oppressive forces that are "built into the structure" (Galtung, 1969: 171), which create power imbalances and social injustices, thus placing groups of individuals in positions of vulnerability and risk. Such structures are violent because they are harmful to people. Farmer and colleagues (2006) define structural violence as the "social structures – economic, political, legal, religious, and cultural – that stop individuals, groups, and societies from reaching their full potential" (p. 1686). These structures also determine who becomes ill, and who is able to access health care services.

Tomlinson and colleagues (2010) suggest that structural factors are particularly significant in poorer countries, where the social, economic and political realities of inequality, low income and poor resources may be more constraining on individual behaviours. This shall be explored in Chapter 5, which looks at poverty and inequality and its relation to health and physical and mental health problems. The remaining chapters in this book explore other social and structural factors that influence and shape individual health and illness (culture, gender and sexuality). For now, let's briefly consider some of the structural factors that play a role in HIV risk behaviour.

An individual level of knowledge about HIV risk and prevention may be shaped by access to such information through the availability of radios for the transmission and reception of HIV prevention messages, and access to health care services (Mann, Tarantola, & Netter, 1992). This may be affected by the countries' ability to provide such resources, which is determined by global economic and political forces. For example, MacDonald (2005) highlights the failure of facilitating access to affordable antiretroviral (ARV) treatment to the millions of people in Africa dying of AIDS. The United States of America was heavily criticized for stalling attempts by the World Trade Organization to relax pharmaceutical patents in order that poorer African countries might have access to cheaper, generic antiretroviral treatment (see, for example, Dyer, 2004). Antiretroviral treatments were available to the majority of HIV-positive persons in developed countries many years before ARVs were available to persons in Africa. ARVs reduce the viral load in the blood. Thus, lack of ARV treatment and the resulting high levels of viral load increase the risk for the onward transmission of HIV. Furthermore, with poorer health care in sub-Saharan Africa, other sexually-transmitted infections remain untreated, increasing the risk for HIV infection (Fleming & Wasserheit, 1999). Poku

(2005) argues how development policies of global financial institutions such as the International Monetary Fund and the World Bank may have negative consequences for individual health in poor countries. He provides the example of how Kenya was advised to introduce a small service user fee for attendees at sexual health clinics, as a measure for encouraging market-led development rather than state-led development. After a nominal service user fee of $2.15 was introduced, attendance fell by 35–60% (Poku, 2005: 43). The result is that sexually-transmitted diseases go untreated, increasing the risk for HIV transmission. These issues need to be considered in the historical context of colonialism and exploitation of Africa, and post-colonial conflict, political instability and resulting economic decline (Poku, 2005).

As the above suggests, poverty is a key structural determinant of HIV risk. Tomlinson and colleagues (2010) explore the relation between poverty, food insecurity and HIV risk. There are different relational paths that this can take. Poverty may create food insecurity for individuals, families and communities. Inadequate availability of food results in poor nutrition and consequent impaired immunity. This increases vulnerability to disease, including HIV. Persons who are already HIV-positive may have a faster deterioration in health and progression to AIDS. Women may be particularly at risk in such contexts. A woman living in poverty and struggling to provide food for her children may engage in transactional sex as a survival strategy (Gillespie, 2006; Weiser et al., 2007). For example, in a study of sex workers in Nigeria, 35% of participants reported that they had decided to engage in sex work as a result of poverty and food insecurity (Oyefara, 2007).

Tomlinson and colleagues (2010) emphasize the importance of structural factors in the context of HIV/AIDS in concluding that safe sex "is only marginally an issue of individual choice or reasoned action in a context within which risky sexual encounters that are detrimental in the long term may constitute the only available means of gaining access in the short term to food and money, and to avoiding physical abuse" (p. 978). The theory of planned behaviour considers social factors that might influence individual behaviours. However, as mentioned earlier, the theory of planned behaviour takes a cognitive approach by conceptualizing these social variables as control *beliefs* and *perceived* behavioural control. This emphasizes a cognitive process on the part of the individual, and does not capture the sorts of social and structural forces that shape behaviour, as mentioned above.

We can likewise consider structural factors that influence health behaviours of people with disabilities. For people with disability, structural barriers to health care may be a significant problem. For example, for persons with physical disabilities, access to health care may be prevented by facilities that are not accessible for wheelchair users, and medical equipment that is not designed for persons with disabilities (Becker, Stuifbergen, & Tinkle, 1997). Persons with disabilities are also more likely to have lower levels of education and employment, and are more likely to live in poverty than persons without disabilities (Elwan, 1999). This may be a structural barrier to health where a disabled person may struggle to cover the cost of transport in order to access health care services, and the cost of medical care itself (Smith, Murray, Yousafzai, & Kasonkas, 2004). A lack of money was one of the reasons reported by caregivers of disabled children for under-utilizing available services in South Africa (Saloojee, Phohole, Saloojee, & Ijsselmuiden, 2007). The relationship between poverty and transactional sex is also an issue for people with disabilities. Poverty may lead some women with disabilities to turn to prostitution as a means to survive, increasing their risk for sexually-transmitted diseases and HIV infection (Smith et al., 2004). Income inequality also places people with disabilities at risk in countries that we would consider to be wealthy. For example, McCarthy (1993) highlights the practice of exchange of sex for money and other material goods in the experiences of women with learning disabilities in institutional settings in England. The barriers faced by people with disabilities in relation to sexual health are explored further in Chapter 7.

Laying the responsibility on the individual

The cognitive-behavioural approach implies that responsibility for health rests with the individual, as a result of his or her decisions and his or her behaviours. The result can be that the individual is blamed and held responsible for their illness. The emphasis made on lifestyle choices (as mediated by attitudes, motivations and intentions), overemphasizes the role of the individual, making them partly responsible for becoming ill or contracting a disease (Davison & Davey Smith, 1995). Galvin (2002) refers to the notion of 'behavioural culpability' as the belief that individuals can make a choice to adopt healthy behaviours and so avoid illness. Persons who fall ill become culpable in that they did not 'choose' health.

Crawford (2006) uses the term 'healthism' to describe a moralizing of the health state. Health is the personal responsibility of the individual, and health is something that must be achieved if one wants to be considered a good citizen. Those who are ill can be held responsible for their ill-health and marginalized as inferior citizens. This can be seen, for example, with regards HIV, where people who contract HIV are held responsible for their illness, are blamed and othered (Crawford, 1994; Petros, Airhihenbuwa, Simbayi, Ramlagan, & Brown, 2006). Many mental health problems are also attributed to the individual, for example patients suffering eating disorders or substance use disorders are often perceived by the lay public as being to blame for their condition (Crisp, Gelder, Rix, Meltzer, & Rowlands, 2000). In this way, medicine and its promotion and moralizing of health behaviours and practices has become a form of institutionalized social control. Crawford links this with neoliberalism (see Box 5.3), where an individual, having personal responsibility for one's health, has the freedom to choose appropriate health resources. This overemphasis on the individual not only simplifies the role of disease aetiology (Davison & Davey-Smith, 1995), but also does not lay sufficient 'responsibility' for the conditions of inequality or poor health resources in which individuals may find themselves.

ECOLOGICAL SYSTEMS THEORY

3.3 Bronfenbrenner's (1972, 1977) Ecological Systems Theory may provide a useful theoretical framework for understanding the role of social and structural factors in health. The Ecological Systems Theory describes four levels of environmental influence (or 'ecologies'), of increasing distance from the individual, that shape and affect behaviour. Bronfenbrenner (1972, 1977) referred to these as: (1) the *microsystem*, which is the immediate environment to the person, which may include the family, peer groups and the immediate occupational environment; (2) the *mesosystem*, which refers to connections between the immediate environmental system, forming an intermediate level of influence, which may include interactions between family members, peers, as well as interactive settings such as the church or workplace; (3) the *exosystem*, which extends the mesosystem and refers to external environments, in which the individual may not be immediately located but which have an indirect influence on them, such as the neighbourhood, the transport system and the health care system; and (4) the *macrosystem*, which refers to the larger social, cultural, economic and political context. Each system has different rules and norms that exert an influence on the individual. The model suggests that changes made in one system or environment will impact on and lead to changes in other systems. This model is usually conceptualized as a series of concentric circles (see Figure 3.3).

Although first conceptualized as a model of human development, it has been very influential and is frequently utilized in public health and by health psychologists as a model for understanding the social and structural issues in health promotion (Stephens, 2008), and has been important in community health psychology for "understanding the 'person-in-context'" (Cornish, 2004: 283). This model enables researchers to consider the broader social and environmental influences on health and health behaviours, and the social and structural factors that facilitate or prohibit health behaviours in a community. Cornish (2004) points out that a strength of the model is that it concretizes the social environment in terms of specific relationships, rather than the social environment being "abstract or remote" (p. 283), as is the case in the biopsychosocial model. Rather than attempting to change individual behaviours, the model provides a framework for facilitating change at a community level, making changes to social structures and social interactions that impact on and lead to changes in other systems, and thus it facilitates health-enhancing or protective behaviours. For example, Faith and colleagues (2007) considered an ecological systems model in reviewing evidence for interventions at the macro-level for addressing obesity in the population, specifically restrictions on access to certain kinds of foods. DiClemente and colleagues (2008) consider the various psychosocial predictors of HIV risk at the level of the individual, the family, the peer group, relationships, and society. The model has also been utilized in clinical psychology, for example to understand the various factors in multiple ecological systems that contribute to the enduring prevalence of post-traumatic stress disorder (PTSD) symptoms following a natural disaster (Weems & Overstreet, 2008; Weems et al., 2010), and investigating the role of

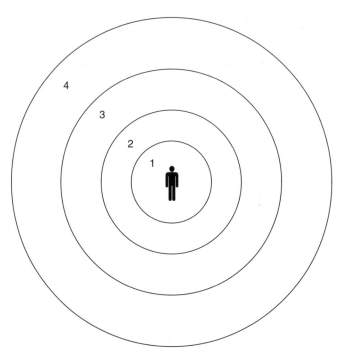

1. Microsystem (e.g. family)
2. Mesosystem (e.g. workplace relationships)
3. Exosystem (e.g. health care system)
4. Macrosystem (e.g. culture)

FIGURE 3.3 The ecological systems theory

family and peer support and community connectedness as protective factors for adolescent suicidality in depression (Matlin, Molock, & Tebes, 2011).

COMMUNITY AND STRUCTURAL INTERVENTIONS

3.4 Interventions that focus on changing individual behaviours do little to address the social and structural conditions that cause ill-health. Health promotion programmes that have as their aim changes to the social and environmental structures that influence health are referred to as structural interventions (Blankenship, Friedman, Dworkin & Mantel, 2006). If we take HIV and poverty and food insecurity as an example, structural interventions would seek to alleviate conditions of poverty and food insecurity that facilitate risk for HIV. Tomlinson and colleagues (2010) identify various structural interventions that have been used to address the problem of food insecurity. For example, often children, especially girls, are taken out of schools in order to contribute to child care and income generation (Bennett, 2003). Thus school-based structural interventions, such as eliminating school fees and school feeding programmes, have health outcome benefits as they facilitate increased enrolment at school, which raises the level of education, providing skills for later income generation, provides the opportunity for health education, and empowers girls. For example, eliminating school fees to promote the increased enrolment of girls in schools improves self-regulation and social-regulation and has been found to increase condom use (Greig & Koopman, 2003). School feeding programmes have been found to lead to increased school enrolment (Bundy, 2005). Farmer Fields and Life Skills Schools for male and female children living without parents (e.g. children orphaned by AIDS) include educational components in life skills, gender relationships and healthy living, with training in agricultural skills, thus aiming to address the long-term health and economic consequences of children living without parents (Drimie, 2006). Basic income grants and disability grants for people living with HIV/AIDS are a structural intervention that provides a source of income where there is none, thus alleviating food insecurity. Such interventions, of course, are dependent on the country's economic resources.

Community-level interventions aim to promote health through collective action, involving community participation and community empowerment. Members of the community are actively involved in identifying the most important health issues and identifying changes that can be made collectively that enable and support behaviour change. Such an approach is opposed to change as driven by 'expert' service providers, favouring a more collaborative approach with a diverse range of community members who hold differing levels of power (Lyons & Chamberlain, 2006). Community approaches to health are often strengthened by a multi-disciplinary approach, which introduces theorizing on social issues from a range of disciplines (Stephens, 2008). Community-level approaches have formed an important part of the response to HIV worldwide. In community-level HIV prevention work, peer-led HIV prevention education has offered a means of combating community resistance to 'expert' opinion. For example, in the early years of the HIV epidemic in San Francisco, the closing of bath houses and messages of abstinence and condom use was met with initial resistance from sectors of the gay community, who interpreted such interventions as oppressive of homosexual liberties (Shilts, 1987). Only with the active participation of the gay community and peer-led interventions could change be brought about. In South Africa, sex workers in an impoverished mining town were empowered to engage in peer-led HIV prevention education among sex workers and mineworkers (Campbell, 2003, 2004). This project aimed to empower women by placing health prevention knowledge in their hands rather than in the hands of experts. It further aimed to encourage social cohesion and consciousness among the community.

Campbell (2003) argues that health psychology has generally provided theoretical and academic contributions to HIV prevention, rather than informing its actual practice. She argues that HIV prevention practice needs to involve approaches that encourage community participation that aims to promote community environments that are health-enabling. Campbell and colleagues (2009) suggest the development of 'AIDS competent communities', which are defined as communities in which members work collaboratively and in support of one another to change the social factors that facilitate or create risk for HIV, which might, for example, include dialogue to reduce HIV stigma, promote safe-sex behaviours among community members, and provide support for HIV-positive community members. These are changes that are identified and brought about by the community themselves, rather than being imposed by outside 'experts'. An example of a community-level and structural intervention for HIV/AIDS is presented in Box 3.1. This involves a multi-level participatory project to promote HIV/AIDS prevention in Siem Reap, a town in Cambodia, situated next to the major tourist site of the Angkor Wat temple. This was an area in Cambodia identified as having a high prevalence of HIV, with a reported 10,000 HIV-positive individuals in a population of just 140,000. The project has elements of participatory, community-led interventions as well as structural interventions. The project is formalized as a non-governmental organisation, known as the Siem Reap Citizens for Health, Educational and Social Issues (SiRCHESI) (see www.angkorwatngo.com).

BOX 3.1

A Spotlight on Research: The SiRCHESI HIV prevention project in Cambodia

Lubek, I., et al. (2002). Collaboratively confronting the current Cambodian HIV/AIDS crisis in Siem Reap: A cross-disciplinary, cross-cultural 'participatory action research' project in consultative, community health change. *Asian Psychologist, 3*(1), 21–28.

Lee, H., et al. (2010). Creating new career pathways to reduce poverty, illiteracy and health risks, while transforming and empowering Cambodian women's lives. *Journal of Health Psychology, 15*(7), 982–992.

Aims: In the town of Siem Reap, near the world-famous tourist site of the Angkor Wat Temple complex in Cambodia, a partnership between academic researchers, health professionals, local citizens, government agencies and non-governmental organizations was formed to collaboratively address the high HIV and sexually-transmitted infection (STI) prevalence rates. There is a reported high number of sex tourists coming to the area each year. These tourists often drink heavily and engage in unprotected sex with sex workers in brothels in the area. Local drinking businesses employ 'beer promotion' women, who are typically underpaid by the international beer companies, are encouraged or even coerced to drink with their customers, and often end up engaging in sex without a condom in exchange for money. A multi-disciplinary, collaborative project was started in order to address the health crisis in this area. The aims of the project were to reduce the incidence of HIV and STIs in the area, and to address the various social inequalities (such as employment and poverty) that fuelled the HIV epidemic.

Methods and interventions: The project utilized the methods of participatory action research. In an initial exploratory study with citizens of Siem Reap, the problems and issues were highlighted and the need for change identified. The citizens (sex workers, beer promotion girls and other local citizens) formed an organization (SiRCHESI), and in partnership with researchers and various stakeholders, aimed to identify the health and social problems in the area, and develop action steps and interventions for change (see Chapter 8 for description of participatory action research). The project included a number of interventions, such as:

1 HIV prevention peer education among sex workers and beer promotion women.
2 Advocacy work with local industries and international companies to improve the working environments of the beer promotion women (for example, advocating for higher wages, prohibiting the coercion of beer promotion women to drink at work, and advocating for businesses to participate in health promotion campaigns.
3 Education and skill development to provide opportunities for the women to find alternative employment. For example, a Hotel Apprenticeship Programme, which provided training in hospitality for beer promotion women, for employment in hotels, and thus safer, healthier work environments.
4 Literacy programmes to improve employability.

Results: The project involves continuous research and data collection in order to evaluate outcomes. Data suggests there have been improvements in the level of HIV knowledge, condom use, reduced alcohol consumption, and increased literacy. Data from behavioural surveys and HIV testing suggest that the HIV incidence rates in the area have decreased since 2001 (Stephens, 2008). Challenges still faced are that of creating sustainable changes and longer-term structural changes on the part of businesses and international companies which continue to operate a profitable business.

Conclusion: This project provides an excellent example of multi-level health promotion that focuses not only on individual factors (e.g. HIV knowledge, condom use), but also on social (e.g. citizen cohesion) and structural (e.g. employment and poverty) factors. Thus, in addition to the traditional HIV-prevention education work, a significant part of the project involves social change, changing the conditions in which high HIV-risk behaviours take place. The success of the project has been in part due to its multi-level, multi-disciplinary partnership, and the 'ownership' of aspects of the project by those who will benefit from it (most notably the beer promotion women). While the project has some important successes, the limitations are the sustainability of the project (although it has been successfully running for some time), which requires considerable resources and input.

Community health psychology arose out of a concern that mainstream health psychology has remained largely silent in its contribution to understanding and addressing health inequalities (Campbell & Murray, 2004). Campbell and Murray argue that although mainstream health psychology has provided an important contribution to understanding individual, behavioural determinants of health, which have been rigorously researched, it has fallen short in translating this knowledge to addressing health inequalities in complex, real-world set-tings. Community health psychology is not only concerned with understanding the social context of health, but is also concerned with facilitating social action and social change. As articulated by Murray and colleagues (2004), community health psychology "begins with an understanding of the social and political dimensions of health and illness and then develops a research and intervention strategy based upon building the strength of the community and challenging the various means of social oppression" (Murray, Nelson, Poland, Maticka-Tyndale, & Ferris, 2004: 331).

While this chapter has tended to focus on health psychology, and the discussion above has been on community health psychology, the importance of considering social and structural factors is also significant for mental health. Family therapists, and feminist family therapists and feminist clinical psychologists, have long recognized the importance of family relationships and gender inequalities in understanding and addressing mental health problems. Community psychology in relation to mental health has been important in considering broader social and political inequalities as factors influencing mental health. For example, Kirmayer, Simpson and Cargo (2003) review literature on social and structural factors influencing mental health among Canadian Aboriginal people, which suggest that the history of oppression has contributed to the increased prevalence of mental health problems among Canadian Aboriginal communities. They go on to review research that suggests the importance of promoting community cohesion and identity and political empowerment for improving mental health. In South Africa, the importance of contextual factors (such as poverty, racism and inequality) has been recognized as an important focus for mental health work, with mental health services benefiting from community partnerships and involvement (Swartz, Gibson, & Gelman, 2002). Participatory community interventions for mental health have included programmes facilitating the development of businesses owned by users of psychiatric services, so as to increase access to employment and income, which is a protective factor for mental health (e.g. Church, 1997). An ambitious preventative community-based project for child mental health is the Better Beginnings, Better Futures project in Canada (Pancer & Foxall, 1998; Peters et al., 2004). The project has been running for over 25 years in eight different communities and involves considerable community participation. The programme includes interventions to assist parents (e.g. home visitors, parent training, play groups), the children (e.g. classroom programmes) and the community (e.g. creating safer parks and streets). The programme documented improvements in health in the home environment (for example, reduced smoking among parents) as well as improved health and school performance among the children, and consequent reduction in prevalence of emotional and behavioural problems among the children of the various communities involved.

In the UK there has also been a growing emphasis on service user involvement in the training of clinical psychologists and the planning of services (Mitchell & Purtell, 2009). Clinical psychologists can also make an important contribution in consulting with and supporting people engaged in community-level programmes, which are often demanding and stressful (Mitchell & Purtell, 2009; see Swartz, Gibson, & Gelman, 2002 for examples of consultative work in the South African context).

Community and structural-level approaches to health interventions do have their limitations. First, the very notion of 'community' is complex and contested, and not easy to define (Nelson & Prilleltensky, 2005). Individuals belong to varying communities, not only geographical ones, but also ones based on identity or membership, and members may construct a community identity in order to define their group identity in contrast to others (Colombo & Senatore, 2005). Thus 'communities' are not homogeneous and may include various 'sub-communities'. More problematically, the term 'community' has often been used to refer to groups of people who are marginalized and disempowered, and in this context 'the community' is referred to as a collection of people for whom charitable deeds should be done (Thornton & Ramphele, 1988). In health psychology, the term 'community' often refers to community as a geographical place (Stephens, 2007), which is often chosen, for practical reasons, over communities of identity (Campbell & Murray, 2004). Stephens (2007) cautions that health psychologists should be more reflective of their constructions and representations of community, because how a particular community is represented may serve to privilege who is included and may reproduce power imbalances by who is excluded. Secondly, it is not always easy to evaluate and quantify outcome data, as changes may occur gradually over time, and results can only be seen after some time has past. For example, in HIV prevention programmes, quantifiable outcome data in the form of reduced HIV incidence rates will only occur after some time has passed. This makes such projects difficult to fund and to keep sustainable, and thus they are often marginalized in health research (Daykin & Naidoo, 1995).

SUMMARY

3.5 As we have seen from the previous chapter and this chapter, although the influence of broader social and cultural factors has been recognized as playing an important role in health and ill-health, most of health and clinical psychology tends to focus on factors in close proximity to the individual, most notably his or her behaviour and lifestyle choices, which may be shaped by such social influences as peer pressure or social demographics as a variable. It is perhaps more of a challenge for psychologists to step out from the immediate environment to consider broader social, structural and political environments, as this moves us on to a multi-disciplinary arena and out of our comfort zone. But as Tomlinson and colleagues (2010) argue in relation to health psychology, for psychology to make an important contribution to addressing global concerns, such as poverty and global health disparities, we need to move away from a focus on the individual and extend ourselves to a wider arena.

FURTHER READINGS

Campbell, C. (2003). *'Letting them die': Why HIV/ AIDS prevention programs fail*. Bloomington, IN: Indiana University Press. This book presents the work of a community-level intervention for HIV/AIDS in a mining community in South Africa. The book provides a critical discussion of traditional HIV-prevention programmes, offering a critique of cognitive-behavioural models of health. Although the project on which this book is based on did not achieve significantly positive outcomes, the book nevertheless uses this 'failure' to analyse the factors important for the success of community-based interventions.

Stephens, C. (2008). *Health promotion: A psychosocial approach*. Maidenhead: Open University Press and McGraw-Hill. This book provides a critical approach to health promotion, with an emphasis on community health promotion. It provides a detailed theoretical framework for community health promotion as well as examples of practice.

Stroebe, W. (2000). *Social psychology and health* (2nd edition). Maidenhead: Open University Press. This book provides a social psychological perspective on health and provides a good outline of the cognitive-behavioural models of health discussed in this chapter.

CULTURE

4

INTRODUCTION

4.1

In 1851 Cartwright published a paper in the *New Orleans Medical and Surgical Journal* where he described what he understood to be some of the diseases particular to the "negro slaves" in the USA. In this paper he argued that the enslavement of African men and women was beneficial to their physical and mental health. For example, he wrote of the African slaves:

> their organization of mind is such, that even if they had their liberty, they have not the industry, the moral virtue, the courage and vigilance to maintain it, but would relapse into barbarism, or into slavery, as they have done in Hayti [*sic*]. The reason for this is founded in unalterable physiological laws. Under the compulsive power of the white man, they are made able to labour or exercise, which makes the lungs perform the duty of vitalizing the blood more perfectly than is done when they are left free to indulge in idleness. It is the red, vital blood, sent to the brain, that liberates their mind when under the white man's control; and it is the want of a sufficiency of red vital blood, that chains their mind to ignorance and barbarism, when in freedom. (Cartwright, 1981 [1851]: 30)

Psychology has a shameful history of what has been termed 'scientific racism', where many studies, observing, for example, differences in performance on intelligence tests, formed the basis of evolutionist arguments distinguishing 'primitive man' (African) from 'civilized man' (European) (Richards, 1997). It is more widely acknowledged that the concept of 'race' is not grounded on biological differences, but rather that it is a socially constructed concept. Rather than such investigations of racial differences, more emphasis is placed on the role that cultural differences may have on human behaviour.

Two predominant approaches to understanding and investigating the role of culture in psychology have been: (1) transcultural research, which aims to investigate whether psychological phenomena occur across different cultures; and (2) cross-cultural research, which proposes that different psychological phenomena exist in separate cultural contexts (Swartz & Rohleder, 2008). This chapter will draw on both strands of work as well as more critical work which considers that any phenomenon can only be considered with reference to issues of diversity and context (Swartz & Rohleder, 2008). The chapter will refer to work from multiple disciplines, particularly disciplines of medical anthropology and cross-cultural psychiatry. Medical anthropology, as a discipline, has been an important contributor to thinking about culture and physical and mental health, as medical anthropology focuses on how clinical presentations and illness experiences are shaped by the cultural and social context in which they occur.

The chapter will first examine how culture may influence the experience of physical illness, by looking at cultural variations in the experience of cancer and pain as two examples. The chapter will then investigate culture and mental health, with a particular focus on cultural influences in the presentation of depression. The role of culture in disordered eating will be discussed, crossing the disciplines of clinical psychology and health psychology, looking at not only eating disorders themselves, but also the role of culture and body image and its influence on disordered eating. The chapter shall then take a brief look at culture and disability, although, as stated in Chapter 1, issues of disability are relevant for physical and mental ill-health. Finally, the chapter will look at culture and health care, focusing on health care as a cultural system and culturally competent health care.

4.1.1 DEFINING CULTURE, RACE AND ETHNICITY

Before proceeding, however, it is important to briefly define some concepts that shall be used in this chapter. First, in work related to culture, reference is often made to the 'western' and the 'non-western' world, or 'western' cultures and 'non-western' or 'eastern' cultures. These are somewhat arbitrary and socially constructed terms, which have historical roots in differentiating European, and Christian, civilization from Asia (prior to the discovery of the Americas). With reference to culture or society generally, 'the west' or 'western cultures' refer to cultures and societies which have origins with European cultures, and where Christianity plays a dominant role. These cultures include the cultures of Europe, North and South America, Australia and New Zealand. 'Eastern cultures' refers to cultures of Asia. The term 'non-western' cultures, as the term suggests, refers to all cultures that are not derived from European, Christian cultures, and include the 'eastern' cultures of Asia, as well as African cultures and indigenous cultures such as native-Americans, the aboriginal peoples of Australia, and the Maori of Polynesia and New Zealand.

Secondly, when discussing issues of culture, two overlapping concepts are that of 'ethnicity' and 'race'. These terms are often used interchangeably. I shall be making reference to all three, but it is worth differentiating what is meant by these terms. Helman (2007a), writing from a medical anthropology perspective, defines 'culture' as "an inherited 'lens' through which individuals perceive and understand the world that they inhabit and learn how to live within it" (p. 13). Helman uses the term "inherited 'lens'" as he refers to culture as a set of guidelines that are transmitted from one generation to another within a certain group of people, by means of its rituals, symbols and language. These guidelines inform the members of that group how to perceive and experience the world and how to behave in it. 'Race' is a term which has historically been used to refer to what are thought to be biological differences which were regarded as distinguishing groups of people. Physical and genetic features, such as texture of the hair, shape of the eyes, colour of the skin, were historically used to classify people as Caucasoid (white), Mongoloid (Asian) and Negroid (black) (Eshun & Gurung, 2009). However, the notion of race as being biologically determined has been generally dismissed (Smedley & Smedley, 2005), and there is an increased recognition that the notion of 'race' is a social construction. We continue to use the term 'race' as a classification to easily describe people and as a reference to identity (Eshun & Gurung, 2009), such as in referring to 'white American' and 'black American'. The term 'ethnicity' is used to refer to a group of people who may share a common ancestry and have similar cultural and physical attributes, such as language, religion, social rituals and norms, values and beliefs (Eshun & Gurung, 2009). Culture, then, is a component of ethnicity. Smedley and Smedley (2005) provide a simple definition for ethnicity as referring to "clusters of people who have common culture traits that they distinguish from those of other people" (p. 17). I shall generally be referring to culture when discussing cultural variations in health and illness, unless studies cited have used the term 'ethnicity' or 'race'.

DIMENSIONS OF CULTURE

4.2 One way in which we can examine differences between cultures is by exploring psychological dimensions that are shared and endorsed by a cultural group, which may differ from the psychological dimensions shared and endorsed by another cultural group. One of the most frequently cited and most influential studies exploring dimensions of culture is that of Hofstede (1984), who identified different dimensions of culture from analysing results of a survey study conducted in 40 different countries measuring differences in social action and manner of thinking about the social world. Hofstede argues that people develop 'mental programs' from childhood, which contain aspects of the culture in which the person is born, and is expressed most clearly by the different values and expectations that people (and nations) hold. Hofstede conducted a survey questionnaire using participants recruited from 40 national subsidiaries of a large multinational business organization. The survey was conducted twice, in 1968 and 1972, and produced 116,000 completed questionnaires. His statistical analysis tried to identify underlying patterns for the whole sample. From his analysis, he identified four different dimensions of culture based on predominant values that were held: power distance; uncertainty avoidance; collectivism–individualism; and femininity–masculinity (see Box 4.1).

BOX 4.1

Hofstede's Dimensions of Culture

Hoftsede (1984) identified four main dimension of culture against which different societies can be compared:

Power distance: This dimension is concerned with how inequality is understood and managed in a society. Hofstede distinguished between two poles in a continuum of low power distance and high power distance. In low power distance, inequality between members of a hierarchy is minimized and there is a greater degree of interdependence. In high power distance, there is a clearer and expected distance between people of different ranks, and there is a greater degree of dependence relationships.

Uncertainty avoidance: This dimension is concerned with how people (and societies) manage the uncertainty of the future. Hofstede argued that people are made anxious about uncertainty and unknown situations, and have a need for predictability in order to minimize this anxiety. Hofstede distinguished between two poles in a continuum of high uncertainty avoidance and low uncertainty avoidance. In high uncertainty avoidance cultures, people tend to be more worried about the future, and so are attracted to strict rules of behaviour, structure, loyalty and truthfulness. There is a fear of failure and less risk-taking. Individuals tend to have higher levels of stress, are more aggressive and more emotionally expressive, and are more intolerant of deviance. In low uncertainty avoidance cultures, there is a greater acceptance of change and personal risk, lower levels of stress and aggression, and relative tolerance.

Collectivism–individualism: This dimension "describes the relationship between the individual and the collectivity which prevails in a given society" (Hofstede, 1984: 148). In this dimension, 'collectivism' refers to societies which hold values of strong social cohesion and integration between members of a group. In collectivist cultures there is a strong sense of loyalty to members of the group, and members are protected by the group. In contrast, 'individualism' refers to societies in which there are loose ties between individuals, and individuals are expected to be responsible for looking after themselves and their own family. Thus this dimension refers to the extent to which you exist and behave as a member of a social group or as an individual. This dimension has received considerable attention in social psychology with regards cultural influences on sense of self, and has often been cited when referring to 'collectivist cultures' (often referring to 'eastern' cultures such as in China and Japan) and 'individualist cultures' (often referring to 'western' cultures such as the UK and the USA).

Femininity–masculinity: This dimension is concerned with differences between the sexes and how this is managed in a given society. Although the two poles of the dimension are referred to as 'masculine' cultures and 'feminine' cultures, Hofstede used the dimension of masculinity as denoting degree of difference between sex roles. A society with high masculinity demonstrates the greatest distinction between the roles of men and women. In high masculinity cultures there is greater emphasis on competitive performance, with the rewarding of success. A society with low masculinity (or 'feminine' societies) has less distinction between sex roles, with more degree of overlap. Low masculinity societies also have a lower emphasis on competition and reward for trying to be better than others.

Hofstede's study, although highly influential, has also been widely criticized (see, for example, McSweeney, 2002) as being too simplistic, and for ignoring or obscuring differences that exist within cultures, and equating 'nations' with 'cultures' (which is problematic given that we live in multicultural societies). However, Hofstede's dimensions of culture have been useful in exploring differences in phenomena between different cultures, including differences in health and illness.

4.2.1 DIMENSION OF CULTURE AND VARIATIONS IN HEALTH AND ILLNESS

Bond (1991) examines differences in cultural values and their association to differences in physical health. Bond explored variation in values between 23 different countries, and simplified this variation statistically into two key dimensions, each having a continuum ranging between two poles. These two dimensions are 'social integration'–'cultural inwardness', and 'reputation'–'morality'.

In the first dimension, 'social integration' refers to the cohesion between groups of people, where there is a value of tolerance towards others and a sense of harmony with others. Other values held are trustworthiness and non-competitiveness, patience and persistence. On the other end of this dimension is 'cultural inwardness', where there are values of cultural exclusivity and superiority, and observed cultural rites and rituals. Bond observed that there were statistical associations between holding values of 'social integration' and problems with the digestive system (such as ulcers of the stomach and neoplasms of the digestive system). There was also increased association with incidences of cerebrovascular disease. There were no significant associations with these diseases and the holding of values of 'cultural inwardness'. Thus it would seem that 'cultural inwardness' is associated with better health than 'social integration'.

In the second dimension, 'reputation' refers to protecting your dignity (not losing 'face'), the possession of wealth and the exchange of gifts and favours. 'Morality' refers to a sense of righteousness and keeping oneself pure. MacLachlan (2006b) conceptualizes this dimension as "appearing good" – "behaving good" (p. 135). The dimension of 'reputation'–'morality' is also associated with differences in diseases. Bond found that the dimension pole of 'reputation' was significantly associated with ischaemic heart disease and heart attacks (myocardial infarction). It was also significantly associated with neoplasms of the digestive system (as with the dimension pole of 'social integration') and the respiratory system (lungs, trachea and bronchi). The dimension pole of 'morality' was significantly associated with cirrhosis of the liver.

These differences also remained when the influence of income (measured as gross domestic product (GDP) per capita) was controlled for. This suggests, then, that some of the variations in diseases can be accounted for by cultural differences. However, it is not clear why these different cultural dimensions are associated with particular diseases.

As suggested earlier, one must be cautious in taking such averaged statistical findings based on broad, large-scale surveys as indicative of actual general differences between cultural groups. Such studies provide stereotypical norms in a given culture and ignore variations within that culture. It would be false to assume that *all* people from the UK have values that suggest 'individualism', for example, so it would be inaccurate to describe the UK as only an 'individualist culture' or Japan as only a 'collectivist culture'. It would also be inaccurate to assume that individual members have a definitive cultural identity. As MacLachlan (2006b) states, "each person represents an amalgam of differing cultural experiences, to which they may give more or less credence than others do" (p. 59). Thus there are variations in the identity and cultural experiences among members of a specific 'cultural group'. However, findings from such studies are useful as they provide some evidence that suggests that differences between cultural groups do exist and, for our purposes, that suggests that culture differences are related to differences in health and illness.

Variations in health and illness are not only accounted for by cultural differences. Other factors may be associated with variations in prevalence of diseases between different societies or groups of people, which are not related to cultural factors. For example, there may be genetically transmitted diseases that are concentrated in certain cultural groups. One such disease is sickle-cell anaemia, which causes reduced supply of oxygen to vital organs in the body, resulting in possible organ failure and brain damage. Sickle-cell anaemia is genetically transmitted via a recessive gene. When two people who have this recessive gene have a child, the child could develop sickle-cell anaemia. The frequency of the disease is highest among people of sub-Saharan Africa, Western Africa, India, Saudi Arabia and Mediterranean countries (World Health Organization, 2006b). Immigrants from these areas will have a higher prevalence rate of the disease than the local population. The disease, however, is linked with geographical origin rather than culture, ethnicity or race (Williams, Lavizzo-Mourey, & Warren, 1994).

CULTURE AND ILLNESS EXPERIENCE

4.3

Culture also plays a role in how people from different cultural groups may have differing experiences and understandings of the same illness. Different cultures may have different explanations for the experience of a disease or illness. Two areas that have received some attention are cultural variations in the incidence of and beliefs about cancer, and cultural variations in the experience and expression of pain.

4.3.1 CANCER

Cancer is a leading cause of death worldwide. Given the varieties of cancer and its widespread prevalence, it is difficult to think that there may be cultural variations in the incidence of cancer. Yet, research has shown that there are variations in the incidence of cancer and variations in types of cancer between cultural groups.

Meyerowitz and colleagues (1998) conducted research in the USA which aimed to explore any links between ethnicity and cancer-related outcomes. They analysed data from the USA National Institute of Health's statistics on racial and ethnic patterns of cancer from 1988 to 1992. They reported the ethnic breakdown for the incidence of different types of cancer, which demonstrated clear, large differences in cancer incidence between different ethnic groups. The researchers found that African Americans had the highest incidence rates for cancer overall, and had higher mortality rates for cancer than whites. Hispanics had relatively low incidence rates of cancer overall, except for high rates of cervical cancer. Similarly, Asian groups (Japanese and Chinese) had low incidence rates for all types of cancer, except stomach cancer. Native Americans have low rates of cancer, while Native Hawaiians have high rates of cancer. The highest rates of five-year survival are for Japanese. Thus cultural differences exist in the type of cancer and its prognosis. Meyerowitz and colleagues further analysed confounding variables related to these ethnic differences in cancer. Included in the conceptualization of ethnicity was status as a minority and consequent socio-economic status. Minority status was associated with lower socio-economic status, which in turn was associated with poorer access to health care. This affects behaviours that affect outcome, such as going for screening tests, adhering to medical treatment and attending follow-up appointments. Thus an important issue here is that much of the overall differences regarding cancer-related outcomes can be accounted for by socio-economic inequality, rather than culture. As Chapter 5 explores, there is a very clear and consistent relationship between socio-economic status and health. It is also often the case that people living in lower socio-economic areas in a country have a minority status as people from a different culture or ethnic background from the majority population.

Where culture perhaps has a greater influence is on people's understanding of the cause and meaning of cancer. Kleinman (1980) used the term 'explanatory model' to refer to the process by which an illness may be understood, interpreted and treated. Explanatory models of illness are held by the professional practitioner as well as the patient (sometimes referred to as 'lay belief'). Dein (2004) reviewed varieties of explanatory models of the causes of cancer in different regions in the world – ethnic minorities in USA and Canada, Africa, Asia, Australia, and the UK. Dein observed a wide variety of explanatory models which differed from metaphysical or spiritual beliefs of cancer, interpersonal explanations and physical or biomedical explanations. Metaphysical or spiritual beliefs of cancer were found in studies from Asia and among some ethnic minorities in USA and Canada (Dein, 2004; Kohli & Dalal, 1998). For example, spiritual causal explanations of cancer were found by Kohli and Dalal (1998) among Hindu women in India who were being treated for cervical cancer. Most attributed the cause of cancer to spiritual beliefs – as being God's will or as a result of karma (punishment as a result of past actions). This belief was also associated with a fatalistic attitude towards cancer as being 'out of their control'. A more recent study from Australia (Shahid, Finn, Bessarab, & Thompson, 2009) also found high degrees of fatalism and associations of cancer with spiritual causes among Aboriginal peoples. In this study, some participants understood cancer as a result of a curse and a spiritual punishment for misdeeds done to others in the past. For many, this resulted in a sense of fatalism about the cancer, with beliefs of cancer being deserved and there being little that can be done about it. This sense of fatalism about the cause and prognosis of cancer has implications for seeking treatment, with individuals delaying or not seeking treatment as the belief is that cancer inevitably leads to death.

Sontag (1991), a philosopher and literary critic, observes how there are particular metaphors that are associated with cancer in western society. Sontag observes that cancer is often considered to be a disease of repression, where the cancer sufferer is characterized as having suppressed and repressed their emotions over many years. Eventually a malignant growth emerges as a result of the repressed emotional energy. Thus associations are made between cancer and psychological character, rather than biomedical causes. Sontag also discusses metaphors of cancer as an 'evil force', a disease that is 'uncontrollable' and 'unrestrained'. She observes how public health discourse often uses metaphors such as the 'war' on cancer, accentuating the metaphor of cancer as an evil force.

4.3.2 PAIN

Pain is perhaps the most common symptom that is presented in clinical practice. There are different types and intensities of pain, which may be a feature of various diseases, as well as injuries and even normal physiological processes, such as menstruation and childbirth. We have all experienced pain in some form or another, and I am sure we have all also observed and made comments about how some people can tolerate more or less pain that others. Helman (2007b) differentiates between 'private pain' and 'public pain'. Private pain, as the name suggest, is the individual's subjective experience of pain, which is unknown to others. Pain that results from within rather than from an injury is 'more' private, in the sense that the cause of pain cannot be observed by others. Public pain is when we signal the experience of pain to others through our pain behaviours, which includes facial and bodily expressions as well as verbal expressions. The extent to which we may keep our pain experience private, and the way in which we may make it public, may be influenced by a variety of factors, including cultural factors.

There has been considerable interest in research exploring cultural and ethnic differences in experience of pain. One important early study was that by Lipton and Marbach (1984), who conducted a study exploring ethnic differences in pain, using a sample from a facial pain clinic in New York. They randomly selected 50 patients attending the clinic, from the five prominent ethnic groups that the clinic served (Black, Irish, Italian, Jewish and Puerto Rican). Participating patients were asked to complete a detailed questionnaire that measured their health-seeking behaviour, their physical experience of pain, the cognitive and emotional aspects of their pain experience, and how their pain interferes will daily functioning. No significant differences were found for two-thirds of the items on the questionnaire, items related to patients' responses, attitudes and descriptions of pain. For example, they did not differ in the degree to which they experienced their pain as 'burning like fire' or 'stabbing or sharp'. Significant differences were found for some description of the quality and intensity of the pain, with differences in pain being experienced as 'a dull ache' or as 'very severe, almost unbearable'. There were also differences in the emotional reaction to pain, with Puerto Rican patients reporting 'losing control' when describing their pain to others, black patients being more likely to think there is no use complaining about their pain and just trying to bear it, and Irish, Italian and Jewish patients being more likely to try hide their pain when they were with friends and family. Differences were also found in the extent to which pain interferes with appetite and ability to work.

Other more recent studies have similarly found cultural differences in the experience of pain. In a study of 1,557 chronic pain patients in USA, Riley and colleagues (2002), found that African American patients reported significantly higher levels of pain unpleasantness and emotional response to pain (depression and fear) than white American patients. However, there were no significant differences in the reported intensity of pain. In a retrospective analysis study of 3,669 white and African American adults with chronic pain, Green, Baker, Sato, Washington, and Smith (2003) found that African American patients with chronic pain reported more pain and sleep disturbances than white Americans, as well as more psychological distress (depression, post-traumatic stress symptoms) associated with pain. The two studies above compared African Americas with white Americans. However, Chang (2009) compares literature on pain among various cultural and ethnic groups in the USA, and found differences in the expression of pain between Native Americans, Mexican Americans, Arab Americans, Elders, Irish-Americans, Jewish and Italian-Americans. Such ethnic differences in pain perception, assessment and treatment are found for acute pain, cancer pain, chronic non-malignant pain and experimental pain (Green, Anderson, Baker, Campbell, Decker, Fillingim, et al., 2003).

One of the few studies that explore cultural variations of pain in the UK (Palmer, Macfarlane, Afzal, Esmail, Silman, & Lunt, 2007) looked at the issue of acculturation and differences in reported musculoskeletal pain among three South Asian groups (people of Indian, Pakistani and Bangladeshi origin) and a European UK group. The study found that widespread pain was more commonly reported by South Asian patients. Some of this difference may be influenced by rate of acculturation, with the greater the extent of acculturation being associated with lower prevalence of reported widespread pain. In a qualitative study (Patel, Peacock, Mckinley, Clark-Carter, & Watson, 2008) of GP experiences of managing chronic pain patients of South Asian origin living in the UK, GPs reported greater challenges in treating patients of South Asian origin (particularly first-generation), whom they reported as presenting more frequently and expressed pain as being more widespread and thus difficult to localize. Many GPs felt that in many cases the pain was psychosomatic. The participating GPs reported that people of second- and third-generation South Asian origin presented similarly to white British patients, suggesting that the presentation of pain may be influenced by degree of acculturation.

It is not clear why there are cultural and ethnic variations in the experience of pain. It is also important to note that these variations are not general and absolute. There is variation *within* cultural and ethnic groups. The experience of pain, and the expression of that experience, may be influenced by cultural or religious norms about what is considered to be normal ways of expressing pain experiences. Helman (2007b) refers to a cultural "language of distress" (p. 189). Different cultures and groups have different ways of expressing suffering and distress to others, whether it is physical or emotional pain. Some cultures value a stoic, restrained expression of distress and suffering (think, for example, of the stereotyped British 'stiff upper lip'), whereas other cultures value an extravagant, overt display of suffering. For example, Zola (1966) studied differences in reactions to pain in a sample of 63 Italian-Americans and 81 Irish-Americans recruited from medical clinics of a Massachusetts hospital. Zola observed how the responses of Italian-Americans were more expressive and expansive than the responses of Irish-Americans, who tended to underplay or ignore their symptoms. Lipton and Marbach (1984) found that there were different 'triggers' for patients' pain experience, with different factors being associated with experience of pain in different groups. Black patients, who had a greater degree of dependency on non-professionals when sick, had a higher expressive and emotional response to pain, and higher levels of interference with daily functioning. Among Irish patients, longstanding friendships with other Irish people were related to non-emotional expression to pain, and a greater reporting of interference with daily functioning. For Italian patients, the length of time that they experienced pain was associated with their response to pain, with chronic pain being associated with a greater emotional and expressive response to pain and interference with daily functioning. For Jewish patients, the higher the level of psychological distress, the greater the emotional and expressive pain response and interference with daily functioning. For Puerto Rican patients, emotional expression of pain and interference with daily function were associated with high levels of psychological distress, longstanding friendships with other Puerto Ricans, dependency on non-professionals when sick, and chronic pain.

Such research suggests that while different cultural groups may experience similar intensity of pain (although some studies do observe differences – for example, Sheffield, Biles, Orom, Maixner, David, & Sheps, 2000) most differences are in the response and expression of pain. This has implications for health care in pain, where clinicians need to be aware of how patients from different cultural groups may express pain in different ways, ranging from stoic expressions of pain, to loud exclamations of pain (Ondeck, 2003). Similarly, as discussed earlier, varying cultural or ethnic beliefs and understandings of cancer and its cause may influence how individuals may seek treatment or the attitudes taken towards treatment (particularly if there is a high sense of fatalism). Up till now the focus has been on physical health. There is a vast amount of literature that has also focused on cross-cultural aspects of mental health, to which we now briefly turn.

CULTURE AND MENTAL HEALTH

4.4

In the medical model of mental ill-health, psychiatric disorders are seen to be universally prevalent, and the symptoms of particular mental disorders are observed across cultures. However, considerable literature exploring cross-cultural variations in mental health observes that differences exist in how emotional distress may be expressed and what symptoms are considered to be normal or abnormal and in which context. A relativist position (as apposed to a universalist position) would argue that how mental ill-health is expressed is relative to the social-cultural context. At issue are differences in what is conceived as 'normality' and 'abnormality'.

For example, in psychiatry and clinical psychology, dissociative states are regarded as a symptom of a number of disorders, such as dissociation related to trauma and dissociative identity disorder. Dissociation is defined as a disturbance or break in the usual functions of consciousness, perception, memory or identity (APA, 2000). However, dissociative states or states of altered consciousness are common features of trance and possession phenomena, which exist as part of shamanic rituals or Christian exorcism practices (Odenwald, van Duijl, & Schmitt, 2007), and are common in many cultures around the world, including western cultures. Such dissociative states would thus be considered non-pathological in socio-cultural contexts in which dissociative phenomena are considered to be part of normal experiences. However, research does suggest that experiences of possession in many cultures are often preceded by periods of stress (see Odenwald et al., 2007). Thus the cultural beliefs in which the experience occurs may inform how the psychological effects of stress may be experienced as spirit possession or as dissociative trauma states. The

DSM-IV, in an effort to take into account non-pathological dissociative states, stipulates that a diagnosis of dissociative or possessive trance disorders may be classified under 'dissociative disorders not otherwise specified', when the trance state is involuntary and not acceptable as part of a normal cultural or religious ritual. The importance is thus whether the behaviour or experience is culturally sanctioned or not. This requires an assessment of the cultural context in which the 'symptom' occurs.

Similarly, hallucinations are regarded as a symptom of serious mental health problems, such as schizophrenia and other psychotic disorders. A person hearing voices or seeing people that are not present in reality would typically be considered as having an abnormal experience by the psychiatrist or clinical psychologist. However, as is the case with dissociative trance states, hearing the voices of one's ancestors or seeing visions may be considered 'normal' experiences in shamanic rituals. Swartz (1998) provides a South African case study example of a Xhosa man, called 'John', suffering from a variety of physical and mental symptoms, including what western psychiatry would term 'auditory hallucinations'. John claimed to be hearing messages sent to him by Jesus, and hearing voices instructing him to slaughter a cow in order to prevent harm happening to other people. Such auditory hallucinations could be indicative of a serious mental health problem. However, in this case, John's mother claimed that John was hearing the voices of his ancestors, which was a (normal) sign that the ancestors were calling him to train to become a traditional healer. In Xhosa culture, *ukuthwasa* refers to "the state of emotional turmoil a person goes through on the path to becoming an indigenous healer" (Swartz, 1998: 165). *Ukuthwasa* is a positive (although emotionally turbulent) state that arises as a result of the person's ancestors calling him or her to become a traditional healer.

I have referred above to mental health symptoms characteristic of metal disorders classified as universally prevalent (dissociative identity disorder or schizophrenia), but cultural differences in mental health can also be explored by means of mental disorders that may be found in particular cultures and not in others, what has been termed 'culture-bound syndromes'.

4.4.1 CULTURE-BOUND SYNDROMES

Culture-bound syndromes are a group of disorders or illnesses that are unique to particular cultures or groups of people. Each disorder represents a cluster of symptoms and behaviours which are recognized by the members of the socio-cultural group in which it occurs (Helman, 2007b). The DSM-IV includes an appendix of 25 culture-bound syndromes (Box 4.2 lists some examples), which it defines as:

> recurrent, locality-specific patterns of aberrant behaviour and troubling experience that may or may not be linked to a particular DSM-IV diagnostic category. Many of these patterns are indigenously considered to be 'illnesses', or at least afflictions, and most have local names. Although presentations conforming to the major DSM-IV categories

can be found throughout the world, the particular symptoms, course, and social response are very often influenced by local cultural factors. In contrast, culture-bound syndromes are generally limited to specific societies or culture areas and are localized, folk, diagnostic categories that frame coherent meanings for certain repetitive, patterned, and troubling sets of experiences and observations. (APA, 2000: 898)

Although the DSM acknowledges that there may be some links with the major diagnostic categories, the culture-bound syndromes have symptom presentations that are unique to specific cultural contexts.

BOX 4.2

Some Examples of Culture-bound Syndromes

Amok is a syndrome described in Malaysia and Indonesia in which a person breaks out into a sudden and unprovoked episode of indiscriminate destructive, violent or homicidal behaviour, followed by fatigue or amnesia, and in many cases ending in suicide. It may be accompanied by persecutory ideas.

Dhat is a syndrome described in India and Taiwan, involving somatic complaints and anxiety related to fear of semen loss in men as well as women (who are also thought to secrete semen).

Koro is a syndrome described in South-East Asia, China and India, where a person presents with an acute panic reaction involving fear that their genitals will suddenly retract into their bodies, resulting in possible death. The onset is sudden and rapid.

Latah is a syndrome described in Indonesia and Malaysia involving a highly exaggerated response to a trauma or fright. The response is followed by echopraxia, echolalia, or a dissociative trance state.

Nervios is the Spanish name given to a syndrome described in South America and Mexico, but similarly described in Egypt, Northern Europe and Greece. The syndrome is characterized by often chronic episodes of extreme sadness, sorrow or anxiety, which induce various somatic complaints such as headaches, nausea, insomnia, fatigue and agitation.

Rootwork is a set of cultural interpretations that ascribe the cause of illness to witchcraft, sorcery, spells or the evil influences of another person. The 'hexed' person, may experience symptoms of anxiety and gastrointestinal complaints, dizziness and weakness, fear of being poisoned or being killed, until the 'root' of the spell has been eliminated. It is prevalent in the southern United States among African American populations and Caribbean societies.

Susto or *espanto* is described in Mexico, Central and South America, and involves an extreme fright, inducing 'soul loss'. Symptoms include agitation, fever, diarrhoea, mental confusion, depression and apathy.

Taijin kyofusho is a culturally distinctive phobia which is prevalent in Japan and resembles social phobia. An individual experiences intense fear that his or her body, parts of their body, or its functions, displeases or embarrasses or is offensive to other people whether by appearance, odour, movement or expression.

In addition to an appendix of culture-bound syndromes, the DSM-IV includes an appendix on making a 'cultural formulation' of a patient's presenting problem, which takes into account the role of the patient's culture in his or her explanation of their illness, the cultural factors related to the patient's environment and level of functioning, and the cultural elements of the practitioner–patient relationship.

Guarnaccia and Rogler (1999) applauded the inclusion of culture-bound syndromes in the DSM-IV, stating the importance of furthering knowledge in these syndromes for the purposes of improving mental health care in an increasingly cultural diverse (American) society. They further argue that by including culture-bound syndromes, the DSM extends its reach and usefulness as an 'international document'. However, there has also been considerable critique about the extent to which the DSM has included culturally-bound syndromes into its nomenclature of disorders. For example, Lloyd (2007) argues that the DSM-IV and ICD-10 are ethnocentric in listing only those conditions that do not occur in the cultural context of the authors (i.e. western cultures) as being culture-bound syndromes. An often discussed example is that of the eating disorders anorexia nervosa and bulimia nervosa, which are listed as a main diagnostic category but have often been argued as being a western culture-bound syndrome (see below for further discussion of this). Similarly, Lopez and Guarnaccia (2000) critique these diagnostic systems as having a western bias, and rendering culture-bound syndromes as 'exotic' by including them in an appendix, with little elaboration of assessment and diagnosis. They further argue that the DSM provides an incomplete discussion of the role that culture plays in the expression of psychopathology. The syndromes are merely described briefly, with no detailed diagnostic category provided, as is done with the 'main' disorders listed in the DSM. Swartz (1998) also observes how the classification of these culture-bound syndromes may be dependent on who is recording them, which may relate to the practices and interests of mental health professionals and anthropologists researching and writing about particular parts of the world. Furthermore, it has been argued that the concept of a culture-bound syndrome can be applied to all disease classifications, as all diseases have to exist within a cultural context. No syndrome can be culture-free (Lloyd, 2007).

Despite the inclusion of culture-bound syndromes in the DSM and in the ICD-10, few textbooks on clinical psychology include any detailed coverage of these. This accentuates a western bias and the marginalized status of such syndromes. Yet there are many important debates concerning culture-bound syndromes as being discrete syndromes or as variants of existing 'major' disorder categories. One much debated cross-cultural variant of distress is that of the varying presentations of depression.

4.4.2 CULTURE AND DEPRESSION

Depression is one of the leading causes of disease burden in the world (measured in disability adjusted life years (DALYs)), with an estimated 121 million people suffering depression worldwide (WHO, see www.who.int/mental_ health/management/depression/definition/en/). Depression is one the most commonly prevalent mental disorders. For example, in the UK, symptoms of depression and anxiety are the most common mental health problems, and are found to be prevalent in 15.1% of people surveyed nationally, with more than half of these presenting with mixed anxiety and depression (McManus, Meltzer, Brugha, Bebbington, & Jenkins, 2009).

The DSM-IV defines depression as a minimum two-week period of consistently low mood or loss of interest and pleasure in daily activities, accompanied by at least four additional symptoms from a list including change in appetite or weight, change in sleep behaviour, psychomotor agitation, loss of energy, concentration difficulties, feelings of guilt or worthlessness and suicidal thoughts (see Box 4.3 for DSM-IV-TR diagnostic criteria).

BOX 4.3

DSM-IV-TR Diagnostic Criteria for Depression

A. For a diagnosis of depression, the following symptoms must be present for at least a two-week period:

  1 Depressed mood or loss of interest or pleasure in daily activities

  Plus four or more of the following:

  2 Significant weight loss or weight gain not attributed to dieting; or increase or decrease in appetite
  3 Psychomotor agitation or retardation
  4 Insomnia or hypersomnia
  5 Loss of energy or fatigue
  6 Feelings of worthlessness or inappropriate or excessive guilt
  7 Difficulties concentrating
  8 Recurrent thoughts of death or suicide.

B. Symptoms cause significant distress or impairment in social or occupational functioning.
C. Symptoms are not due to a general medical condition or effects of a substance, or not better accounted for by bereavement.

(APA, 2000: 356)

The prevalence and incidence rate of depression varies across nations. The WHO World Mental Health Survey Consortium (Demyttenaere et al., 2004) reported 12-months prevalence rates of depression in 14 different nations ranging from low rates of 0.8% in Nigeria and 1.7% in Shanghai, China, to high rates of 8.5% in France and 9.6% in USA. Lower rates were reported in the countries surveyed in Asia and Africa as compared to countries in Europe and the Americas. A number of other studies similarly report variations in prevalence of depression between countries, with lower rates of depression typically reported in non-western countries (Eshun & Caldwell-Colbert, 2009). Some of these differences may be attributed to inconsistencies in epidemiological prevalence studies. Taking depression in countries in Africa as an example, Tomlinson and colleagues (2007) observe how there are limited epidemiological studies of depression in African countries. They further state how studies on depression often rely on standardized assessment measures that have been primarily validated for psychiatric patients in western countries, and may not be wholly translatable to other cultures. They observe how there are no equivalent terms for 'depression' in many African languages, and experiences of distress may be expressed in other forms, such as through somatic complaints. For example, research on depression in Zimbabwe (Patel, Abas, Broadhead, Todd, & Reeler, 2001) has found that somatic complaints, such as fatigue and headaches, are the most common presentation for depression. Most patients understood their illness as resulting from "thinking too much", an explanatory model also observed in Uganda (Okello & Ekblad, 2006). Swartz (1998), writing from South Africa, also observes how in the context of limited resources and facilities for psychiatric care, people with mental illness come to the attention of health care professionals when they present with behaviours that were causing problems for others. Thus, a person who may be unhappy, but causing little problems for others, may not be seen. Tomlinson and colleagues (2007) thus argue that depression in countries in Africa may be more common that previously thought.

According to the DSM criteria, a key symptom for diagnosing depression is the person's mood, expressed by a sad mood or loss of interest or pleasure. Frequently, depressive symptoms also include somatic complaints, such as headaches and other sorts of aches and pains. In fact, a majority of patients with common mental disorders (depression or anxiety) may present with physical complaints (Kroenke, 2003). A considerable body of research suggests that there is some cultural variability in how people experience depression and how it may present. Differences centre on whether depression manifests predominantly through mood symptoms, or predominantly through somatic symptoms. Draguns (1997) reviews cross-cultural studies on symptomatology of depression, which suggest that the vegetative symptoms of depression (sad mood, fatigue, lack of energy and tension) may be universal whereas the feelings of guilt may be related to cultural differences. Such studies find that non-westerners tend to report more somatic complaints whereas westerners reported additional feelings of guilt.

There has been considerable debate and research on this discrepancy between depression and mood and depression and somatization. Much of this research has focused on the differences in presentation of depression among Asian cultures, and on the differences between the DSM diagnosis of depression and the diagnosis of *shenjing shuairuo* (or neurasthenia). *Shenjing shuairuo* is a diagnosis included in the Chinese Classification of Mental Disorders and is included as a culture-bound syndrome in the DSM-IV. The disorder, prevalent in China, is characterized by various somatic complaints, including physical and mental fatigue, headaches, dizziness, pains, concentration difficulties, memory loss and sleep disturbances. Other symptoms include sexual dysfunction, gastrointestinal problems, irritability or excitability and other signs suggesting a disturbance of the autonomic nervous system (APA, 2000: 902). Some of these symptoms parallel symptoms of depression (such as fatigue, sleep disturbances, concentration difficulties, irritability).

Kleinman (1988) suggests that the way in which people experience distress (what he terms 'illness' as differentiated from 'disease') differs between cultures, and thus psychiatric disorders may differ in their presentation between and within cultures. For example, Kleinman (1982) makes the argument that major depression and *shenjing shuairuo* are similar. He bases this argument on his study that found that 87% of a sample of patients in China who had been diagnosed with *shenjing shuairuo* met the DSM criteria for major depression disorder, and furthermore responded well to antidepressant medications. Chang and colleagues (2005), however, argued that *shenjing shuairuo* has little to do with depression, but rather could be easily reclassified as a type of somatoform disorder according to DSM-IV classification. The arguments that are made here is that the neurasthenia and depression (or somatization) are two forms of expression of the same underlying disease. Shweder (1991) makes a criticism of favouring western disease concepts such as depression over neurasthenia, arguing that depression can just as reasonably be argued to be a form of neurasthenia (or *shenjing shuairuo*). Thus neurasthenia is the underlying disease and depression is an "emotionalized neurasthenia" (MacLachlan, 2006b: 97).

CULTURE, BODY IMAGE AND DISORDERED EATING

4.5

Eating disorders, particularly anorexia nervosa and bulimia nervosa, have been proposed as being culture-bound syndromes particular to western societies, and linked to western notions of beauty and the ideal body (for example, Prince, 1985; Swartz, 1985). Anorexia nervosa refers to a condition of self-starvation and refusal to maintain normal body weight. Bulimia nervosa refers to an illness characterized by recurrent episodes of binge eating followed by purging behaviours or fasting in an effort not to put on weight. Both disorders have significant implications for physical health as disordered eating may lead to inadequate nutrition.

Historically, eating disorders have been found to be most prevalent among white women living in western cultures (Wildes, Emery, & Simons, 2001). However, research has suggested that eating disorders are prevalent in many parts of the world, although the prevalence may be lower (Hood, Vander Wal,

& Gibbons, 2009). In a review of the research evidence on culture and eating disorder prevalence, Keel and Klump (2003) conclude that anorexia nervosa may not be considered a culture-bound syndrome, but that bulimia nervosa may be culture-bound. Keel and Klump suggest that access to food within given societies may determine the presence of binge eating. They further argue that while restricting food intake and self-starvation may have been present throughout various cultures, the associated obsessions with weight that are included as criteria in the DSM may be particular to western cultures.

A large number of studies have attempted to investigate the links between disordered eating with concerns about weight as related to western ideals of the female body image (this is discussed further in Chapter 6). For example, studies investigating changes in the weight and body mass index of *Playboy* centrefolds have shown that the average weight and body mass index of centrefolds have decreased over the past decades (Garner, Garfinkel, Schwartz, & Thompson, 1980; Voracek & Fisher, 2002). This thin ideal is not shared by all cultures. For example, Hispanic and African American cultures in the USA have been found to favour a larger, more curvaceous body size ideal (Crago, Shisslak, & Estes, 1996; Winkleby, Gardner, & Taylor, 1996).

Orbach (2009) argues that western society is increasingly becoming more body conscious, suggesting that we experience 'body anxiety' from early in our lives, as we are increasingly concerned with the shape, form, aesthetics and 'normality' of our bodies. This is transmitted to children by parents, among whom the first concerns are whether the new-born infant has all 10 fingers and 10 toes and that everything is anatomically correct. Orbach also observes how there has been a significant rise in cosmetic surgery as we seek bodily perfection. In the USA, approximately $1.3 million was spent on cosmetic surgery in 2000; a 225% increase since 1992. This increased further to $14 billion being spent on cosmetic surgery in 2007. Such concerns about the body also include concern about body shape and weight, with the slim body, particularly for women, being the ideal.

The increase in prevalence of eating disorders among non-western cultural groups has been argued to be due to cultural change, with western acculturation and resulting western ideals of body image increasing vulnerability for disordered eating (Miller & Pumariega, 2001). For example, in a prospective study comparing two samples of all ethnic Fijian school girls recruited at two secondary schools in an area of Fiji (Becker, Burwell, Gilman, Herzog, & Hamburg, 2002) found that the exposure of western media influenced the rate of disordered eating. In their study, 63 participants took part in the baseline study in 1995 one month after television had been introduced in the study area. The participants completed a questionnaire that included questions related to body image, binge eating and purging behaviours. A second study was conducted three years later on 65 participants. The researchers found that while the reported rate of binge eating had not significantly changed (although it decreased slightly), the percentage of participants who reported self-induced vomiting to control weight had increased significantly from 0% to 11.3% over the three-year period. These findings must be treated with some caution, as two different samples were used, and it appears that the questionnaire was modified for the 1998 study, so the two samples may not be comparable. However, the findings do suggest a change in attitudes, corresponding to the arrival of television media. Acculturation and vulnerability to eating disorders has also been researched within western societies. For example, in the UK, Bhugra and Bhui (2003) conducted a survey study with a sample of 266 teenagers at a multicultural school in east London. Results indicated higher rates of disordered eating among Asian respondents, which may be explained by excessive fasting being interpreted as being related to religious practices, rather than as a weight-loss practice. The researchers further found that bulimic eating behaviours may be associated with culture change. However, it was not clear whether disordered eating was associated with acculturation, or whether it was a result of trying to manage stress associated with being in a different culture. In a multicultural society, ethnic minorities may find themselves caught between two cultural ideals (see Box 4.4).

BOX 4.4

A Spotlight on Research: Culture, body image and weight

Gardner, K., Samsam, S., Leavey, C., & Porcellato, L. (2010). 'The perfect size': perceptions of and influences on body image and body size in young Somali women living in Liverpool: A qualitative study. *Diversity in Health and Care, 7*, 23–34.

Aims: The research literature suggests that adult Somalis living in western countries are likely to be overweight. Some of the reasons given for this include the cultural acceptability of larger body sizes as well as changes in diet. This study aimed to explore perceptions of body image and influences on body image among young Somali women living in Liverpool, UK.

Methods: The study adopted qualitative methods of data collection. A sample of 13 women between the ages of 18 and 28 were interviewed in small focus groups. During the focus groups, visual body silhouettes were used as prompts to initiate discussion about body size and body image, healthy bodies and diet. Two follow-up focus groups with eight of the original participants were conducted to discuss major themes that emerged from the first round of focus group interviews, as a means of gaining responded validation of the working analysis. The data were analysed using thematic content analysis, where quotes from the interview transcripts were selected and coded to emerging themes.

Results: Findings indicated that the participating Somali women wished to be a smaller body size, and described the perfect, healthy body size as slim but toned. The participants spoke about societal pressures to fit into perception of a thinner body size as ideal, and commented, for example, how jeans were made to fit smaller skinnier body shapes that their 'African', larger bodies did not comfortably fit into.

(Continued)

(Continued)

Participants spoke about being caught between the pressures of Somali culture, which favoured larger body sizes, and western culture, which favoured slimness. Most of the pressure came from older Somali women, and family and friends back in Somali, who viewed slimness as unhealthy and a sign of illness. One participant, who was slim, spoke about how upsetting it was to be criticized as being too skinny by older Somali women. Participants also spoke about Somali traditional diets and eating practices, which resulted in weight gain, and which western society considered in some cases to be unhealthy. The participants also spoke about their perception that these ideals are gradually changing in the migrant Somali community.

Conclusion: The authors highlight the position of young Somali women as caught between two competing cultures. They discuss this in relation to obesity and associated health problems such as diabetes. They conclude that there is an increasing awareness among young Somali women about the importance of a healthy diet and a healthy body weight, yet there remains pressure to conform to cultural ideals which favour a larger body size.

What this study is able to show, is how the participating Somali women negotiate, understand and make sense of issues related to health and body size in a context where they are caught between two competing cultural ideals. Using qualitative methods, the study is interested with the participants' subject experiences in a context of transformation or change (living in and adapting to a new culture).

Although not related to eating disorders, the issue of western cultural influence on body ideals is also evident through other body-related health issues. For example, Orbach (2009) also comments on the rise in cosmetic surgery in non-western cultures that suggests a preference for western body ideals, for example the insertion of a western, more rounded eyelid shape among Korean girls, or skin-bleaching among African Americans. This may suggest that western body ideals may influence perceptions of success and belonging in an increasingly globalized and multicultural world, with the western celebrity of television and films being increasingly seen as ideals.

CULTURE AND DISABILITY

4.6 People with disabilities are perceived as distinct in all societies, but different societies may have differing meanings and values associated with different types of disability (Groce, 2005). For example, people with visual impairments may be more socially included than those with mental health disabilities, as mental health problems may carry more associations with fear and stigma. The experience and understanding of disability may vary across cultures, as different understandings exist as to the cause of disability. As we have briefly observed earlier, different cultures hold different explanatory models about illness and disease. These obviously extend to explanatory beliefs about disability.

4.6.1 CAUSAL BELIEFS ABOUT DISABILITY

In many societies the birth of a child with a disability may be understood as divine punishment as a result of parental sin (Groce & Zola, 1993). Likewise, disability acquired later in life may be seen as a divine punishment for the breaking of some taboo on the part of the individual or the community. Disability may be seen as a curse from God or a god, and the person with disability may be approached with a sense of fear (e.g. Hanass-Hancock, 2009). In cultures with beliefs about reincarnation, disability may be seen as a punishment for wrong deeds committed in a previous life incarnation (Miles, 2002). For example, in interviews with South Asian parents of children with autism, Jegatheesan and colleagues (2010) reported how some parents held beliefs about reincarnation and karma in relation to their child's autism. For example, one woman in their study commented that she believed that because her son had autism this meant that he was on his "last rebirth" (Jegastheesan, Miller, & Fowler, 2010: 102). Gabel (2004) in a study of South Asian parents' cultural beliefs about their child with a learning disability found that beliefs about reincarnation and karma were important explanatory models for understanding their child's disability. One woman was reported as saying: "If your body is mentally retarded that is a god's gift, so you have to suffer it. In last birth you must have done something bad" (p. 18). While this may seem alien to some readers, consider the more subtle forms that such beliefs may take in western, Christian societies, where one may view disability as 'part of God's plan' or the 'will of God'.

Disability may also be understood as being the result of witchcraft (Groce & Zola, 1993); a curse placed on the individual or family. As Groce and Zola observe, such beliefs often result in the individual or family being held accountable for the disability. Associated with this are possible beliefs of contagion, where the disability may be 'caught' by others who come too close. For example, in such contexts, pregnant women are discouraged from coming into contact with a person with disability for fear that their child may be born with a similar disability (Groce, 2005). The result is stigma and shame for the family of a person with disability. Such beliefs may also influence expectations as to the extent of participation for persons with disabilities in societies. Parents may regard investment in the child's education as unnecessary, or societies may regard it inappropriate that an individual with disability is made to work rather than stay home under the care of their parents (Groce & Zola, 1993).

4.6.2 DISABLED WITHIN A CULTURAL CONTEXT

The social model of disability (discussed in Chapter 2) emphasizes social and environmental barriers as central to the understanding and experience of disability. We tend typically to draw on a medical model of disability to think of blindness, deafness and physical impairments as disabilities, but if we adopt a social model of disability, other conditions can be included as a disability. An example here is that of albinism, a genetic condition that results in the person having little or no skin, hair and eye pigmentation. Albinism results in the person having sensitive skin, easily burnt by the sun, and low or poor vision. However, a person with albinism in a predominantly Caucasian society will not stand out as much as a person with albinism would in an African country (Braathen & Ingstad, 2006). In a qualitative study of the experiences of persons with albinism in Malawi (Braathen & Ingstad, 2006), participants spoke of the stigma associated with albinism, referring to beliefs held by the community of albinism as contagious, or as people with albinism being referred to as 'ghosts'. Participants spoke about people with albinism being treated by others as an oddity or something to be feared, and at times shunned or mocked. All of the participants understood albinism as being caused by the will of God. Similar experiences of stigma were reported by people with albinism in Zimbabwe and in South Africa (Baker, Lund, Nyathi, & Taylor, 2010; Lund, 2001). As a result of such stigma, persons with albinism in many African countries are often excluded from education and employment (Baker et al., 2010). Such is the fear of people with albinism in some of the more rural contexts in countries in southern Africa, fuelled by the belief that albinism is caused by evil spirits, that some anecdotal reports exist of babies born with albinism being killed at birth (Baker et al., 2010). Such anecdotal reports point to an extreme response, but it is important to also reflect that persons with albinism in these same countries also live in a context of love and acceptance, particularly within their families (Braathen & Ingstad, 2006).

If we adopt the social model for considering deafness as a disability, central to such an understanding are the barriers to communication which exclude people who are deaf from full participation. However, this may also be relative to context. An interesting anthropological study was that of Groce (1985) of a community in Martha's Vinyard in the USA which had a higher than average prevalence of deaf persons living there. Groce observes how the deaf members of the community were perceived and treated as equal members of the community, which was aided by the ability of all members of the community (not just the families) to communicate using sign language. Thus no communication barriers existed which prevented deaf persons being excluded. In this context, and if we adopt the social model of disability, there was minimal experience of disability. Consider this in relation to communities with which we may be more familiar, where most of us are not able to communicate in sign language.

We have so far looked at the role of culture in the experience and prevalence of physical and mental ill-health, and disability. This has implications for professionals diagnosing and treating patients coming from different cultures than their own. It is important to be aware of alternative cultural explanations that people may have for their illness experiences. This leads us on to the need to consider culture and ethnicity in relation to health care.

4.7 HEALTH CARE AS CULTURAL

4.7.1 THE CULTURAL SYSTEMS OF HEALTH CARE

Kleinman (1980, 1988) considers medicine, and health care, as being a special kind of "cultural system" (Kleinman, 1980: 24). By this he means that each country has a system of health care that is informed by the country's social and cultural context, and is integrated into that society to become a "socially organized" response to disease (Kleinman, 1980: 24). The health care system is the system of interconnected relationships, involving responses to illnesses from the persons who are experiencing illness and the people who are treating illnesses, as well as the institutions that are related to disease and illness. Kleinman distinguishes between disease, which he defines as biological, and illness, which he defines as subjective, experiential suffering. The health care system, with patients and healers being key components of this system, thus involves the interface between disease and illness and the response to this. Kleinman (1980) argues that in order to properly research and understand disease and illness in any society, one should start with developing an under-standing of the health care system. This requires a holistic view of the system, the component interrelationships and institutions, and the social cultural con-text in which health care occurs. Kleinman, from ethnographic studies in China, has developed a tripartite model of health care, which involve three interconnected subsystems: the professional sector, the popular sector and the folk sector.

The professional sector

The professional sector, as the name suggests, comprises the organized medical professions, which in the majority of cases is scientific medicine. Kleinman (1980) also includes professionalized indigenous medicines in certain societies (such as Chinese herbal medicine in China and Ayurvedic medicine in India). The professional system has tended to dominate the more formal aspects of the health care system. It is the more organized system, and the most powerful and most funded system. In the UK, the professional sector includes the National Health Service (NHS) and private medical care.

There are measures of control that determine what counts as professional medicine and what does not. Professional bodies give legitimacy to certain professions, while others are marginalized and considered as outside medicine. There is also a hierarchy of professions, where professions associated with biomedicine are the most highly regarded. When it comes to physical health, doctors and surgeons are higher in the hierarchy than nurses. In mental health, psychiatry dominates over clinical psychology. The dominance of the medical profession has also resulted in the common perception that health care and medicine refers only to the professional sector, with research in health care focusing generally on the professional sector and neglecting proper consideration of the other sectors.

The popular sector

This is the largest subsystem of the health care system and includes the lay or non-professional environment in which illness is first experienced, defined and responded to. This sector includes the values and beliefs of not only the individual and his or her family, but also the social network and community. This, then, is the self-treatment health care at the family and community level. Most illnesses are first treated, or even entirely treated, at this level. When we are feeling like we are ill or that something is wrong with our physical or mental health, we usually first turn to others for help – our family and friends. The individual or the family, or in consultation with friends, may decide on the meaning and severity of the symptoms and arrive at some understanding and diagnosis of the illness experience, and decide on a course of action. This is made by relying on shared understandings of how certain illnesses are experienced, previous experience of illness, general knowledge and beliefs about health and ill-health. This may be knowledge that is influenced or learnt through family and friends, across the generations or in current time, or through media. In recent years, the internet has provided a source of immediate information related to ill-health (for example, www.symptomchecker.com). People can input symptoms felt and gain some information about possible meanings of those symptoms and advice that they can then include in their assessment of their illness.

Helman (2007b) includes self-help groups as a component of the popular sector. There has been a fast rise in the numbers of self-help groups since the Second World War, and these have provided support for individuals in their experience of illness. This is a source of shared information and advice and source of support for shared suffering, or what Helman (2007b) refers to as "communities of suffering" (p. 109). Self-help groups are to be differentiated from support groups, which are often initiated by professionals for the benefit of patients. Support groups, then, would span the boundaries of the professional and popular sector (Swartz, 1998). Included here are self-help books and the more recent rise of books where people share accounts of their illness, trauma or mental health experience. People draw on these as further sources of information and understanding, and thus support in managing their illness. Self-help books might be developed by professionals (and thus come *from* the professional sector) but are used by the individual within the boundaries of the popular sector.

Kleinman (1980) observes that the popular notion is that professionals have organized health care for lay people whereas it is lay people who organize and plan their use (or not) of health care. It is the lay person who decides at what point to consult a doctor, which doctor and where, and it is the lay person who decides whether to comply with treatment or not. The popular sector may be considered the point of entry and exit to the other sectors within the health care system. Treatment typically starts in the popular sector, and may from there proceed to the professional and/or folk sector (discussed below), and return to the popular sector, where treatment is evaluated and further decisions made.

My discussion so far has been on practices of healing that occur within the popular sector, but MacLachlan (2006b) points out that the popular sector may include beliefs that are "anti-health promotion ideas" (p. 203). He includes here ideas about AIDS being unpreventable, and AIDS denialism. We might also consider here the tendency to defend ourselves against notions of risk by attributing health risk to certain others and not ourselves (discussed in Chapter 2). So, for example, HIV is an issue for gays, prostitutes and drug addicts, and not a risk for 'normal' people (Joffe, 1999; Rohleder, 2007).

The folk sector

The folk sector comprises the non-professional and non-bureaucratic specialists. It includes secular and spiritual or sacred elements, although Kleinman (1980) argues that the boundaries of the two overlap. The spiritual or sacred elements may include faith healing, shamanic healing or healing through sacred rituals. This would include healing through prayer. Secular forms of healing would include herbal healing, traditional treatments, exercise, and symbolic healing. Herbalism in this sector is differentiated from the professionalized herbal medicine, such as Chinese herbal medicine or Ayervedic medicine, which has organized itself in ways similar to scientific medicine.

Someone from the UK or USA might think of folk sector healing as referring to the practices of indigenous populations in other countries. Swartz (1986, 1998), writing from a southern African context, argues that when it comes to indigenous healing, there may be a misunderstanding in relation to sophistication, where it is perceived that all 'unsophisticated' Africans choose to make use of the folk sector, and the more 'sophisticated' Africans make use of the professional biomedical sector. However, folk remedies for healing exist in all societies, and with modern societies becoming increasingly multicultural, individuals may make increasing use of healing practices from other cultures, which have gained in popularity. Thinking about the UK, for example, in addition to formal medical treatment (professional sector), a person's illness may be treated at home (popular sector) using, for example, traditional, long-established remedies that are considered good for the improvement of health (e.g. chicken soup for colds) or the use of over-the-counter medicine for treating common ailments. So, while the self-care may at times be medical, it still takes place within the boundaries of the home (the popular sector). Additionally, a person suffering from an illness may seek treatment using herbal medication, so-called 'alternative' therapies such as acupuncture or reflexology. Family and friends may pray to their god for the health of loved ones. These are all components of the folk sector. In recent decades (from the 1970s onwards), there has been a rise in the so-called 'new age' movement, with people making increasing use of 'alternative' healing practices, such as crystals, essential oils and spiritual meditation. More and more people have combined practices (including biomedicine) to maintain a healthy lifestyle – healthy mind, body and spirit.

The health care system also includes the way people, both healers and patients, use the various subsystems and act within them. People take on different social roles as they move in and out of the various subsystems. Thus they may be the 'sick family member' in the popular sector, the 'patient' in the professional sector and the 'client' in the folk sector. Each sector has its own social cultural norms, for example the language used and the customs of interaction. In the professional sector, the person experiencing illness may be more passive in his or her role as 'patient' in relation to the role of 'expert' of the professional. This has long been recognized and there has been a desire to alleviate this, with the emphasis on patient-centred care and service user involvement.

4.7.2 HEALTH CARE AND CLASHES OF PERSPECTIVES

A biomedical approach to health and ill-health is, as one would expect, the dominant perspective of the professional health care subsystem, which typically has tended to neglect a holistic view of health care. With its emphasis on science and reductionism, disease is understood in terms of underlying biological factors, which are addressed biologically or with the aid of technology. From this perspective, disease, as Kleinman (1980) points out, is seldom understood in terms of social problems. The professional system, with its emphasis on the biomedical, often neglects the other subsystems. In terms of Kleinman's differentiation between disease and illness, this may result in a clash between the perspective of disease and the perspective of illness. Kleinman (1980) further points out that, as the biomedical approach is ethnocentric in terms of its western origin, the redevelopment of health care provision in non-western countries, particularly developing countries, is often modelled on the idealization of a biomedical, professional model of health care. Again, this may result in a clash between disease and illness experience (see Box 4.5).

BOX 4.5

A Clash of Two Cultures in a Treatment of a Hmong Child in the USA

When working in a multicultural context, there may be a clash between the explanatory models of illness of the health care professionals and that of their patients. An example of such a clash is offered by Fadiman's ethnographic study, which is detailed in her award-winning book, *The spirit catches you and you fall down* (Fadiman, 1997). The book gives a detailed account of a Hmong child being treated by American doctors. The case involved the refugee Hmong family from Laos, living in California, and the family's young daughter who was diagnosed with severe epilepsy by doctors at a California hospital, where she received medical treatment.

FIGURE 4.1   Lia with her mother, Foua Yang
© Anne Fadiman (reproduced here with permission)

Fadiman conducted hours of interviews with the child's doctors, her family and members of the Hmong community, as well as making observations of the family. The book gives an account of the ongoing clash between the biomedical views of the doctors and the child's family and the Hmong community, who understood her seizures as being caused by her soul fleeing from her body. In Hmong culture this condition is referred to as *qaug dab peg* which means 'the spirit catches you and you fall down'. This refers to the body of the person collapsing/falling to the floor when the spirit or soul is stolen away from the body. Hmong culture also understands this condition as a possible sign that the child might eventually become a spiritual healer. The study observes a lack of understanding between the doctors and the family over the illness and how it should be treated. For example, according to Hmong understanding of the body and the soul, procedures such as taking blood samples and anaesthesia could cause the soul to flee the body, and thus make the condition worse. Thus, while such procedures seemed reasonable and necessary to the doctors, they were seen as "sadistic" (p. 43) by the child's family. Cultural and language barriers created considerable difficulties in facilitating proper communication between the doctors and the child's family. The consequences are tragic, with the doctors eventually having the child removed from her family. Later the child was

(Continued)

(Continued)

returned to the family who, upset with the doctors, cared for her at home. The child later suffered a massive seizure, which left her in a persistent vegetative state. You may probably immediately think that the child's family is to blame for what happened. However, Fadiman is careful not to make any apportion of blame. Fadiman describes both parties (the doctors and the family) as compassionate and caring, and focuses on not only the language barriers, but also the cultural differences in understanding the nature of the body and how the body should be treated. This cultural clash created considerable miscommunication and lack of understanding which had direct consequences for the child's care.

It may often be the case that some cultural explanations of illness or illness experiences are seen as less important or are not taken seriously. Yen and Wilbraham (2003a, 2003b) conducted a study in South Africa to explore how culture in relation to mental ill-health is understood and constructed by mental health professionals. They used discourse analysis as a method to explore how psychiatrists, psychologists and traditional healers talk about culture and mental health problems. What they found in their analysis was that discussions around 'cultural illnesses' particular to African patients were constructed as being less severe forms of distress of western psychiatric disorders. They further found that African culture was often constructed as being more primitive than western culture. In this way, psychiatrists and psychologists were able to disqualify the contributions of cultural understandings of illnesses and the role of traditional healers, and thus re-inscribe the view that the DSM psychiatric disorders are universal.

4.7.3 CULTURAL COMPETENCE IN HEALTH CARE

Culture and ethnicity are often associated with disparities in diagnosis of illness and disparities in health care treatment. We have seen above how there are reported cultural and ethnic disparities in the diagnosis and experience of illnesses, such as cancer and pain. Disparities in diagnosis of mental problems have also been found. For example, African Caribbean men and women in the UK are much more likely to be diagnosed with schizophrenia that white English men and women (McLean, Campbell, & Cornish, 2003). Similar disparities are found for ethnic minority groups in other countries, for example for African Americans in the USA (Bresnahan et al., 2007). Haasen and colleagues (2000) reported a 19% misdiagnosis rate for psychosis for Turkish migrants with mental health problems in Germany, compared to 4% for the German population studied. They further found that the rate of misdiagnosis was not strongly associated with proficiency in language, suggesting that the difference may be influenced by cultural factors during the process of diagnosis and evaluation.

McLean and colleagues (2003) reviewed literature regarding disparities in mental health care for ethnic groups in the UK, and observed a number of disparities that may suggest that ethnicity and race influence treatment in health care services. For example, they found that:

- African-Caribbean people experience higher rates of involuntary detainment in secure psychiatric facilities, and have greater police involvement in sectioning.
- Minority ethnic groups are more likely to not be offered psychotherapies.
- Minority ethnic groups tend to be prescribed higher drug dosages.
- African-Caribbean patients are more likely to be perceived as potentially dangerous.
- Black service users report lower rates of satisfaction of mental health care than white service users.

McLean and colleagues argued that various forms of social exclusion (cultural, institutional and socio-economic) may contribute to these disparities. Cultural exclusion arises out of the dominance of western psychiatric culture, which may result in misunderstandings, furthered by language and cultural communication barriers (such as in the study by Fadiman outlined earlier). Institutional exclusion refers to difficulties in taking up services, which may result in users coming to the service in circumstances of crisis. This may reinforce the stereotype of African-Caribbeans having more serious mental health problems and stereotypes of dangerousness. Minority groups may also feel marginalized in institutions that are not sufficiently equipped to cope with the unique service needs of members of minority groups (for example, language interpretation). Socio-economic exclusion refers to the relationship between lower socio-economic status and poorer mental health (explored in Chapter 5), where there is a disproportionate location of minority ethnic groups in low socio-economic groups. The various forms of social exclusion in relation to mental health care and disparities in treatment of ethnic minorities may also be as a result of the impact of explicit or implicit racism on the part of professionals in mental health care settings (Bhui, 2002). McLean and colleagues (2003) sought to investigate the experiences of mental health care services of African-Caribbeans, focusing on their interaction with mental health care services and experiences of inequality (see Box 4.6).

BOX 4.6

A Spotlight on Research: African-Caribbean interactions with mental health care services in the UK

McLean, C., Campbell, C., & Cornish, F. (2003). African-Caribbean interactions with mental health services in the UK: Experiences and expectations of exclusion as (re)productive of health inequalities. *Social Science and Medicine*, 56, 657–669.

(Continued)

(Continued)

Aims: This study explored the experiences of mental health care services of African-Caribbeans in a town in the South East of England. The study aimed to investigate local perspectives about interactions between the African-Caribbean community and health services, interactions through which possible inequalities are experienced.

Methods: The study employed a case study methodology, using a small town as a site of investigation to explore the interactions there as a single case study. A combination of individual and focus group interviews were conducted with a total of 30 individuals, comprising members of the various professional, non-professional and African-Caribbean stakeholders. Data were analysed by means of thematic coding.

Results: The authors present extensive findings which can only be partly discussed here. Some of the key findings indicated that the African-Caribbean stakeholders generally had a predominantly negative perception of the mainstream mental health care services in the area, while a service that was ethnic-specific and focused on issues of cultural identity and civil rights was highly praised. Mental health problems were immediately associated with issues of racism and social exclusion. Participants reported feeling excluded from and mistreated by mainstream mental health care as a result of cultural differences, with many behaviours or language use understood as normal for African-Caribbeans being misinterpreted as deviant. For example, loud verbal expressions with associated hand gestures were perceived and interpreted as being threatening by the mental health care services. Participants spoke about how they felt that the only difference that seemed to be acknowledged was skin colour, with little regard being given to cultural differences. Participants also perceived themselves to be stereotyped as mad and dangerous, and different treatment regimes were given to them, by a mental health care service that was predominantly white and Eurocentric. The participants gave various possible strategies that could be implemented in order to improve services so as to make them more culturally sensitive. Such strategies included building partnerships with informal social networks, through which mental health prevention and care information could be disseminated, thus improving overall access.

Conclusion: The authors conclude that cultural and institutional exclusion seemed to characterize the experiences of African-Caribbeans of their interaction with mainstream mental health care services. As a result, African-Caribbeans felt discouraged about accessing such services. Experiences of racism and other general social exclusion increased vulnerability to poor mental health as well as decreased access to health care services. Social exclusion was thus a key, everyday experience which was "keenly felt and talked about" (p. 667) by African-Caribbean community members.

This study, only briefly presented here, is an exemplary example of qualitative research that not only explores in depth the subjective experiences of the research participants, but also aims to theorize the social phenomenon under investigation. In this case, the role that various forms of social exclusion play in contributing to the different experiences of an ethnic minority group in accessing and receiving mental health prevention and care services. It gives a detailed account of how culture and ethnicity plays a central role in the experience of social exclusion and associated mental health care issues.

The importance of the interaction between members of the minority group and interactions with health care services has also been highlighted by Dixon-Woods and colleagues in relation to general health care in the UK. Dixon-Woods and colleagues (2005) reviewed literature on access to health care by vulnerable groups in the UK, and indicate that there exist disparities in the utilization and receipt of general health care in the UK. However, research findings are not consistent, and they highlight the difficulties around defining, operationalizing and researching access to health care, which make such findings difficult to interpret conclusively. They suggest the notion of 'candidacy' as a useful term for understanding access to health care. They use the term 'candidacy' to refer to the degree of legitimacy that a person has for medical attention, which is jointly negotiated between the health service and service user. Service users may have cultural expectations of what would be an appropriate use of services, as do the providers of such health care services. The review highlights how access to health care for people of ethnic minorities may be affected by this interaction, where people from ethnic minorities may feel alienated from an organization that treats them in an insensitive and stereotypical manner.

Cultural competence has increasingly been promoted in health care as a needed component of the professional–patient interaction (Brach & Fraser, 2000) as a way of reducing socio-cultural barriers that may impact on health care. There are various definitions of cultural competence, which have included components such as knowledge about specific cultures and cultural practices, and communication skills across language barriers. Betancourt (2004) argues that an emphasis on mere knowledge about cultures often results in stereotypical assumptions about individuals from other cultural groups. Betancourt (2004) defines cultural competence as "the implementation of the principles of patient-centred care, including exploration, empathy, and responsiveness to patients' needs, values, and preferences" (p. 953). This emphasizes a dialogical process of co-constructing health care needs. However, being 'culturally competent' or 'culturally sensitive' may be a challenging task. For example, Kai and colleagues (2007) conducted focus group interviews with a total sample of 106 health professionals from various disciplines in England. The participants expressed considerable uncertainty and anxiety about their competency in providing a culturally appropriate and sensitive health care service. Many participants in their study felt anxious about being inappropriate and coming across as potentially racist. This then becomes a barrier in engaging the patient, as the professionals' anxiety hampers their ability to be flexible and creative in their thinking and actions.

Working across culture and ethnicity means working with issues of difference, which for many of us creates an anxiety, as it deals with issues of prejudice (whether conscious or unconscious) and othering. This may be especially salient in societies where there has been a history of inter-group conflict. People may be reluctant to talk about issues of difference, in the interest of appearing politically and culturally correct (e.g. Leibowitz, Rohleder, Bozalek, Carolissen, & Swartz, 2007). In discussing a cultural-sensitivity course for psychiatric residents at a training institute in the USA, Willen, Bullon and Good (2010) reflect on how cultural-sensitivity courses that reduce content to knowledge-based components may not be taken seriously, with courses being met by "eye-rolling" and comments that they are "'p.c.' bunk" (p. 249). On the other hand, the authors also observe that courses which provide a greater exploration of difference by focusing on differences within the group may stir up powerful and uncomfortable emotions in participants, and this needs to be properly acknowledged and responded to by both educators and participants.

SUMMARY

4.8 This chapter highlights how many health and illness states are relative, which challenges the universalist assumptions of the medical model. While it is the case that some diseases and conditions occur across different cultures, differences may exist in how this is understood and experienced. Different explanatory models exist for physical and mental health and disability, which influence how the sufferer may be perceived and treated, and how the illness experience is approached. These are all important considerations for working in a multicultural context, which we are increasingly required to do. Providing effective health care not only requires delivering care and treatment within the framework (usually medical) in which such care is situated, but also requires the integration of possible alternative, cultural perspectives. This chapter has only touched on some issues. However, the influence of culture on health and illness is a vast field, and below I have recommended some texts that explore these issues further.

FURTHER READINGS

Eshun, S., & Gurung, R.A.R (2009). *Culture and mental health: Sociocultural influences, theory and practice*. Chichester: Wiley-Blackwell. This is an edited text containing 14 chapters on various aspects of culture and mental health, including separate chapters on specific mental disorders.

Helman, C.G. (2007b). *Culture, health and illness* (5th edition). London: Hodder Arnold. This is a leading, international textbook for medical anthropology. It is written in an accessible style and addresses the various complex interactions between cultural and social factors and health and illness.

MacLachlan, M. (2006b). *Culture and health: A critical perspective towards global health* (2nd edition). Chichester: John Wiley & Sons. This book provides an excellent, comprehensive coverage of culture and health, including both physical and mental health.

SOCIO-ECONOMIC STATUS

5

INTRODUCTION

5.1 Almost half of the world's population live on less than US$2 a day (Marks, 2004). The disparity in people's income and standard of living across the globe is astonishing. Have a look at the website www.globalrichlist.com/ for a rough estimate of where you fall in the world in terms of income earned. We are all familiar with images of people from some of the poorest regions of the world living in desperate conditions, and the consequences this has for life chances.

Traditionally, poverty has been understood in reference to income and gross national product. Increasingly, poverty has come to be understood in reference not only to income, but also to human rights and development. Amartya Sen (1999) argues that income inequality affects the life that people are able to lead, defining poverty not just in terms of economic resources, but instead in terms of 'human capabilities', where, for example, people living in poverty may not have the ability or freedom to make social and political demands with regards to things like education and health. Thus poverty should be seen as "a deprivation of basic capabilities" rather than just low income (Sen, 1999: 20). Thus the notion of power is central to a definition of poverty. Prilleltensky (2003) understands poverty in terms of the lack of power that an individual or groups of people have in benefiting from "vital entitlements" (p. 22). Poverty can be differentiated in terms of absolute poverty, where people have very few resources and live in desperate conditions, and relative poverty, where individuals may be living on incomes that are below a society's national average. Those living in absolute and relative poverty experience powerlessness and social exclusion, and may be excluded from access to resources that contribute to health and well-being (Prilleltensky, 2003).

Rather that using the term 'poverty' to discuss health inequality, it is more common to refer to the term 'socio-economic status' (SES), which makes comparisons between people living in various levels of poverty and wealth. There is a consistently observed relationship between socio-economic status and health, known as the 'health gradient'. As socio-economic status decreases, mortality and morbidity increases. This health gradient can be observed globally and within countries. It is not just a dualistic matter that the poor have worse health than the rich, but rather that there is a consistent health gradient as one moves up and down the SES hierarchy. Thus health improves as SES increases (Adler & Snibbe, 2003).

This chapter will discuss this health gradient in relation to physical and mental health and disabilities. Both global and national health disparities will be looked at, thus focusing on both global poverty and relative poverty within nations. Much of these studies are epidemiological (see Box 8.1), which describe the SES health gradient and associated factors. The chapter will also briefly explore the experience of homelessness and associated health issues. From here, the chapter will examine some explanations for these SES health disparities, looking at not only theoretical and empirical explanatory models, but also lay understandings of SES health disparities. Finally, the chapter will look at how SES may affect the doctor–patient interaction, where in many cases the doctor comes from a higher SES than the patient.

5.2 SES AND DISEASE

5.2.1 GLOBAL HEALTH DISPARITIES

If we look at the top causes of death, according to the World Health Organization (2008), between high-income countries and low-income countries, we can observe notable differences in the causes of death, which are strongly associated with conditions of poverty (see Table 5.1).

Among the top causes of death in developing countries are conditions related to poverty, most notably diarrhoeal diseases, which are typically caused by contaminated drinking water and poor sanitation. Other causes, such as tuberculosis, neonatal infections, prematurity and low birth weight, are also associated with conditions of poverty, such as malnutrition and low immunity, and poor health care services. In contrast, among the leading causes of death in high-income countries, are many diseases associated with lifestyle factors (for example, lung cancers and diabetes).

Africa has the greatest disease burden globally while spending the least proportion on health, and this is compounded by the continent's continuing struggle to face the problems of inadequate nutrition, poverty, and wars and conflicts (Aikins & Marks, 2007). We should also take note of the number of deaths listed in Table 5.1. These numbers are not very meaningful when we do not have the size of the population against which comparisons can be made. However, many of these deaths (in the millions) are for causes which are easily preventable with adequate health care, such as diarrhoeal diseases, tuberculosis,

TABLE 5.1   Leading causes of death in high- and low-income countries

Causes of death in high-income countries[1]	Number of deaths	Causes of death in low-income countries[2]	Number of deaths
Ischaemic heart disease	1.3 million	Lower respiratory infections	2.9 million
Cerebrovascular disease	0.8 million	Ischaemic heart disease	2.5 million
Trachea, bronchus, lung cancers	0.5 million	Diarrhoeal diseases	1.8 million
Lower respiratory infections	0.3 million	HIV/AIDS	1.5 million
Chronic obstructive pulmonary disease	0.3 million	Cerebrovascular disease	1.5 million
Alzheimer and other dementias	0.3 million	Chronic obstructive pulmonary disease	0.9 million
Colon and rectum cancers	0.3 million	Tuberculosis	0.9 million
Diabetes mellitus	0.2 million	Neonatal infections	0.9 million
Breast cancer	0.2 million	Malaria	0.9 million
Stomach cancer	0.1 million	Prematurity and low birth weight	0.8 million

[1] Defined as countries with a gross national income per capita of $10,066 or more
[2] Defined as countries with a gross national income per capita of $825 or less

Source: World Health Organization (2008). *The Global Burden of Diseases: 2004 Update*. Geneva: WHO, p. 12.

and malaria. This points to a post-colonial global inequality in health care, with health care provision in the world's poorer countries being dependent on the wealth of the world's richer countries (MacDonald, 2005). For example, in Chapter 3 we looked briefly at how some of the HIV/AIDS-related mortality may be attributable to the failure on the part of the richer nations and pharmaceutical companies of facilitating access to affordable antiretroviral (ARV) treatment to the millions of people in Africa dying of AIDS (MacDonald, 2005).

The website *World Mapper* (www.worldmapper.org) has developed some fascinating world maps where countries are re-sized according to different types of statistics, including health statistics. These maps give an effective graphic representation of global disparities of different indices. For example, in Figure 5.1, this re-sized map represents approximate differences in health expenditure across the world.

As is clearly represented, public health expenditure is vastly greater in the developed countries of the Northern Hemisphere, with far less public health spending in developing countries of Latin America, Asia, and Africa in particular. Contrast this to the re-sized world map depicting deaths as a result of cholera (Figure 5.2), which is not only preventable with proper sanitation and vaccination, but is also easily treatable with oral rehydration therapy. In this map, Africa appears almost like the only region in the world, with the Americas and Europe barely featuring.

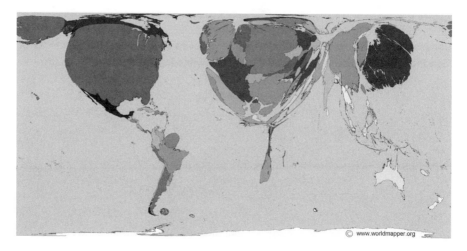

FIGURE 5.1   Public health spending

© Copyright SASI Group (University of Sheffield) and Mark Newman (University of Michigan). Used with permission under the Creative Commons Licence: http://creativecommons.org/licenses/by-nc-nd/3.0/.

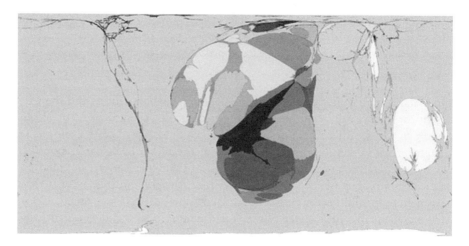

FIGURE 5.2   Deaths by cholera

© Copyright SASI Group (University of Sheffield) and Mark Newman (University of Michigan). Used with permission under the Creative Commons Licence: http://creativecommons.org/licenses/by-nc-nd/3.0/.

If we take a map depicting differences in life expectancy (Figure 5.3), clear differences can be observed, with the regions of Africa and Latin America being significantly more reduced. Similar disparities exist in terms of life expectancy, with life expectancy being shorter for people living in poorer countries. These global health disparities reflect health differences as a result of poverty and deprivation, but health disparities also exist in terms of relative poverty and socio-economic inequality within high-income countries.

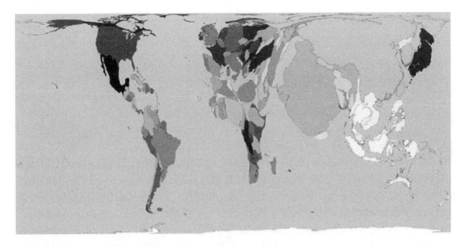

FIGURE 5.3 Life expectancy

© Copyright SASI Group (University of Sheffield) and Mark Newman (University of Michigan). Used with permission under the Creative Commons Licence: http://creativecommons.org/licenses/by-nc-nd/3.0/.

As Coburn (2004) observes, rich people tend to live longer and have healthier lives compared to the poor. This is an observation made in all societies, as well as when we consider global comparisons (as we have seen). Let's now look at epidemiological statistics from the UK to look at this socio-economic health gradient at a national level.

5.2.2 HEALTH AND SES IN THE UK

According to The Poverty Site (www.poverty.org.uk), a website which provides statistics about poverty and social exclusion in the UK, an estimated 13.5 million people or 22% of the UK population were living in households below the 60% household income threshold in 2008/2009. That is 60% or less of the average household income in the UK for that year. This figure had increased since 2004/2005. In 2008/2009, the number of people living below the 40% threshold of household income was estimated at 5.9 million (9.8% of the population), which is the highest number since records began in 1979. According to the website, the UK has a slightly higher proportion of its population living in relative low income than the average for Europe. London has the highest proportion of people living in relative low income than any other region in the UK. The website provides comparative statistics for various demographic factors, such as gender and ethnicity, and indicates differences in the proportion of people living in relative low income. Women are only slightly more likely to live in relative low income households than men, indicating that the gender gap is decreasing. However, significant differences exist with regards ethnicity, with an estimated two-fifths of people from ethnic minority groups living in relative low-income households. This is double the number of white people living in low-income households. The percentage of people from different ethnic groups living in low-income households are broken down as follows:

- 70% of Bangladeshis live in low-income households
- 60% of Pakistanis
- 50% of black Africans
- 30% of Indians and black Caribbeans
- 20% of white people.

As discussed in Chapter 4, issues of cultural and ethnic differences in health, illness experience and health care are compounded by these socio-economic inequalities.

Along with these socio-economic inequalities, there has been consistently observed associated differences in health. In the UK, the recently published Marmot Review (Marmot, 2010; see Box 5.1) provides recent statistics on health inequalities in the UK. One key indicator of socio-economic health inequality is the difference in life expectancy between people living in low SES as compared to those living in high SES. The review reports a difference in life expectancy of seven years between those living in poor areas to people living in rich areas (see Figure 5.4). More significantly, when looking at disability-free life expectancy (that is living a life of relative good health), there is a difference of 17 years between people living in poor areas compared to people living in rich areas (see Figure 5.4). Thus people living in poorer areas will live shorter lives, with more time of that life spent living with a disability. We shall return to

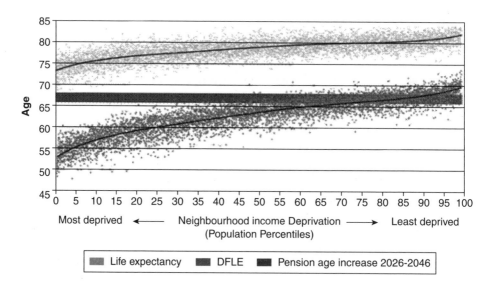

FIGURE 5.4   Life expectancy and disability-free life expectancy (DFLE) at birth by SES in England 1999–2003

Source: Marmot, M. (2010) *Fair society, healthy lives: The Marmot review*. Strategic review of health inequalities in England post-2010. London: University College London; adapted from data from the Office for National Statistics licensed under the Open Government Licence v.1.0 (graph reproduced and adapted with permission)

discussing SES and disability below, but what we are referring to here is the disabling effects of poor health.

The review observes that some of the key health behaviours that contribute to the development of chronic illnesses – smoking, unhealthy diet, lack of physical exercise and obesity – all follow the social gradient. That is that health behaviours, such as smoking, are more prevalent in lower SES households than in higher SES households. Consumption of alcohol, on the other hand, rises as SES rises, although people from lower SES show more problematic drinking and higher rates of admissions to hospital for alcohol-related health conditions. Social factors, such as education and unemployment, affects self-esteem and self-efficacy which in turn affects both mental health (see below) and physical well-being, and has been associated with increased health risk behaviours, such as smoking, problematic drinking and reduced exercise.

In Chapter 3 we have seen how individual health behaviours are shaped by structural factors, such as poverty and unemployment. A focus on individual behaviour and lifestyle alone can easily become victim-blaming. This is congruent with the notion of 'healthism' (Crawford, 2006), where health is moralized, and people are held responsible for their own ill-health. The Marmot Review highlights the importance of tackling social inequalities in order to improve health. According to the review, inequalities in life chances are determinants of health inequalities, which are shaped from birth. An individual's birth and early childhood living experiences lays the foundation for their whole life. For example, mothers living in disadvantaged circumstances are more likely to have babies of low birth weight, which in turn is associated with "poorer long-term health and educational outcomes" (Marmot, 2010: 60). Early childhood deprivation also negatively affects cognitive development. The review argues that "if the conditions of daily life are favourable, and more equitably distributed, then they will have more control over their lives in ways that will influence their and their families' health and health behaviours" (p. 38). Thus the review is concerned with matters of social justice, which the report argues should become the main focus of health intervention.

BOX 5.1

The Marmot Review

The Marmot Review website (www.marmotreview.org/) is an informative and useful website centred around the Marmot Review discussed in this chapter. The website provides a full and summary version of the report, which can be freely downloaded, as well as updates and relative links to supplementary information. The website provides an invaluable link to all sorts of resources relevant to issues of health inequalities. For example, there is a link to an interesting blog written by Professor Sir Michael Marmot, which includes comments on topical issues related to health inequalities. There is also an extensive list of links to external websites of various governmental and non-governmental organizations related to health and social inequalities.

As with physical health problems, there are also some observed SES and mental health disparities. Although people in all SES backgrounds may experience mental health problems, particularly common mental health problems such as depression and anxiety, epidemiological data show that a mental health gradient exists in relation to SES.

SES AND MENTAL HEALTH

5.3 Mental health problems account for 11.1% of the total burden of diseases in low and middle income countries, with depression being the leading neurospychiatric cause for burden of disease (Patel, 2007). The work of Desjarlais and colleagues in 1995 was an important contribution to understanding the distribution of mental health problems across the world, with a particular focus on lower income countries in Africa, Asia, Latin America, and the Pacific. It was the first time that the burden of mental health problems across the world was systematically surveyed.

Desjarlais and colleagues (1995) found that approximately 75% of people diagnosed with schizophrenia live in less developed countries. Interestingly, however, sufferers in low-income countries were found to have a higher rate of recovery after a first episode of schizophrenia than those in higher income countries. One would think that because of better mental health care resources in wealthier countries this would not be the case. It is difficult to speculate as to why this may be so, but we could consider socio-cultural norms and how sufferers may be more socially included in more 'collectivist' cultures, usually associated with some countries of Africa, Asia and Latin America, compared to sufferers who may be more socially excluded and stigmatized in more 'individualistic' cultures, usually associated with countries in Europe and North America (see Chapter 4 for further discussion of collectivist and individualist dimension of culture). Desjarlais and colleagues (1995) also suggest that this may be partly explained by variations in diagnosis, between brief psychosis and chronic schizophrenia, which may have a lot to do with psychological and environmental factors, such as social support, and differing explanatory models for causes of illness. Less variation between poorer and richer countries were found for more common mental health problems, such as depression and anxiety.

In a review of 11 epidemiological studies from six low- and middle-income countries, Patel and Kleinman (2003) found an association between indicators of poverty, particularly low levels of education, and common mental health problems (depression and anxiety). In reviewing articles exploring the links between poverty and common mental health problems, they go on to conclude that factors associated with poverty – feelings of insecurity, vulnerability and hopelessness; social upheaval and change; low levels of education and illiteracy; gender-based violence; and co-morbid poor nutrition and poor physical health – are stronger explanatory factors for the risk of common mental health problems among the poor than level of income alone. They further point out that poor mental health (and physical health) leads to a deepening of poverty as a result of the direct and indirect economic costs of poor health. More recently, Lund and colleagues (2010) conducted a review of studies investigating poverty and common mental health problems, and observed variations in the strength of association of different dimensions of poverty with common mental health problems. They found consistent significant associations between level of education, social class, socio-economic status, financial stress, housing and food insecurity. Less consistent associations were found for employment, level of income, and consumption, as these may be affected by other issues. For example, with regards to level of income, Lund and colleagues observe that factors such as income insecurity, or the stress of living with a low income, may be stronger predictors of poor mental health, rather than low income as a specific variable.

Mental health problems in low-income countries in particular have tended to be overlooked, as more emphasis is placed on communicable diseases (such as HIV and tuberculosis) and economic development. However, epidemiological data indicate the significant contribution that mental health problems, particularly depression, has on the burden of diseases in all countries (WHO, 2008). For this reason, various authors have highlighted the importance of the need to address mental health problems in tackling global health inequalities, poverty and development (e.g. Lund et al., 2010; Miranda & Patel, 2005; Prince et al., 2007).

As with physical health, the prevalence of mental health problems is higher among people from lower SES in middle- and high-income countries. An association with SES and mental health problems was found for a variety of mental health problems, including psychotic disorders, mood disorders and suicide, substance abuse, and personality disorders (Murali & Oyebode, 2004). According to The Poverty Site (www.poverty.org.uk), adults in the poorest fifth of the income distribution in the UK are doubly at risk of developing a mental health problem as those adults on average incomes. Payne (2000), analysing survey data on poverty and social exclusion in Britain, found that over half of the survey's respondents who reported having a mental health problem were among the 26% of the British population who were found to be living in relative poverty in Britain in 1999. Thus poor mental health was found to be disproportionately prevalent among the poorest.

The association between SES and mental health can be observed in relation to changes in SES. For example, in Belgium, Lorant and colleagues (2007) conducted a longitudinal study investigating the association between changes in SES circumstances and depression. A total sample of 11,909 took part an average of 4.6 times in data collection waves over a seven-year period. Depression and SES were measured using a standardized scale. The results of this study indicated that a worsening of SES circumstances was associated with increases in depressive symptoms and cases of depression (that is scores on a scaled measure of depression that would indicate a diagnosable depression). Similar findings were found from a longitudinal study in the UK, which observed an association between decreases in income and worsening psychological well-being (Benzeval & Judge, 2001).

Some association between mental health and SES has also been found in terms of improvement in SES. For example, Costello and colleagues (2003) found that improved SES among Native-American families was associated with some improvements in child psychopathology. Research indicates that, in all classes, negative life events in particular are associated with the emergence of mental health problems, but that people from higher SES experience a greater number of positive life events than people from lower SES, which may act as a protective factor in the development of mental health problems (Rogers & Pilgrim, 2005). However, the effects of growing up in poverty on the sense of a social self may prevail despite changes in SES. For example, a study by Tuason (2008) with a group of Filipinos who had moved out of poverty and a group of Filipinos who had remained in poverty showed few differences, with both groups expressing negative feelings of self-esteem in relation to the experience of living or having lived in poverty (see Box 5.2).

BOX 5.2

A Spotlight on Research: The experience of living or having lived in poverty

Tuason, M.T.G. (2008). Those who were born poor: A qualitative study of Philippine poverty. *Journal of Counseling Psychology, 55*(2), 158–171.

Aim: For many psychologists working on health care, they are often required to work with service users who are poor. Yet relatively little attention is paid to the experience of poverty. This study aimed to explore the psychological experiences of living in poverty and deprivation among two different groups of people living in the Philippines: one group of Filipinos who grew up poor and remained poor, and a second group of Filipinos who grew up poor but became "materially successful" (p. 159).

Method: This was a qualitative study, drawing on social constructionist and critical paradigms. Purposive sampling was used to recruit the two groups of participants, recruited both in the Philippines and in the USA. A total of 25 participants took part – 13 Filipinos in the group who had remained poor and 12 Filipinos in the group who had become wealthier. Eleven of the participants were women, and 14 were men, aged between 25 and 73, with a mean age of 45. All self-identified as having grown up poor. All participants were interviewed individually for between 90 and 120 minutes. Data was analysed using grounded theory (see Chapter 8).

Results: More similarities than differences were found in the two groups of participants' experience of poverty. In recalling their experience for poverty, all participants expressed negative feelings, such as shame, self-pity, loneliness, anger, envy at others who were richer, resentment, fear, pain and hopelessness. For example, one woman is quoted as saying:

> For us who do not have much money, there are no options. We are pitiful, that is true ... . We just stay here and hope to survive. This is poverty; this is how it is for us. (p. 165)

Both had reported dreams of a better life, but those who had remained poor tended to come across as more fearful and feeling more hopeless than those who had become rich. Many attributed the cause of their poverty to their parents, for example for having married early, having too many children, being uneducated, unable to provide for the family, and in some cases substance abuse. Participants also attributed the cause of poverty in some cases to socio-cultural factors, such as limited resources. Many of the participants who had become richer reported being angry with their parents for having been unable to provide for the family. Those participants who had become richer had experienced a "chance event" which had provided access to education and the chance to migrate out of poverty. Those who had become richer tended to express more positive feelings, such as pride and contentment, and regarded their experience of growing up in poverty as having built character. But most continued to have negative feelings, such as shame and anger. All reported usually coping through hardships by seeking help from others, faith in God, and persevering through education and work. Many of those who had remained poor spoke of just getting by and living from day to day. For example, one woman is quoted as saying:

> Through the mercy of God, we survive. We are able to get by, we do not go hungry ... things are okay. Provided you are good in praying to God, whatever hardship becomes lighter. For instance, if we only have egg and rice to eat, then that is okay. We get by. We survive. (p. 167).

Conclusions: The reported experiences and feelings of both groups of participants were similar, with all expressing mostly negative feelings associated with their experience of living or having lived in poverty. Tuason points out how those who had become richer continued to express negative feelings, such as self-pity and anger, indicating that although the actual experience of deprivation is in the past, most who had become richer "continue to cope with poverty internally" (p. 167), and reflects an "internalized sense of social class" (p. 167). Tuason notes the participants' causal explanations of poverty as attributed to familial factors as surprising, with fewer references made to socio-cultural and structural factors.

This study provides experiential data of what the psychological experience is of poverty, and furthermore shows how experiences of childhood poverty are internalized and continue to impact on the sense of self and the emotions of those who have had the opportunity to move out of poverty. It reflects the epidemiological data which indicate higher prevalence of mental health problems in lower SES groups. Qualitative studies such as these offer us a picture of the lived experience of participants, which is not ordinarily captured or paid attention to.

While lower SES may affect access to appropriate health facilitating resources and health care, mental health care services in developed countries, such as the UK and the USA, are dominated by service users from lower SES backgrounds (Rogers & Pilgrim, 2005). Futhermore, many such patients in psychiatric services are there as a result of being detained and treated involuntarily according to mental health care laws. Rogers and Pilgrim (2005) thus raise the suggestion that we may conceptualize such mental health care "as part of a wider state apparatus which controls the social problems associated with poverty (what has been increasingly called the 'underclass')" (p. 53). Rogers and Pilgrim also review research findings that indicate that poor patients are more likely to be given a diagnosis such as schizophrenia, while wealthier patients are given a less stigmatizing diagnosis of depression or bipolar mood disorder. Poorer patients are also more likely to be given biological/medical treatment, while wealthier patients are more likely to be referred for psychotherapy. This echoes to some extent the critiques from the anti-psychiatry movement which viewed 'mental illness' as a label to categorize and control problems of social living (see Chapter 2).

SES AND DISABILITY

5.4 According to the World Health Organization's *Global Burden of Diseases* report (WHO, 2008), the prevalence of moderate and severe disabilities are higher in low- and middle-income countries than in high-income countries, and highest in countries in Africa. In developing countries, people with disabilities may be particularly at risk of poverty, and it has been estimated that people with disabilities make up between 15% and 20% of the poor in low-income countries (Elwan, 1999). Groce (2003) argues that young people with disabilities may be "among the poorest and most marginalized of all the world's young people" (p. 3), with an estimated 80% of the world's youth (under the age of 24) with disabilities living in low-income countries. Persons with disabilities are also disproportionately represented among lower socio-economic classes in higher income countries. For example, according to The Poverty Site (www.poverty.org.uk), approximately one-third of all disabled adults in the UK, aged 25 years to the age of retirement, live in low-income households. This is double the rate of non-disabled adults of the same age range. The biggest reason for this difference is that disabled adults are less likely to be in paid employment.

In a comprehensive review of the literature on disability and poverty, Elwan (1999) concluded that poverty exacerbates the risk of disability, due to associated poor sanitation, inadequate nutrition, and poor health care, which increases the risk for disabling diseases. In a review of research findings on the impact of poverty on disabilities, Park and colleagues (2002) note how conditions of poverty contribute to the development of disabilities for children. For example, poor nutrition during pregnancy has been found to increase risk for later learning disabilities in the child. Poverty also limits access to material resources that enhances the cognitive development of children. In a longitudinal study of households with children aged 3–18 years with a disability in the

USA, Fujiura and Yamaki (2000) found that households defined by poverty and single-parent families showed an increased risk for disability compared to households living at the poverty threshold or above. In impoverished contexts, many disabilities are as a result of *"preventable* impairments" (Emmett, 2006: 210, italics in original) caused by injuries, and peri-natal, maternal and communicable diseases. Malnutrition, poor sanitation, limited access to health care, limited health education and knowledge, inadequate housing, dangerous living and work conditions, violence, and natural disasters are cited as the leading causes of disabilities in low-income countries (Emmett, 2006). The WHO estimates that up to 50% of hearing impairments and 70% of blindness in children in lower income countries is either preventable or treatable (Department for International Development (DFID), 2000).

Elwan (1999) further concluded that poverty was a consequence of disability. She found that people with disabilities were more likely to be unemployed or have poor employment, have lower income and less material assets than the general population. This was observed across countries. Elwan further found that people with disabilities have lower levels of education than the rest of the population. For example, Hanna and Rogovsky (1991) found that disabled men and women received less formal education in the USA than non-disabled men and women, with many more disabled men and women not graduating from high school compared to men and women with no disabilities. Similarly, in Malawi (Munthali, Mvula, & Ali, 2004) and in South Africa (Loeb, Eide, Jelsma, Toni, & Maart, 2008) people with disabilities had lower levels of education and lower literacy levels than people with no disabilities. Groce (2003) found that many disabled children and adolescents may be excluded from school, as education may be regarded as being unnecessary for the child who is seen as not being able to learn, or the child may be perceived as a disruption to the class, and schools may be physically inaccessible to children with visual and physical disabilities. This lower level of education increases vulnerability to inadequate employment. In low-income countries, in conditions of scarce resources, parents may choose to exclude their disabled children from education in favour of putting their non-disabled children through education, with the expectation that the educated, non-disabled child will guarantee a job.

The socio-economic status of people with disabilities also affects an individual's ability to access health care services. For example, in Zambia, women with physical disabilities struggle to access health care services due to lack of assistive devices and suitable transport (Smith, Murray, Yousafzai & Kasonkas, 2004). It has been estimated that only 2% of people with disabilities in developing countries are able to access appropriate rehabilitation and basic services (DFID, 2000). Barriers to accessing services have been indicated for people with disabilities generally as facilities are not always designed with access by people with disabilities in mind (e.g. Anderson & Kitchin, 2000), but this may be compounded by low socio-economic status, as a result of lack of money for transport.

Disability grants assist in raising some households out of conditions of poverty, providing a source of income for people who are excluded from employment. In lower income countries, a disability grant may offer a much valued, at times only source of income for whole households. In the context of a community mental health service in South Africa, MacGregor (2006) observed how patients with mental health problems presented particular "nerve narratives" that conceptualized the strains of living in conditions of social deprivation, while at the same time presented a medicalized discourse with the expectation of receiving a disability grant for psychiatric disability. For many of the clinic attendees observed, the receiving of the grant was often the most primary concern. With regards HIV/AIDS, the issuing of a disability grant (AIDS is considered to be a disability) presents various dilemmas and challenges. Swartz, Schneider, and Rohleder (2006) discuss the complicated implications for households living with lower incomes of receiving a disability grant for HIV/AIDS in the context of South Africa. When an individual is symptomatic with AIDS, and is disabled as a result, he or she may receive a disability grant. However, when that person is treated with antiretroviral treatment, their health may improve, making them able to work and thus no longer eligible for a disability grant. The impact of this loss of income is significant in the context of large rates of unemployment. There have been suggestions that this may result in a perverse incentive to remain ill in order to obtain a disability grant, although there is no clear evidence for this (Swartz, Schneider, & Rohleder, 2006).

HOMELESSNESS AND HEALTH

5.5 Homeless people have a variety of backgrounds. While many people who are currently homeless may have come from lower SES backgrounds, others from educated and employed backgrounds have become homeless following a life event which changed their material circumstances (Flick, 2007). The cause of homelessness, particularly in developed countries, is a controversial political issue. Some arguments are based on individualist, neoliberal views (see Box 5.3) where homelessness is attributed to the 'fault' of the individual; to "individual fecklessness and/or personal deficits or defects" (Rogers & Pilgrim, 2003: p. 123). Others argue that homelessness is a product of SES and structural inequality.

Fitzpatrick (2005) adopts a critical realist approach (see Chapter 2) to examine causal explanations for homelessness in the UK. In other words, instead of exploring homelessness in terms of statistical definitions and statistically associated causal factors (the positivist approach) or homelessness in terms of its meanings and social representations where homelessness is constructed as a social problems through which certain people are thus socially excluded (the social constructionist approach), he takes a critical realist approach that argues that any interpretations or representations of homelessness are mediated through the individual, material and structural realities of conditions of homelessness. Fitzpatrick explores both individual factors and structural factors that explain homelessness, rather than one or the other, as has usually been adopted. Fitzpatrick argues that homelessness in the UK can be understood by means of four intersecting levels of causation: the individual level, which includes individual attributes such as substance abuse, confidence and personal resilience; the "patriarchal and interpersonal structures" (p. 13), which facilitate problems such as domestic violence and child abuse; housing structures, such as land ownership, residential segregation, inadequate housing; and economic structures, which includes socio-economic status and social welfare policies.

A report by FEANTSA, the European Federation of National Organizations working with the Homeless, on the health status of people who are homeless (FEANTSA, 2006), indicates that a number of mental and physical health problems and experience of disability occur at a higher frequency among people who are homeless. People who are homeless may have multiple health needs, including severe mental health problems (such as schizophrenia and severe personality disorders), substance abuse, untreated injuries and wounds, ulcers, chronic foot problems, poor dental hygiene, respiratory diseases, tuberculosis and so on. People who are homeless have a lower life expectancy than the general population, with death as a result of accident or violence and suicide being almost double for persons who are homeless (FEANTSA, 2006; Flick, 2007). Many people who are homeless may have learning disabilities and physical disabilities, some of which were acquired as a result of rough living and exposure to extreme cold (resulting in possible loss of limbs due to frostbite) (FEANTSA, 2006).

A lot of research has explored the mental health problems associated with homelessness, particularly schizophrenia, suicide ideation and substance abuse, which are more prevalent in people who are homeless. For example, in France, Cougnard and colleagues (2006) found that nearly one out of three homeless subjects (32.7%) presented with a psychotic disorder, a higher proportion than that found in non-homeless subjects (15.7%). Females who are homeless have higher prevalence of serious mental health problems than males (Martens, 2002). In the USA, Fitzpatrick and colleagues (2007) found a rate of suicide ideation of 30% among people who were homeless, compared to rates of suicide ideation of 3% in the general population. Severe mental health problems may be a contributing factor in the pathway towards homelessness, as a result of a social drift (discussed further below) and decreasing social support. Homelessness among people with mental health disabilities may have also been caused by deinstitutionalization of mental health care. In France, Cougnard and colleagues (2006) found that homelessness in some cases was the possible consequence of a break in contact with mental health services, with resulting untreated severe mental health problems (such as psychosis).

5.6 EXPLAINING SES HEALTH INEQUALITIES

5.6.1 NEOLIBERALISM AND HEALTH INEQUALITIES

Coburn (2004) argues that health disparities are not associated with income inequality alone, but rather that income inequality is one of various social conditions and inequalities which impact on health. He argues that income inequality is the consequence of broader "changes in class structure which have produced not only income inequality but also numerous other forms of health-relevant social inequalities" (p. 43). As Carroll and Smith (1997) note, in countries such as the USA and the UK, there has been an observed increase in income inequality which has been accompanied by an increase in health inequality. Coburn (2004) stresses the important role that neoliberalism (see Box 5.3) has played, which has resulted in the undermining of the welfare state (p. 44), leading to increased social and income inequalities and social fragmentation. This in turn results in people having reduced access to health-protecting resources, such as education, employment and health care. As argued by Coburn (2004: 45): "Families or individuals in market oriented societies have to rely on individually acquired market-related assets (such as income) to determine the degree to which they can access health-related societal resources (private health insurance versus public provision, private education/housing, etc)". In Chapter 3 we saw the example provided by Poku (2005) of when a service user fee of $2.15 was introduced at sexual health clinics in Kenya in an effort to encourage market-led development, there was a 35% to 60% drop in attendance.

BOX 5.3

What is Neoliberalism?

Neoliberalism refers to an economic, social and political ideology that stresses the benefits of a market-driven economy, where the individual is seen to benefit from being free to pursue free markets and trade and private ownership of property. According to Coburn (2000), the basic assumptions of neoliberalism are:

1 that markets are the best and most efficient allocators of resources in production and distribution;
2 that societies are composed of autonomous individuals (producers and consumers) motivated chiefly or entirely by material or economic considerations;
3 that competition is the major market vehicle for innovations (p. 138).

In neoliberalism, the individual is seen to have autonomy and consumer choice, with the role of the state being to facilitate such practices. The state acts as a facilitator and regulator of the market, rather than a venturer into such markets (Harvey, 2007).

The result in many countries has been increased privatization and the "withdrawal of the state from many areas of social provision" (Harvey, 2007: p. 3). While individuals are ensured freedom of consumer choice and investment in the marketplace, the risk falls on the individual rather than on the state. Thus failures are attributed to the individual. In neoliberalist economies, labour is reduced to a mere commodity (Harvey, 2007). Coburn (2000, 2004) shows how the rise of neoliberalism in developed countries and in the global economy has resulted in a decline of welfare state provision, with resulting rise in social and income inequalities.

Coburn (2000, 2004) also argues that neoliberalism, with its emphasis on the individual versus the collective, influences social cohesion as well as encouraging competitive markets, and this may negatively affect trust and reciprocity and so decrease social cohesion. This decreased social cohesion in turn affects an individual's health and well-being. Wilkinson (1997) points out the importance that the person's status in society has as a relationship of relative earnings rather than their material standard of living. Low social status is associated with increased stress, low self-esteem and poorer psychological well-being, which in turn affects physical health. In a recent review of the empirical work on SES and health inequalities, Wilkinson and Pickett (2009) observed a strong association between health inequality and income *inequality*, rather than national income. They argued that this inequality (which Farmer (2004) would consider as a form of structural violence – see Chapter 3), results in poor psychological well-being for people, as they become more stressed, anxious, untrusting, ashamed and depressed.

5.6.2 SOCIAL CAPITAL AND VARIATIONS IN HEALTH

There has been increasing attention given to the concept of 'social capital' as a way of explaining socio-economic health inequalities. Social capital refers to the degree of interpersonal and community engagement in a society. Putnam and colleagues (1993) used the concept of social capital to argue that successful societies (they used civic life in Italy as a case study) was characterized by the levels of trust between members of a society, its norms and social and institutional networks. They highlight the importance of community identity, networks, and engagement, interpersonal trust, and interpersonal reciprocity as contributing to improvements in the health, the economic success and efficiency of a community or society.

The concept of social capital has been investigated in relation to health (for example, Gillies, Tolley, & Wolstenholme, 1996; Lomas, 1998). Campbell and colleagues (1999) conducted a qualitative study comparing the community engagement in two low SES communities in England; one characterized by relatively high levels of health, and the other with relatively low levels of health. They investigated the different aspects of social capital – interpersonal trust, community engagement, perceived citizen power, local community identity, and local community facilities – in relation to levels of health. Their analysis indicated that the community with relatively higher levels of health was characterized with having higher levels of interpersonal trust, community engagement and perceived citizen power. The community with relatively lower levels of health was characterized as having higher levels of local community identity and community facilities. They thus argued that interpersonal trust and community engagement in particular was facilitative of good health. Although the community with lower levels of health had higher community identity and facilities, community-level *networks* were more prevalent in the community with higher levels of health. The Marmot Review explains the link of social capital to health as follows:

> Social capital describes the links between individuals: links that bind and connect people within and between communities. It provides a source of resilience, a buffer against risks of poor health, through social support which is critical to physical and mental well-being, and through the networks that help people find work, or get through economic and other material difficulties. The extent of people's participation in their communities and the added control over their lives that this brings has the potential to contribute to their psychosocial well-being and, as a result, to other health outcomes. (Marmot, 2010: p. 30)

Survey studies from other regions in the world, for example Latin America (Sapag & Kawachi, 2010), China (Yip, Subramanian, Mitchell, Lee, Wang, & Kawachi, 2007), and Thailand (Yiengprugsawan, Khamman, Seubsman, Lim, & Sleigh, 2011), have found some support for the importance of social capital and health, in particular the aspect of interpersonal trust. Scheffler and colleagues (2008), in a study of social capital and coronary heart disease, found that high levels of social capital in a community were associated with significantly lower levels of recurrence of acute coronary events. However, this was found for those living in low-income areas only, with no association between social capital and health found in higher income areas. This was explained by the finding that the influence of social capital on risk for disease was mediated by the level of psychological distress, with those people experiencing increased psychological distress and low social capital being most at risk.

Campbell (2001) outlines some of the criticisms that have been made against social capital as an aid to explaining health inequalities. Rather than being an explanatory concept, social capital has been critiqued as being a descriptive concept that is vague and poorly defined. Important criticisms have been made of the dangers of using social capital as an explanatory model, as justification for reduced welfare spending. This approach would see spending on encouraging community members to engage with and participate in local services as beneficial for health and well-being, which is cheaper than reducing material and income inequality. It places the responsibility on the individual community members (who needs to become more engaged) rather than on the state.

However, Campbell (2001) cautions that the importance of social capital as an explanatory aid does not negate the importance of material deprivation, and rather social capital can be seen as a mediating mechanism between material deprivation and health outcomes. Gillies and colleagues (1996) argue that material poverty is the primary cause of health inequalities, but that poverty also undermines community cohesion. They thus stress the importance of social development as well as economic development in addressing the effects of poverty on health.

5.6.3 THE CYCLE OF POVERTY AND HEALTH

As we have seen earlier, poor health and disability is a consequence of poverty. But poverty is also a consequence of poor health and disability. A sociological perspective on the relationship between poverty and health is represented by two competing explanatory theories: the explanatory theory of social causation and that of social selection.

The explanatory theory of social causation suggests that people of lower SES develop poorer physical and mental health as a result of the material and environmental conditions of living in poverty. This theory stresses poverty as the cause for poor physical and mental health. For example, with regards to mental health, social causation theory suggests that emotional distress is caused by material deprivation, adversity and stress (Cockerham, 2011). The focus here is on the development of mental health problems as a result of the environmental and social stresses of living in low SES circumstances. As we saw earlier, there are many factors associated with poverty, such as sense of insecurity and hopelessness, social upheaval, change and violence (Patel & Kleinman, 2003), which cause significant stress for individuals resulting in mental health problems. Also relevant here is the social fragmentation and disintegration that occurs as a result of poverty, with consequent reduction in social capital.

Social selection theory, on the other hand, suggests that there is a higher prevalence of physical and mental health problems, and disabilities, in lower SES populations because people with poor health and disability tend to become increasingly socially and economically excluded and thus 'drift' downwards on the SES continuum (Cockerham, 2011). This is also known as the social drift hypothesis. Health may also facilitate an upwards drift. For example, individuals from low SES backgrounds who have good mental health may be upwardly mobile, "leaving behind a 'residue' of mentally ill persons" (Cockerham, 2011: 141).

It has become generally understood that the relationship between poverty and health is a cyclical one, and that poor health may lead to declining SES, which in turn negatively impacts on health. This has been referred to as a vicious cycle of poverty and health, and has been discussed with regards physical health, mental health and disability (see Figure 5.5).

SES inequality is also compounded by other social factors, such as ethnicity and gender. The impact of SES may differ in terms of the degree of social

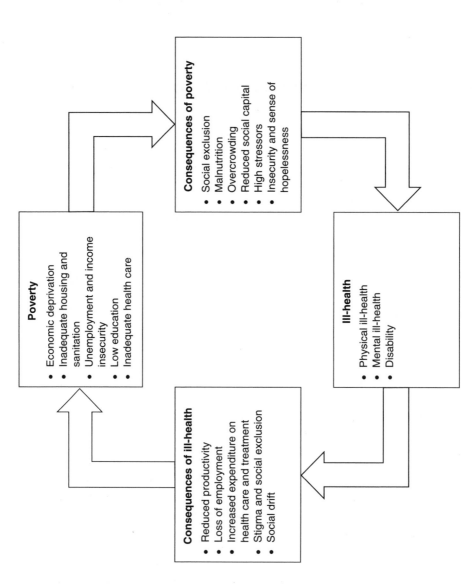

FIGURE 5.5 The vicious cycle of poverty ill-health

exclusion or meaning of social status. For example, Tiffin, Pearce, and Parker (2005) investigated the effect of SES on psychological well-being throughout the life course in a 50-year longitudinal study in the UK. They found that SES at birth had an impact on mental health at age 50, but that this impact differed between men and women. They concluded that women were more sensitive to having experienced SES disadvantage in childhood, whereas men were found to be more sensitive to a lack of having achieved socio-economic success. This points to the importance that gender roles and gender representations may have (see Chapter 6).

We have looked mostly at objective indicators of SES and health and illness, and theoretical models for understanding these SES health disparities. Equally important, however, is to consider how the lay public might understand or even recognize SES health disparities.

5.6.4 LAY UNDERSTANDINGS OF HEALTH INEQUALITIES

Chamberlain (1997) has highlighted the important contribution that qualitative research can make in understanding the experience of socio-economic health disparities, and the meaning of health that different people have at different places of the SES continuum. Some attention has been given to lay understandings of health inequalities. Chamberlain (1997) reviewed qualitative interview studies exploring lay understanding of health inequalities among people from low SES positions and high SES positions, noting differences in people's understanding of health and health-related practices which differed with regards the socio-economic context in which people were placed. For example, Chamberlain discusses studies that have found differences in where distress is located in the body, with people from working-class backgrounds understanding distress in terms of bodily symptoms (aches and pains), and middle-class people understanding distress in mentalistic terms (stress and worry).

Blaxter (1997) combined an analysis of data from a survey study of British participants with qualitative research findings on attitudes about the causes of health and illness. She found that there was little discussion about health inequalities, particularly among people from lower SES positions. Most explained the causes of health and illness in terms of individual factors, rather than environmental risk factors. Blaxter goes on to caution how the methods used in asking people to talk about health may silence representations of health inequalities. Blaxter distinguishes between public and private representations and accounts that individuals have and how the way questions are phrased in interview and survey studies may tap into different types of accounts. This was observed in a study by Popay and colleagues (2003) who explored lay understandings of health inequalities in four localities in the UK. They paid attention to how different methods of collecting data and the way that questions were asked may elicit differing types of accounts (see Box 5.4).

BOX 5.4

Spotlight on Research: Lay understandings of health inequalities

Popay, J., Bennett, S., Thomas, C., Williams, G., Gatrell, A., & Bostock, L. (2003). Beyond 'beer, fags, egg and chips'? Exploring lay understandings of social inequalities in health. *Sociology of Health & Illness, 25*(1), 1–23.

Aim: This study aimed to explore lay understandings of the causes of heath inequalities, and how these lay explanations may vary among people living in differing socio-economic areas. The study also aimed to explore how different methods of collecting data and questions used may influence how the lay understandings are generated and reported.

Method: The study took place in two cities in the North West of England. In each city two localities were selected – one relatively disadvantaged and one relatively advantaged. Thus the study involved four different localities. Data were collected by means of a postal survey of a random sample of people living in these four localities. Two thousand people were selected as possible respondents across the four localities and were provided with a survey questionnaire, which included one open-ended question on causes of health inequalities. A total sample of 777 people completed the survey questionnaire, representing a response rate varying from 35% to 56% across the four localities. Further data were collected by means of in-depth interviews with a purposively selected sub-sample of survey respondents. Fifty-one people were selected to take part in an interview, purposively selected to reflect a social diversity of respondents. Of these, 19 respondents took part in a second interview focusing on health inequalities. These interviews made use of prompt materials to initiate and aid discussion.

Results: The majority of responses to the open-ended survey questions related to place-specific factors as causes of health inequalities, which included things such as housing, traffic, crime, access to facilities and pollution. The second most common type of response related to individual factors, such as behaviours, lifestyles and attitudes. The third most common type of response was factors related to macro-structural causes, such as poverty and unemployment. Those respondents living in areas of relative disadvantage were more likely to explain health inequalities in terms of place-specific causes, whereas those respondents from areas or relative advantage were more likely to explain health inequalities in terms of individual factors. In responses where a combination of factors were indicated, place-specific factors still tended to predominate.

Results from the 19 respondents interviewed showed some interesting differences. At first, respondents from the more deprived areas tended to challenge the findings linking health inequalities and SES which were presented to the interviewees, whereas respondents from the affluent areas did not dispute these health inequalities. For example, one respondent is reported as saying:

> People in areas where they've got more money and professional backgrounds ...
> it kind of puzzles me in a way to say that the men are living longer because

heart disease is the biggest killer I think in this country and I would have thought that men who were in high powered or stressful jobs ... would be perhaps only on a par with a lower working class person in that respect. (Popay et al., 2003: 11)

The researchers felt that many of the respondents from the deprived areas were initially rejecting the perceived labelling of people from different areas in terms of poor and good health. As one woman is quoted as saying: "they are making out that it's all like scum and they're all dying" (p. 13). However, as the interviews progressed, respondents began to talk about their lived experiences of health inequalities, drawing on complex causal explanations related to place factors, individual factors and macro-structural factors. For example, respondents referred to the effects of low income, poor living conditions, crime, poor housing, the physical and social environment, and social cohesiveness on health. Stress was highlighted by most respondents as the key mediating factor between disadvantage and ill-health. While discussing the effects of disadvantage on health, participants from disadvantaged backgrounds also stressed issues of coping and control, in so doing reconstructing an acceptable moral identity (p. 18). People from more affluent areas did not seem to need to refer to a moral identity in this way.

Conclusions: The results indicated that people tended to place more emphasis on place-specific factors as explanations of ill-health, with less reporting of macro-structural factors, such as SES inequality, as explanatory factors. However, during the interviews, after an initial rejection of macro-structural explanations for health inequalities, these factors featured more prominently in respondents' accounts of their lived experience of health.

The authors suggest that the emphasis made on area and place (by naming the specific localities) made in the survey and interview resulted in a greater emphasis made by respondents on place-specific factors over other factors, but that these factors also had a "lighter 'moral' load" (p. 21), and thus were easier emotionally to refer to.

The interesting part of this paper is that attention is given to how different questions and methods of collecting data may elicit different accounts of lay understandings. In the interviews, respondents were gradually able to account for macro-structural causes of health inequalities, but reveal how doing so carried connotations of moral labelling (poor as inferior and "scum"). However, it must be noted that the interview data were preceded by responses collected by means of a survey questionnaire and a first interview (the paper reports on qualitative data from the second interview). It needs to be considered that the respondents were given considerable prompts (both explicit and implicit) to perhaps facilitate the incorporation of SES inequality as an explanation into their understanding of health inequalities.

SES AND THE PROFESSIONAL–PATIENT INTERACTION

5.7

In many countries, SES determines access to adequate health care. Access to health care differs depending on the health care system. For example, in the USA different health care systems exist for patients with or without health care insurance, and research has shown that those patients with no health care insurance receive poorer health care (Morrison & Bennett, 2009). Recent health care reform in the USA aims to maintain public and private health care systems but improve access to health care insurance for poorer families in an effort to make health care more equitable. In the UK, with the existence of the National Health Service, access to health care is more equitable; however, disparities have been shown in the type of intervention or frequency of medical and surgical procedure received between patients from lower SES and patients from higher SES (see Morrison & Bennett, 2009). Access to health care in many countries is also dependent on the ability to afford time off from paid employment, covering the cost of travel, and other practicalities, which may cause more difficulties for people from low SES communities.

It is often the situation that a health care professional, due to their professional status or background, work with patients who come from lower SES backgrounds. This is particularly so in public health care systems. This class difference may influence the consulting relationship between the professional and client (as is the case with other types of differences, such as culture, gender and sexuality discussed in the other chapters). Professionals, coming from higher SES backgrounds, have generally not been exposed to the experience of poverty, and generally issues of poverty and class are neglected in professional trainings, thus professionals may hold biased assumptions of their patients from lower SES backgrounds reflective of broader class socialization (Rogers & Pilgrim, 2005).

Research suggests that there are differences in how patients from lower SES are treated by health care professionals. For example, research indicates that patients from lower SES groups, are given less information by health care professionals during their interactions, and have shorter consultations that those from higher SES (Lyons & Chamberlain, 2006). Interactions with patients of low SES are often characterized by less positivity and emotional warmth on the part of the health care professional, and a less participatory style of consultation (Willems, De Maesschalck, Deveugele, Derese, & De Maeseneer, 2005). With regards mental health professionals, they may conceptualize the distress of patients living in poverty in biological terms, rather than social-psychological terms (Rogers & Pilgrim, 2005). Research has found that mental health clinicians tend to interpret lower scores on psychometric tests of poorer patients as indicative of greater psychopathology than with the similar scores of richer patients, despite evidence showing that performance on psychometric tests are significantly affected by conditions of poverty (Rogers & Pilgrim, 2005). Such differences in the patient–health care professional interaction may be compounded by cultural issues. In Chapter 4, disparities were explored in the treatment of patients from ethnic minority groups, many of whom come from lower SES communities.

Interactions may involve discriminatory and judgemental attitudes. For example, Renedo and Jovchelovitch (2007) conducted a qualitative study of health professionals' representations of homelessness and how this may impact on their professional interactions with clients who are homeless. They found that contradictions existed in their representations of homelessness, for example with humanizing representations which focused on the whole person and human dignity of the homeless versus a victimizing representation in which homeless people were 'othered' and pitied, and viewed as powerless and voiceless. These differing representations can enhance or undermine the health of their homeless clients, as clients are treated either with understanding or with judgement.

SUMMARY

5.8 This chapter has explored the SES health gradient both at a global level and at a country level. Most of the studies referred to here have been epidemiological studies, which have provided reliable indicators of this SES health gradient. We have also looked at different explanations for this disparity. Central in all these explanations is the issue of power inequality and social exclusion, of interest to critical psychologists (see Chapter 2). This power dynamic is also played out in the doctor–patient interaction, when often the doctor is from a higher SES background compared to the patient. Marks (2004) argues how central to understanding and tackling SES health inequalities is the analysis of power and promotion of social justice, and that these should be at the heart of a critical health (and clinical) psychology approach to health inequality. As Marks points out, this takes us outside the field of psychology and into economics, politics and human rights. But as many people have argued, tackling the significant global social problems, such as poverty, requires a multi-disciplinary approach.

FURTHER READINGS

Desjarlais, R., Eisenberg, L., Good, B., & Kleinman, A. (1995). *World mental health: Problems and priorities in low-income countries*. New York and Oxford: Oxford University Press. Although this book is now quite dated, it nevertheless provides a detailed investigation of mental health problems around the world, particularly in low-income countries. The observations made and issues raised remain relevant.

Dodd, R., & Munck, L. (2002). *Dying for change: Poor people's experience of health and ill-health*. Geneva: World Health Organization and World Bank. Very often literature on SES and health focus on statistics and the experiences of people living in poverty are rarely presented. This report by the WHO and the World Bank provides a presentation of peoples' experiences and perspectives of poverty and health, drawing on data from a large qualitative study involving 60,000 poor women and men from 60 different countries.

Rogers, A., & Pilgrim, D. (2003). *Mental health and inequality*. Basingstoke: Palgrave Macmillan. This book, written by a sociologist and a psychologist, explores SES inequality and mental health. The book also takes into account other social divisions, such as age, gender and race, when exploring inequality in mental health.

Wilkinson, R., & Pickett, K. (2009). *The spirit level: Why more equal societies almost always do better*. London: Penguin Group. This book highlights the importance of SES inequality in relation to health, mental health and social well-being. It is accessible in its style, drawing on 30 years worth of epidemiological research.

GENDER

6

INTRODUCTION

6.1 There are so many gender-based clichés that we bandy about daily: women are bad drivers; men only have sex on their minds; women are nurturers; men are better at maths; women are more emotional than men; men are stronger, women are weak. Then we stigmatize those men and women who do not fit our stereotypes. So women bosses are 'bitches', male nurses are the source of jokes (think of the character Greg Focker in the movie *Meet the Parents*). We have so many ideas of how men should behave and how women should behave. We constantly reflect on our differences, and like to think that many of these differences are innate: men and women are *just* different. Some of these notions are supported by research that claims scientific evidence for differences between men and women and their behaviours and capabilities. However, some have contested this science of sex differences (Fine, 2010).

When it comes to health, we have similar notions: men are tougher and more robust than women. Women look after themselves more than men. It is more acceptable for men to have a beer-belly than it is for a woman. There are disparities and differences in health in relation to gender. While many differences are a result of biological differences (and having different anatomical structures), other differences relate more to social constructions of gender and gender-based relationship differences. This chapter shall explore some of these issues, looking at the role of gender (both femininity and masculinity) in relation to physical health, mental health and disability. The existence of a health gender gap shall be discussed in terms of morbidity and life expectancy. Some of these differences will be explored in relation to masculinity and men's health, which is receiving increasing attention. The social constructions of femininity and masculinity shall then be explored in relation to health risk behaviours – smoking and drinking – with some interesting changes in behaviours being observed. The chapter will then look at two issues which overlap clinical psychology and health psychology – sexual health and sexual disorders, and gender, body image and eating disorders. Gendered mental disorders are explored in relation to depression and anxiety, but we shall also look at the diagnosis of borderline personality disorder as a particular gendered disorder. As clarified in Chapter 1, when speaking of physical illness and mental health problems, we are also often referring to disabilities. However, the chapter shall close by looking at some issues of gender and disability more broadly. But before we proceed, it is important to clarify what is actually being referred to with the term 'gender'.

6.1.1 DEFINING GENDER

Social scientists distinguish between 'sex' (as referring to biological differences) and 'gender', which refers to socially constructed entities. This approach views 'gender' as referring to representations of masculinities and femininities that are social-cultural. Differences exist in how similar phenomena may be represented for men and for women. These refer to differences that do not exist *within* the individual, but rather as part of an "*unnatural* social categorization system" (Clarke & Braun, 2009: 236). For example, behaviour that may be represented as "assertive" in men, may be represented as being "pushy" in women.

Gender is also normatively constructed as being a dual category – male or female – which excludes transgendered persons who may wish to identify as neither. Male and female dualism is regarded as 'normal' whereas transgendered individuals are regarded as 'abnormal', and may be persuaded to undertake gender reassignment surgery.

Constructions of gender also dictate what is appropriate and inappropriate gender behaviour. Butler (2006) argues that gender is performative, where gender refers to what you *do*, rather than what you *are*. According to Butler, the 'realities' of differences in masculinity and femininity are created and maintained through activities that we view as differentiating the two genders, such as girls 'preferring' the colour pink and playing with dolls, and boys 'preferring' the colour blue and playing with toy guns. These do not represent intrinsic differences between male and female, but rather are socially constructed practices which are seen as producing a gendered reality. As Butler argues: "There is no gender identity behind the expressions of gender; [gender] identity is performatively constituted by the very 'expressions' that are said to be its results" (Butler, 2006: 34). These gendered practices and performances also maintain gender inequalities. Connell (2009) argues that gender is power-based, in which men are privileged over women.

Many studies have observed health disparities in relation to sex (males and females), which do not necessarily reflect on the issues of gender (that is masculinities and femininities). This chapter will draw on both as it is epidemiological studies that have permitted us to observe clear, statistical differences in health, which can be further explored in terms of notions of 'gender'. Although I have differentiated between sex and gender here, I shall make use of the term 'gender' in most cases, for ease of reading.

6.2 GENDER DISPARITIES IN HEALTH

6.2.1 GENDER DIFFERENCES IN HEALTH AND ILLNESS

Epidemiological studies in many societies have suggested that women live longer than men, but have poorer health than men (Doyal, 2000). For example, Figure 6.1 shows statistics of life expectancy among men and women in the UK, over the period 1980 to 2007, showing improved life expectancy for both men and women over this period, but also showing a relatively stable difference between men and women (although the gap is closing).

The leading cause of death in the UK for both men and women is heart disease, although it is lower for women than for men (Office for National Statistics, 2010). Other leading causes of death for men were lung cancer, cerebrovascular disease and chronic lower respiratory disease. For women, other leading causes of death were cerebrovascular disease (more than for men), dementia and Alzheimer's disease, and influenza and pneumonia (Office for National Statistics, 2010). Violence and accidents are another leading cause of death, more so for men than women.

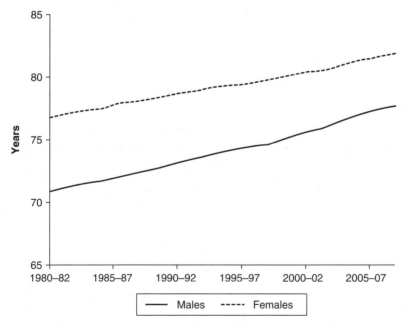

FIGURE 6.1 Life expectancy at birth, UK, from period life tables, 1980–1982 to 2007–2009

Source: Office for National Statistics licensed under the Open Government Licence v.1.0.
(www.statistics.gov.uk/CCI/nugget.asp?ID=168)

The leading causes of death for men and women worldwide are presented in Table 6.1. The leading cause of deaths for men and women worldwide are similar, with the notable exception that more men than women die as a result of road traffic accidents, and more women die of diabetes and maternal conditions (complications during pregnancy and childbirth).

Certain diseases and illnesses may be attributed to biological sex differences. Obvious examples include prostate cancer for men and ovarian cancer for women. Biological sex differences have been found to contribute to differences in the causes and incidence of many diseases, including tropical infectious diseases, sexually transmitted diseases, coronary heart disease and tuberculosis (Doyal, 1998, 2000). For example, in the case of malaria, women may be more prone to infection with malaria during pregnancy as a result of a compromised immunity, and malaria during pregnancy is one of the major causes of maternal death (Doyal, 1998). With sexually transmitted disease, women are more prone

TABLE 6.1 Leading causes of death for men and women worldwide

Men		Women	
Cause of death by category	**%**	**Cause of death by category**	**%**
Cardiovascular diseases	27.2	Cardiovascular diseases	31.7
Infectious and parasitic diseases	19.4	Infectious and parasitic diseases	18.8
Cancers (with lung cancer being the highest)	13.3	Cancers (with breast cancer being the highest)	11.6
Unintentional injuries (e.g. traffic accidents)	7.7	Respiratory infections	7.3
Respiratory infections	6.7	Respiratory diseases	6.6
Cause of death by specific cause	**%**	**Cause of death by specific cause**	**%**
Ischaemic heart disease	12.7	Ischaemic heart disease	12.5
Cerebrovascular disease	8.5	Cerebrovascular disease	10.9
Lower respiratory infections	6.5	Lower respiratory infections	7.1
HIV/AIDS	4.8	HIV/AIDS	4.9
Chronic obstructive pulmonary disease	4.7	Chronic obstructive pulmonary disease	4.9
Tuberculosis	3.4	Diarrhoeal diseases	3.2
Diarrhoeal diseases	3.1	Malaria	2.5
Trachea/bronchus/lung cancers	3.0	Tuberculosis	2.0
Road traffic accidents	2.9	Diabetes mellitus	2.0
Malaria	2.0	Maternal conditions	1.9

Source: World Health Organization (2004). *World health report 2004 – changing history*. Geneva: World Health Organization.

than men as a result of women having a larger genital surface area of the vagina and thus larger area of mucosa, which is exposed to their partner's secretions during sex (Doyal, 1998). But differences in health are also influenced by the social constructions of gender and resulting gender inequality and gendered relationships (Doyal, 2000).

6.2.2 GENDER, MASCULINITY AND HEALTH DISPARITIES

Gender inequalities have been shown to be related to both physical and mental health (Doyal, 1998). As we saw in Chapter 5, poverty is one of the most important contributing factors to poor health, and women are more likely to be living in conditions of poverty. Women are often disadvantaged in the workplace, affecting their quality of life and physical and mental health (Annandale & Hunt, 2000). Such gender inequalities and power differentials in gender relationships have been recognized as playing a major part in the spread of HIV/AIDS (Jewkes, 2009). This shall be discussed further below.

Until fairly recently, concerns about the gendered aspects of health have tended to focus on women, with less attention given for how social constructions of masculinity may influence men's health (Doyal, 2000). There has, however, been some recent attention given to masculinities and health (for example, Gough & Robertson, 2010; Lee & Owens, 2002). As suggested above, men are more likely to die as a result of violence and accidental or occupational injuries than women (Doyal, 1998). Of course some violence is gendered, such as domestic violence and rape. Death as a result of occupational hazards may be partly attributed to traditional constructions of the male as the breadwinner, and their likelihood to be employed in more dangerous jobs (for example, as miners, fire fighters and construction workers) than females (Doyal, 1998). Such differences focus on the gender *roles* of men, but as Courtenay (2000) argues, men hold health-related beliefs and partake in health-enabling or risk behaviours as a means of demonstrating masculinity. For example, men, often constructed as tough, strong and fearless, may also feel compelled to partake in risky physical activities as a means to prove their masculinity. The influence of constructions of masculinity for health are also reflected in the statistics showing that men are more likely to die as a result of violence or be killed in road accidents or dangerous sports (Doyal, 2000). Courtenay (2000) argues that men may hold health beliefs or partake in health risk behaviours as a demonstration of power, for example as not appearing weak, emotional or vulnerable, and being seen to have physical control. Courtenay (2000: 1389) states:

> In exhibiting or enacting hegemonic ideals with health behaviours, men reinforce strongly held cultural beliefs that men are more powerful and less vulnerable than women; that men's bodies are structurally more efficient than and superior to women's bodies; that asking for help and caring for one's health are feminine; and that the most powerful men among men are those for whom health and safety are irrelevant.

As Courtenay suggests above, men are less likely to seek help and health care than women. In doing so, they are not only partaking in a health practice, but are also demonstrating masculinity, and rejecting what are constructed as feminine ideals. Men have been found to think of health as belonging to the women's domain, and may as a consequence have limited knowledge about men's health problems, such as prostate cancer (Cameron & Bernardes, 1998). Furthermore, illness may be feared by men, as it may be seen to challenge their masculinity, reducing them to a 'marginalized masculinity' (Cameron & Bernardes, 1998). These notions also differ across cultures. For example, in a qualitative study from the UK exploring the help-seeking behaviour of white and South Asian men who have had cardiac chest pain (Galdas, 2010), the majority of white men interviewed spoke about initial concerns about appearing weak when they first noticed their chest pains. They felt the need to display a high tolerance for pain, and delayed seeking help, partly out of concerns about appearing like a 'hypochondriac' to their peers. Many did not disclose their pain to others as a result of these concerns. In contrast, none of the South Asian men interviewed had concerns around appearing weak, and saw their chest pain as a legitimate reason for seeking help. They placed greater value on wisdom and responsibility as important male attributes.

Men's health is often depicted as being in a state of 'crisis' (Lyons & Willott, 1999; see also Gough, 2006), where *all* men are portrayed as being unhealthy, and traditionally not concerned about their health. Lyons and Willott (1999) observed how media representations of men's health may often depict men as passive and helpless when it comes to looking after their health, and thus be in need of women to look after them. This maintains the stereotype of health being the women's domain, and not the concern of men. In a more recent study, Gough (2006) similarly observes how media representations of men's health depict men as unconcerned about health, and not always psychologically capable of seeking help (they are depicted as emotionally repressed and invulnerable). Gough observed a slight shift away from the portrayal of women as best able to assist men with their health, to a focus on services being required to adapt in order to reach out to the needs of men, thus maintaining their 'masculinity'. In his study of media representations of men's health, masculinity is essentialized, with all men merged into one, unhealthy group. Men who may represent marginalized masculinities are not included. Not *all* men are emotionally repressed, unconcerned about their health and helpless when it comes to seeking help.

Some of these constructions of masculinity and femininity and their relation to health behaviours are reflected in a qualitative study exploring lay understandings of gender disparities in health (Emslie & Hunt, 2008). Most of the 45 men and women taking part in the study drew on socio-cultural explanations for why women live longer than men, rather than biological explanations. These are demonstrated in some of the participants' quotes below:

> I think they [women] cope with things more easily ... they would talk about it. I feel as if men, I know they do hide a lot of things ... I suppose it's just pride ... or it's a man thing. (p. 812)

> Being a young man is, I think, is very dangerous to your health. ... Playing sports ... going out drinking ... threats of violence. (p. 812)

> I don't know if it comes back to the sort of old sort of rules of being macho ... that ... illness is a weakness ... whereas with women, it's not any big deal. (p. 813)

One area in which we can observe health risk behaviours as influenced by constructions of gender is in alcohol consumption, smoking and drugs.

6.2.3 GENDER AND HEALTH RISK BEHAVIOURS: SMOKING AND DRINKING

Research has shown that in most societies men are more likely than women to smoke and to drink alcohol in excess (Waldron, 1995). This increases men's vulnerability to heart disease and other health problems, such as lung cancer and liver damage. There are cultural variations in attitudes towards drinking and smoking, and what is considered 'normal' consumption, when such consumption should take place and by whom (Helman, 2007b). Drinking alcohol and smoking may be part of social rituals, such as champagne at celebrations in many western cultures. These cultural meanings around 'normal' and 'abnormal' drinking and smoking also involve notions of gender.

According to World Health Organization estimates (MacKay & Eriksen, 2002), more men than women smoke worldwide, with the gap between men and women who smoke being greater in developing countries. According to these WHO statistics, 35% of men and 22% of women in developed countries smoke, and 50% of men and 9% of women in developing countries smoke. Smoking has traditionally been represented as a masculine activity, with cigarette advertising often portraying cigarette smoking as manly. A woman smoking is often represented as being unfeminine (although media have depicted the image of the seductive woman smoking a slim cigarette, or the powerful, sexy woman smoking a cigar). Over the past decades there has been an observed change, with an increasing number of women smoking. An early study in the USA (Reeder, 1977) observed an increase of women smokers, particularly among employed, better educated women, thus associating the rise in smoking with women's changing gender roles. Smoking was thus seen as a possible "indicator of increased social power and/or independence" (Reeder, 1977: 194). As the WHO statistics quoted above indicate, these representations of gender and smoking may vary across cultures. In a survey study of women's attitudes towards gender and smoking in Vietnam (Morrow, Ngoc, Hoang, & Trinh, 2002), only 6.3% of the 2,020 women participants self-reported as current smokers (much less that that reported in men in national surveys in Vietnam). The women surveyed generally indicated that smoking by women was inappropriate, with many indicating that women smokers were associated with having "loose" morals. In contrast, smoking by men was regarded as being normative. Low rates of smoking among women in Vietnam were perceived by the majority of participants as being due to social disapproval, with many younger women indicating that smoking for them was "forbidden".

Similarly, drinking alcohol is often constructed as being a masculine activity, and research indicates that men drink more alcohol than women (Ahlström & Österberg, 2004/2005; Wilsnack, Vogeltanz, Wilsnack, & Harris, 2000). For example, in a survey study in Moscow (Jukkala, Mäkinen, Kislitsyna, Ferlander, & Vågerö, 2008), responses indicated that men drank more than twice as much alcohol (converted into a measure of grams of pure ethanol) than women per occasion. In this study, 29.6% of men were found to be binge-drinking compared to 5.9% of women. The study found associations between men binge-drinking and experiencing economic strain. Women, on the other hand, were found to be less likely to binge-drink when experiencing economic problems. The study also found that level of education was strongly associated with binge-drinking. Jukkala and colleagues (2008) further concluded that women's drinking tended to occur in the context of socializing with friends, while men's drinking occurred "everywhere".

Public drinking is viewed by many men as a means of symbolizing masculinity (De Visser & Smith, 2007; Kaminer & Dixon, 1995; Peralta, 2007). For example, in qualitative interview studies with men, participants have been found to define public drinking as a masculine activity, as typical among 'mates', and contrasted it with women drinking as unnatural and inferior (Kaminer & Dixon, 1995). All-men nights out drinking was also depicted as forming part of a heterosexual masculine identity, and as an opportunity for expressing heterosexual masculinity and the disparagement and subordination of women and non-normative masculinities, such as 'nerds' and gay men (Gough & Edwards, 1998; Kaminer & Dixon, 1995). In a qualitative study with 78 male university students in the USA, public drinking was found to be viewed by the male students as being the embodiment of masculinity, where masculinity is constructed in terms of a tolerance and capacity to drink, whereas minimal drinking is viewed as a sign of weakness, femininity and homosexuality (Peralta, 2007).

However, there has been an observed increase in drinking among women (Allamani, Voller, Kubicka, & Bloomfield, 2000; Lyons & Willott, 2008). In many western societies, women are entering domains which have been previously male-dominated, and have increased opportunities for engaging in leisure activities which have traditionally been seen as male activities, such as frequenting bars and pubs (Day, Gough, & McFadden, 2004). In a study of media representations of women's drinking in the UK, Day and colleagues (2004) reported that while there was an acknowledgement that women were drinking more alcohol, and that more feminine drinking places (such as café-bars) had become more popular, there was little recognition that women may drink for pleasure, and rather women's drinking was more regularly depicted negatively, with women drinking being represented as "unfeminine, risking their health, and even emasculating" (p. 171).

Data from nine countries in Europe (Allamani et al., 2000) indicate that women have increased their intake of alcohol in recent decades, and the authors find an association between women's increased alcohol intake and women's increased levels of education and increased involvement in paid workforce. In a more recent comparative study (Rahav, Wilsnack, Bloomfield, Gmel, & Kuntsche, 2006) of gender differences in alcohol consumption across 29 countries, men's drinking was reported to be more prevalent than women's, and involved more heavy drinking. However, findings indicated that the extent of the gap between prevalence of men's drinking and women's drinking was associated with the modernization of the country and women's social positions. The greatest gender differences were found in countries such as Sri Lanka and Mexico, with countries such as Iceland and Finland having a much smaller gender difference gap. Lyons and Willott (2008) conducted a qualitative study exploring New Zealand women's understanding of their drinking behaviours, and showed how women's increased drinking behaviours may be a reflection of women's changing social positions (see Box 6.1).

BOX 6.1

A Spotlight on Research: Women's changing social positions and alcohol consumption

Lyons, A.C., & Willott, S.A. (2008). Alcohol consumption, gender identities and women's changing social positions. *Sex Roles, 59,* 694–712.

Aims: In light of a recent marked increase in the alcohol consumption of young women in many western countries, this study aimed to explore contemporary constructions of gender, particularly femininity, in relation to alcohol consumption. This research drew, in part, on the work of Butler, who views gender as performative, to explore if changes in drinking behaviour is reflective of changes in women's social positions and changes in constructions of femininity.

Methods: This was a qualitative study using focus groups as a way of collecting data. Eight friendship groups were interviewed, comprising a total of 32 participants (16 of whom were female). Friendship groups (i.e. groups of acquaintances) were recruited from worksites in the city of Auckland (New Zealand) and by word of mouth. Seven of the groups were mixed sex and one was all-female. The interview data were analysed using primarily discourse analysis (see Chapter 8 for description of discourse analysis).

Results: All participants spoke about drinking large amounts of alcohol as being a pleasurable, fun activity and part of a "big night out" on a weekend. Heavy drinking was depicted as normative for both men and women in these friendship groups, although women reported drinking a little less than men overall. Participants attributed the increase in women's drinking to increasing gender equality. Heavy drinking was also spoken about as being part of the cultural identity of being a New Zealander. Although both men and women drank to excess, there were gender differences in who drank what. Men primarily drank beer, whereas women primarily drank wine and spirits. Drinking beer was seen as a "what guys do" (p. 701). Thus men drank

(Continued)

(Continued)

beer because it was associated with what was normative for men, rather than because of enjoying the taste of beer. Women who drank beer were perceived by some participants as being of a lower class. Some men, however, viewed women drinking beer as "cool". Participants understood the changing roles of women as being more financially independent, and delaying childbirth or choosing not to have children, as giving them more freedom to go out and drink. There were some gender differences in terms of places to drink, with the pub being seen as a more masculine place to drink, and cafés and bars being seen as more feminine or gender equal places. Not all women who drink were seen favourably, with older women drinking or very drunk women being seen unfavourably. Both men and women recognized the vulnerability of drunken women to being sexually attacked by men, whereas there was little worry about drunken men.

Conclusions: Men and women were enacting versions of masculinity and femininity in their drinking behaviour. There were differences in what was drunk by men and women, how it was drunk and where. Although drinking was seen as part of a pleasurable, fun night out, there was a "feminization of binge drinking" (p. 708) as women tried to assert a feminine identity to traditionally masculine behaviour.

The strength of this study is that it provides an in-depth exploration of men and women's understanding of drinking behaviours, and links these to broader sociocultural constructions of gendered behaviour and expectations, which have changed over time. This goes beyond observing trends or patterns of behaviour, providing insight into the different meanings of drinking behaviour, and how constructions of gender are incorporated into these meanings.

GENDER AND SEXUAL HEALTH

6.3 Sexuality has for a long time been subject to social mores and control, and it is perhaps the aspect of our lives that causes most anxiety and, in some cases shame. It is also the arena in which gendered power relationships are played out. Both male and female sexuality, particularly with regards the reproductive system, has always been a focus of health care (Doyal, 2001). Women's reproductive health has been most medicalized as women have been more in need of reproductive health care than men. In the past few decades, our sexual lives have increasingly become the focus of medical attention, with the advent of HIV/AIDS and, more recently, the release of Viagra and the increased medicalization of sex. A critical perspective of sexual dysfunctions and transmission of HIV highlights how the biomedical model may rest on gendered assumptions of what is normal and abnormal, and also does not give attention to the role that gender relationships have in the transmission of sexually transmitted diseases.

6.3.1 SEXUAL DIFFICULTIES AS SEXUAL DYSFUNCTIONS

The DSM-IV-TR defines a sexual dysfunction as characterized by "a disturbance in the processes that characterize the sexual response cycle or by pain
associated with intercourse" (APA, 2000: 535), where the sexual response cycle
is conceptualized (by Masters and Johnson, 1966) as a linear progression from
sexual desire leading to sexual arousal, culminating in orgasm, and leading to
resolution (see Figure 6.2).

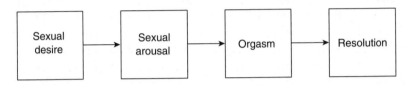

FIGURE 6.2 The sexual response cycle

At each stage of the sexual response cycle, quantifiable physical changes can
be observed, such as changes in blood flow, heart rate, secretion of various flu-
ids and so on. A sexual dysfunction is diagnosable at the various stages of this
sexual response cycle (see Box 6.2)

BOX 6.2

DSM-IV-TR Sexual Dysfunction Disorders (APA, 2000)

Disorders of Desire:

1 Hypoactive Sexual Desire Disorder: persistent or recurring deficiency or absence
   of sexual desire
2 Sexual Aversion Disorder: aversion to and avoidance of genital sexual contact with
   partner

Disorders of Sexual Arousal:

1 Female Sexual Arousal Disorder: Persistent inability to attain or maintain an adequate genital lubrication-swelling response of sexual excitement
2 Male Erectile Disorder: Persistent inability to attain or maintain an erection

Disorders of Orgasm:

1 Female Orgasmic Disorder and
2 Male Orgasmic Disorder: persistent or recurrent delay in or absence of orgasm
   following normal sexual excitement
3 Premature Ejaculation.

The emphasis of the sexual response cycle and the DSM sexual dysfunctions is on genital functionality. With this focus on functional aspects of sex, sexuality has become medicalized and any disruption of normal function is diagnosed as abnormal and, according to a biomedical model, subject to medical intervention. Marshall (2002) points out that what is considered as *dysfunction* is the disruption to the normal function of (hetero)sexual intercourse, which historically has been constructed as essential for a happy (heterosexual) marriage.

A much cited study investigating prevalence of dysfunction among 1,410 men and 1,749 women in the USA (Laumann, Paik, & Rosen, 1999) suggested that sexual dysfunction was more prevalent in women than in men. The survey study asked participants questions about whether they had experienced any problems related to the sexual response cycle for two months or more in the past 12 months. For example, participants were asked if they had experienced lacking a desire for having sex, any anxiety about their sexual performance, trouble lubricating (for women) or achieving an erection (for men), inability to achieve an orgasm, and so on. From the findings of the self-report data, the researchers concluded that "the total prevalence of sexual dysfunction is higher for women than men (43% vs 31%)" (p. 541). The authors conclude that sexual dysfunction, caused by both health-related and psychosocial factors, "warrants recognition as a significant public health concern" (p. 544). This figure is now frequently cited for the prevalence of sexual dysfunction. However, Moynihan (2003) raises concerns about the validity of this figure, given that if respondents answered 'yes' to one of the seven questions asked, they were categorized as having a sexual dysfunction. Bancroft (2002) further problematizes the categorization of women who responded yes to any of these questions as having a sexual dysfunction, when the researchers themselves found an association between the reporting of sexual problems with well-being and problems in the relationship. These findings may be more to do with sexual *difficulties* rather than sexual *dysfunctions* (Moynihan, 2003). As a result, it has been suggested that this finding has contributed to the "overmedicalization of women's sexuality" (Moynihan, 2003: 46). Sexual problems or inhibition may be a normal response to personal or social stresses, rather than a biological, medical problem that requires medical intervention.

Tiefer (2006) argues that the diagnosis of female sexual dysfunction is an example of what has been termed 'disease mongering'. Disease mongering is considered to be the contemporary form of medicalization, and has been defined as "the selling of sickness that widens the boundaries of illness and grows the markets for those who sell and deliver treatments" (Moynihan & Henry, 2006). Tiefer (2006) argues that in recent decades the public has come to desire and expect a rewarding sexual life with 'good sex' constructed as important for happy, fulfilling relationships. However, sex also has a long history of social control and taboo, and very often is related to feelings of "shame and ignorance" (Tiefer, 2006: 436), making it difficult for people to know how to go about achieving the goals of sex as rewarding. This has led to our sexual lives becoming vulnerable to disease mongering, as it takes anxiety about sexual performance that is in large part socially created and converts it into a medical problem that can be treated. Take the success of Viagra as an example. The introduction of Viagra in 1998 was hailed as a 'miracle pill' which would transform our sexual lives. Marshall (2002) describes the introduction of Viagra to the market as "a cultural 'event'" (p. 132), and as a signifier of a new era in sexual performance and sexual relationships. Viagra has become commonplace in our social culture, and has gone beyond just being a pill for achieving an erection to being a pill that will enhance sexual performance and sexual pleasure, for both men and women. In this sense, Viagra has become a lifestyle drug.

Soon after the introduction of Viagra, there were calls for the development of a female Viagra, although it was not clear what a female Viagra would treat (Tiefer, 2006). There was a quantifiable problem that could be treated for men – the failure to achieve an erection, but what exactly should be treated in women was not clear. The treatment of erectile dysfunction can be seen as an incidence of medicalization. Marshall (2002) argues that much of the research on sexual dysfunction is couched as scientific discoveries, but that masks the gendered constructions about what constitutes a normal sexual response cycle, with penile–vaginal intercourse as the centre-piece. For example, she observes how there was a shift from "impotence" to "erectile dysfunction" in the late 1980s, emphasizing an inability to achieve an erection as a physiological problem (a dysfunction) rather than a psychological or emotional problem (Marshall, 2002). Marshall further points to the emphasis placed on research on erectile dysfunction, where the erect penis is seen as central to successful sexual intercourse, with problems of male sexual desire and premature ejaculation getting much less attention. Erectile dysfunction becomes constructed as a mechanical, biological problem that can be easily rectified with medication. Female sexual dysfunction, on the other hand, is more difficult to quantify and has been at times problematized in terms of low self-esteem and insecurity. However, since the 1990s, increased attention has been given to research on female sexual dysfunction and there have been efforts to find a treatment for vaginal lubrication. Moynihan (2003) argues that female sexual dysfunction is a fabricated medical and mental diagnosis, driven by funding for research by pharmaceutical companies who have enjoyed massive profits from the medicalization of sexuality, for example from the market success of Viagra.

Research in sexual dysfunctions have tended to utilize experimental, quantitative methods for measuring the physiological sexual responses in men and women diagnosed as having sexual dysfunction, and in later decades the psychological factors (such as cognitions and affect) that may be associated with the physiological response. Such approaches, however, tend to make a linear model of problems in the sexual response, and do not capture the complexities of men and women's sexual desires and arousal and the relationship between the two (Janssen, McBride, Yarber, Hill, & Butler, 2008). More recently, qualitative research methods have been seen as useful as a method for critiquing the medicalization of sexuality, but also to explore gender differences in sexual response and its complexities. For example, Janssen and colleagues (2008) conducted a qualitative focus group study with 50 male participants (not diagnosed with a sexual dysfunction) with the aim of exploring men's understanding of the relationship between sexual desire and arousal, and the various factors and situations that promote or prevent sexual desire and arousal. The authors found that some of the factors that some men understood as inhibiting sexual arousal, other men understood them as enhancing sexual arousal. Important factors identified related predominantly to emotional or feeling states, including feelings about the self and about the partner, feeling desired by the partner, and feeling emotionally connected with the partner. Emotional states, such as negative or positive mood could act as either an enhancer or an inhibiter. Other factors also included the use of erotica and contextual variables, such as the setting and the use of alcohol. What this points to is the importance men place on psychological and social factors (including the quality of the relationship) for sexual desire and arousal. Furthermore, their study also shows that whether such factors act as inhibiters or enhancers differs between men.

Janssen and colleagues (2008) point to the similarities in their findings with those of a qualitative focus group study of women, conducted by Graham, Sanders, Milhausen, and McBride (2004). Women participants in Graham and colleagues' study similarly discussed the importance of emotions and feelings and the quality of the relationship, as well as contextual factors. Similarly with the study on men, women differed in understanding such factors as either inhibiters or enhancers for sexual desire and arousal. One notable difference is the women's report of concerns about their reputation and concerns about pregnancy and contraception as important factors associated with sexual desire and arousal. Such findings challenge the medical model of sexual dysfunction, with the focus on the genitals, which tends to marginalize the role of psychological, relationship and contextual factors. These findings also challenge the tendency to focus on differences *between* men and women, with women's sexual responses often understood as being more complex, and rather highlight the need to consider "differences *among* men and women" (Janssen et al., 2008: 262). Although the difference regarding women's concerns about reputation and pregnancy suggest a gender difference based on different constructions of morality and responsibility in relation to male sexuality and female sexuality, women's sexual behaviours are subject to moralizing and denigration, so that women who are perceived to 'sleep around' are called 'slag' and 'slut', whereas their male counterparts are not similarly denigrated with these words (Cameron & Kulick, 1993).

The current proposals for the next edition of the DSM (the DSM-V) is to collapse some of the sexual dysfunction disorders into each other, and provide less of an emphasis on biological factors, with more consideration given to psychological and contextual factors (see www.dsm5.org). For example, consideration is being given to collapse the DSM-IV disorders of Hypoactive Sexual Desire Disorders for females and Female Sexual Arousal Disorder into one disorder – Sexual Interest/Arousal Disorder in Women – which includes various specifiers, including partner factors, relationship factors and cultural factors. Similarly, these specifiers will also be included for the diagnosis of erectile dysfunction and other sexual disorders. Thus psychological and contextual factors affecting the achievement of an erection is taken into account, giving less emphasis to erectile dysfunction being perceived as biologically caused.

6.3.2 GENDER, POWER RELATIONSHIPS AND HIV

Global HIV/AIDS epidemiological statistics suggest that women are more vulnerable to HIV infection than men. As mentioned earlier, some of this vulnerability is due to biological factors, such as women having a larger surface area of mucosa in the vagina than men have in their penis, exposing the women to more of her partner's secretion during sex (Doyal, 1998), thus increasing the area of exposure for the possible transmission of HIV. There are a number of social-cultural factors that play a possibly more important role, which shall briefly be explored here.

Women are more likely to live in conditions of poverty, and are more likely to be portrayed in some cultures as being less entitled to resources than men, which may push women into taking sexual risks in order to meet their basic survival needs (Boesten & Poku, 2009). As we have seen in various chapters of this book, women may be compelled to enter into sexual relationships, often high risk sexual relationships, in exchange for economic support. Furthermore, a very important factor to consider is the problem of gender-based violence. A multi-country research study by the World Health Organization (2005) indicates that violence against women, including physical and sexual violence, is widespread across many parts of the world and is associated with poor mental health and physical, sexual and reproductive health outcomes. Young women under the age of 19 are particularly at risk for physical and sexual violence. In this study, a total of 24,000 women in 10 countries were interviewed. The report highlights that a difficulty in addressing this problem is that such violence is often normative, and thus is seen as 'normal' for many of the women interviewed. For example, one woman from Bangladesh is quoted as saying:

> My husband slaps me, has sex with me against my will and I have to conform. Before being interviewed I didn't really think about this. I thought this is only natural. This is the way a husband behaves. (WHO, 2005: 10)

In the study, between 10% and 20% of women interviewed at sites in Bangladesh, Ethiopia, Peru, Samoa and the United Republic of Tanzania felt that women did not have the right to refuse sex with their partners under *any* circumstances. Few women across all countries felt that they were able to refuse sex with their partners based on her preference (i.e. not wanting to have sex). Furthermore, the threat of violence makes it difficult for women to negotiate safe sex (Jewkes, 2009; Jewkes, Levin, & Penn-Kekana, 2003). Research has also shown that men who commit violence against their partners tend to not use condoms and are more likely to be HIV-positive (Jewkes, 2009). Women engaged in sex work in order to meet their basic living needs are further marginalized and stigmatized, increasing the risk for violence at the hands of men who may attempt to assert their authority over women who are seen to have transgressed traditional gender norms (Campbell & Gibbs, 2009).

A difficulty with focusing on women as vulnerable to HIV is that it does have the potential to reinforce stigma and social constructions of women as 'dirty' and 'diseased', and as the vectors of HIV and other sexually transmitted diseases (Lawless, Kippax, & Crawford, 1996). Change must also address how men may be pressurized into behaving in gender-normative roles. Inequality in sexual relationships, and resulting risk for HIV, particularly for women, needs to be seen as a component of hegemonic masculinities in which male behaviours reproduce and maintain demanded-for male dominance (Connell, 2009). Men may engage in behaviours that place them at risk for HIV, such as having multiple sexual partners, having sex without a condom, and even sexual violence, as "markers of successful masculinity" (Lindegger & Quayle, 2009: 43). However, as Lindegger and Quayle point out, these constructions of masculinity are not fixed and can, and indeed have been in recent years, challenged. Challenging constructions of 'traditional' masculinities presents difficulties as men fear being perceived as having marginalized masculine identities.

From this brief discussion we can see how factors other than biological ones play an important role in the transmission of HIV. Thus, while the medical model would focus on biological vulnerability, the large body of research on gender and HIV points to the significant importance of social-cultural factors. The position that women have in many societies in the world shape the course that their lives take, with potentially serious consequences for health and longevity (see Box 6.3).

BOX 6.3

Video Clip: The Girl Effect

www.girleffect.org/video

This three-minute video is part of a campaign, The Girl Effect, launched by the Nike Foundation and partners in 2008, which highlights how for many girls around the world their position as girls and women in society places them at significant risk for HIV. The video is not a documentary, but presents a simple, clear, visual message that highlights the importance of intervening in a girl's life chances before she reaches the age of 12. The campaign highlights the importance of education for helping girls out of conditions of poverty and dependence, and resulting HIV risk.

The HIV epidemic as a gendered epidemic can also be observed in relation to prevention campaigns. Susser (2009), for example, argues that HIV prevention work has centred on the use of male condoms as the primary means of preventing

HIV. However, there is also such a thing as the female condom. The female condom, which fits inside the vagina, is inserted by the woman, and is under the control of the woman. Far less research and research funding have been provided towards developing and improving the female condom as a preventative measure in HIV. Susser (2009) discusses research findings that suggest that women would prefer using a female condom as a preventative measure against HIV, and that they were more likely to be able to use the female condom than try to persuade their male partners to use a male condom. Yet the female condom is not widely or freely available. More recent attention to male circumcision as reducing the risk of HIV infection for men highlights for Susser the focus on protection that is within men's control over protection that is within women's control.

GENDER, BODY IMAGE AND DISORDERED EATING

6.4 There has been a well-documented observed change in media representations of the ideal female body in western cultures over recent decades. For example, a study by Voracek and Fisher (2002) estimated the body mass index of *Playboy* centrefolds from December 1953 to December 2001, and reported an observed decrease in BMI over this period below average population levels. Of course such a study has to be treated with caution as they draw on estimated BMI using measures that may not be accurate. However, representation of slimness as the female body ideal is well documented (Grogan, 2000). Furthermore, images are usually digitally enhanced, and thus not a realistic representation of human bodies. Much attention has been given to how these socio-cultural constructions of thinness can be thought of as a causal factor for body anxiety (Orbach, 2009) and disordered eating (see Chapter 4 for discussion of this in relation to cultural differences). Adolescent girls have been found to report higher levels of pressure of socio-cultural attitudes of ideal body image than boys (Halliwell & Harvey, 2006). Socio-cultural ideals of thinness as an ideal aspect of femininity are internalized, and create greater pressures on girls than on boys to lose weight. In a qualitative interview study by Ahern and colleagues (2011), the women participating in the study immediately associated thinness with an ideal body type. However, they also expressed some ambivalence and conflict about the 'normality' of thinness, reporting feeling pressurized by media representations of thinness as ideal, and having concerns about health. These concerns, however, did not translate into a rejection of thinness as ideal. I am focusing here on body image ideals, but eating disorders in women must also be understood in terms of women's social roles, roles which may be oppressive, and thus eating disorders among women may be understood as a battle for autonomy (Orbach, 2005), and as "expressive of a *multiplicity* of societal concerns and dilemmas" facing women (Malson, 2000: 370).

Eating disorders are significantly more prevalent in females than males, and thus the majority of research has focused on body image, weight concerns and eating disorders among women, with far less attention placed on men. However, ideal male body images in the media have also changed. While for women the body ideal has been an increasing emphasis on slimness, for men, the body ideal has been an increasing emphasis on muscularity, athleticism, low body fat and minimal body hair (Drummond, 2010). For example, Pope and colleagues (1999) studied representations of the male body in popular action toy figures over a 30-year period, and found an increased muscularity in the figures over time. Leit and colleagues (2001) investigated changes in body image in *Playgirl* centrefolds from 1973 to 1997, and found that on aver-age the *Playgirl* centrefold has lost body fat but gained muscle over this time. It has been shown that muscularity in men is perceived by women and men as masculine, and that men feel more masculine and powerful when they gain more muscle (McCreary, Saucier, & Courtenay, 2005). The importance of muscularity is strongly linked to strength and sport. Sport and athleticism are important components of representations of masculinity, with males who do not take part in sports, particularly 'masculine' sports, being marginalized as un-masculine or gay (Drummond, 2010). However, as Drummond points out, not all men conform to this ideal of muscularity and athleticism, rejecting such norms by deliberately over-consuming food and alcohol. These men are now facing attack from anti-obesity discourses.

In a qualitative study involving in-depth interviews with men of all ages about their body image concerns (Drummond, 2010), the importance of mus-cularity as an indicator of strength and masculinity was a dominant theme. The men interviewed pointed to the important influence that media has on their body concerns and body image ideals. The men interviewed further talked about the importance of muscularity, not only as an image of masculin-ity, but as enabling masculine behaviour, such as being competitive or physi-cally active. This reflects Butler's (2006) notion of gender as performative. For the men interviewed, body fat was a sign of loss of control, which was depicted as un-masculine. The concerns around body fat were associated with "body aesthetics" and having a body that was "ripped" and "cut" (Drummond, 2010: 209), rather than concerns about health. Similarly, Sloan, Gough, and Conner (2010), in interviews with men who were partaking in healthy behaviours, such as exercising and not smoking or drinking, emphasized such behaviour as important in relation to being active, partaking in sport as well as aesthetic concerns, rather than as concerns about health. These body image concerns may be private, as men are reluctant to talk about body image, as this may be perceived as a concern for women or gay men (Hargreaves & Tiggemann, 2006).

Body concerns and dissatisfaction in males may not be limited to muscularity, but also with other characteristics of the body, in particular weight, penis size, and height (Tiggemann, Martins, & Churchett, 2008). Among the 200 partici-pating heterosexual men in Tiggemann and colleagues' (2008) study, many desired to be taller and slimmer, more muscular, have more head hair and less body hair, and have a larger penis. Representations of muscularity as ideal have been found cross-culturally. For example, in a study investigating body ideal among men in the USA, Ukraine and Ghana, all participants reported wanting to be more muscular, as this was perceived by the men as making them more powerful and attractive to women (Frederick et al., 2007).

This emphasis on muscularity as the masculine ideal, has been found to make men exposed to such images feel depressed and unsatisfied with their body image (for example, Agliata & Tantleff-Dunn, 2004). As with women, body dissatisfaction in men is associated with low self-esteem, depression, disordered eating, and the use of performance-enhancing substances (Olivardia, Pope, Borowiecki, & Cohane, 2004). Homosexual men have been found to have greater concerns about body weight and shape, leading to restrained eating, than heterosexual men (Conner, Johnson, & Grogan, 2004).

The importance of body image in the impressions that others have of us is shown by Dittmar and colleagues (2000), who found that body characteristics were rated as more important than personality by both men and women participants when they described their ideal in the opposite sex. For men, ideal body characteristics in women included attractiveness, long hair and being skinny but still voluptuous (rather an impossible task!). For women, ideal body characteristics in men included an athletic, trim body, with a thin waist and muscular upper body.

GENDER AND MENTAL HEALTH

6.5

As with physical health, gender differences are found in the incidence and experience of mental health problems. Controversially, many of the mental disorders listed in the DSM have differential gender prevalence. These gender differences are purported to be supported by research evidence. However, Hartung and Widiger (1998) argue that the evidence indicating gender differences in prevalence may be complicated by biases in sampling. For example, they suggest that studies that rely on clinic population samples may be gender biased as a result of differences in willingness to seek treatment between men and women. Sample biases may also exist as a result of co-morbidity with other disorders, which increase the likelihood of referral to a clinic. Hartung and Widiger further argue that differential gender prevalence may be as a consequence of biases in the diagnostic criteria used.

6.5.1 GENDER AND COMMON MENTAL HEALTH PROBLEMS

Depression and anxiety, the two commonest types of mental health problem, are more common among females than among males in most countries of the world (Desjarlais, Eisenberg, Good, & Kleinman, 1995; WHO, 2008). In a recent cross-national survey of gender differences in depression in 23 European countries (Van de Velde, Bracke, & Levecque, 2010), women reported higher levels of depression than men in all 23 countries. While research has looked at biological explanations for the gender differences in prevalence of depression, socio-cultural factors have been found to play perhaps a more important role. A lot of research has departed from the medical model to explore psychosocial factors that are associated with the gender disparities. These include: women's employment status, marital status, role as carers, and the strain of having multiple roles, gender role socialization, representation of women which are often derogatory, and sexual violence (Ussher, 2000a). In a review of research investigating contributing factors to gender differences in prevalence of depression (Piccinelli & Wilkinson, 2000), adverse childhood experiences, a history of anxiety and depression in childhood and adolescence, adverse experiences related to socio-cultural gender roles, and vulnerability to adverse life events and poorer coping skills were found to be most important in accounting for gender differences. This echoes arguments made that victimization is an important contributing factor to the development of depression and other mental health problems, such as post-traumatic stress disorder (PTSD) in women (Hamilton & Jensvold, 1992).

In a cross-national survey study of mental health problems and their correlations with gender (Seedat, Scott, Angermeyer, Berglund, Bromet, Brugha, et al., 2009), it was found that women had higher prevalence of anxiety and mood disorders than men, while men had more externalizing problems, such as substance dependence, than women. This was found across all 15 countries surveyed and across all age group cohorts. However, the researchers found a narrowing of prevalence rates between men and women in more recent cohorts, particularly for depression and substance abuse, which the researchers found were related to changes in traditional female roles. These changes were measured in terms of: (1) the ratio of women to men with work experience before the age of 35; (2) the ratio of women to men achieving equitable median level of education; (3) the ratio of the average age at marriage for women and men; and (4) the proportion of women in each cohort who used contraception before the age of 25.

However, research also suggests that depression may be under-diagnosed in men (Emslie, Ridge, Ziebland, & Hunt, 2006). Men may find it difficult to acknowledge and seek help for depression as this runs counter to masculinity stereotypes of strength, invulnerability and emotional control. This is depicted in the old cliché: "boys don't cry". Research has shown that common stereotypes held for men are that they are less likely to experience emotions such as sadness, distress and fear than women, but more likely to experience anger and pride (Plant, Hyde, Keltner, & Devine, 2000). There are few studies that explore the experiences of men with depression. One of the first qualitative studies with 14 men diagnosed with depression (Heifner, 1997) reported the men to describe themselves in terms of stereotypes of masculinity – as strong, in control, and able to handle problems themselves. This was at odds with the expression of vulnerability, and the men spoke about the sense of emotional isolation and disconnectedness with others with whom they could express fears and vulnerability.

Experiencing depression felt like a loss of control and a sign of weakness, which men felt they had to keep private. A more recent study from Canada (Oliffe, Robertson, Kelly, Roy, & Ogrodniczuk, 2010) similarly reported on men's understanding of their depression in relation to notions of masculinity (see Box 6.4). For men diagnosed with depression, reconstructing their sense of a masculine identity becomes an important part of recovery (Emslie et al., 2006).

BOX 6.4

A Spotlight on Research: Masculinity and depression

Oliffe, J.L., Robertson, S., Kelly, M.T., Roy, P., & Ogrodniczuk, J.S. (2010). Connecting masculinity and depression among international male university students. *Qualitative Health Research, 20*(7), 987–998.

Aims: This qualitative study aimed to explore the experiences and understanding of depression among international male students at a Canadian university. The study aimed to link notions of masculinity, particularly marginalized (minority groups) masculinity and depression.

Methods: Fifteen men between the ages of 19 and 28 years who self-identified as having depression were interviewed individually. The majority (13 men) self-identified as Asian, with one self-identified as Latino and one as Middle-Eastern. All had been resident in Canada for less than three years. The participant's presentation of depression was measured using the Beck's Depression Inventory. Interviews lasted between 1 and 1.5 hours. Interviews were analysed using an interpretive inductive approach.

Results: In their understanding of the causes of depression, some men attributed it to genetic factors (having inherited it from a parent) or biological factors, most notably as being caused by emotionality, which many attributed as being a female trait. Other men also understood depression as caused by life events, and with stresses of being an international student, with pressures to achieve academically, and loneliness from being far away from home.

As men who were depressed, their "emotionality" signalled for them a form of weakness that went against constructions of masculinity. The participants reported a reluctance to disclose their depression, particularly within their home country, which was perceived as being less understanding of depression (among men) than Canada. Participants spoke of the perceived (or actual) stigma that being a man with depression has. For example, one participant was quoted as saying:

> Men have a dominant position in our society and usually it's better to be a tough person, a strong person, rather than to worry the whole family. They are usually labeled as the breadwinner, so I think this is one of the main reasons that keeps people away, especially men, from seeking help because when they are going for advice they may lose face, right?—so it is kind of a shame for them to get help. (p. 992)

(Continued)

(Continued)

Along with conceptions of weakness, participants also spoke about shame and a sense of failure as a man with depression. The researchers suggest that some of the participants attempted to reclaim some of their 'lost masculinity' by reference to "fighting" and self-managing their depression. Some men spoke about becoming angry (in the context of depression) as a way of showing power.

Conclusions: The authors highlight how constructions of masculinity are both by-products and strategies for dealing with depression. Masculine constructions of strength, control and autonomy, were threatened by depression, which implied vulnerability and weakness. However, some sense of control and autonomy could be retained as the men spoke of "fighting" and coping with depression on their own, without seeking help or taking medication. The authors point to the difficulties that this may cause when it becomes a struggle for men to maintain this "resilience", which may drive more damaging behaviours, including the possibility of self-harm and suicide.

Important in this study is not only that it provides an account of the lived experiences and understanding of depression in men, which few studies do, but that it raises some important considerations for health care for men with depression. The reticence for men to seek help, because it challenges constructions of masculinity that have become threatened, may result in self-damaging behaviours. This highlights the importance of considering gender in understanding and treating depression, and perhaps why depression may be under-diagnosed in men.

Epidemiological studies influenced by the medical model of psychopathology, observes gender differences in prevalence of mental disorders, but often do not consider the context in which this prevalence occurs. As Brown (1992) argues, often comments as to higher prevalence of certain disorders among women are made in a "conceptual vacuum" (p. 215), where the meaning of this higher prevalence is not always interrogated. Such an approach medicalizes women's experiential distress, so that distress caused by biological factors or dysfunctional thoughts or life stressors can be medically treated (Ussher, 2010). Cosgrove (2000) argues that the medical model relies on essentialist thinking, and for the meaning of gender differences in diagnosis to be properly understood we require alternative paradigms, such as social constructionism and phenomenology. However, Ussher (2010) cautions that a social constructionist approach that views psychiatric diagnosis as a "gendered practice that pathologizes femininity" (p. 13) may in part dismiss women's 'real' experience of distress. Let's take a psychiatric diagnosis – borderline personality disorder – and have a look at how social constructions of gender roles and the lived experiences of women influence the higher frequency of diagnosis.

6.5.2 BORDERLINE PERSONALITY DISORDER

Borderline personality disorder (BPD), is one of ten personality disorders listed in the DSM-IV, and is characterized by an enduring pattern of instability and inconsistency in interpersonal relationships, self-image and affects, and behaviour, which is marked by impulsivity (see Box 6.5 for DSM-IV diagnostic criteria). People diagnosed with BPD are understood as having failed to develop a coherent sense of self. The term 'borderline' derives from psychoanalytic classifications of mental health problems belonging to the psychotic and the neurotic range, the term 'borderline personality' denoting a mental health problem which sits at the margin (the borderline) between psychotic and neurotic illness.

BOX 6.5

Diagnostic Criteria for Borderline Personality Disorder (APA, 2000: 710)

A pervasive pattern of instability of emotions, self-image and interpersonal relationships, as well as marked impulsivity, as indicated by five or more of the following:

- A preoccupation with abandonment, with consistent efforts to avoid either real or imagined abandonment
- Instability in self image or sense of self
- Recurrent pattern of unstable and intense interpersonal relationships, with feelings alternating between idealization and devaluation
- Impulsivity and impulsive behaviour that can be damaging for the self (e.g. promiscuity)
- Recurrent suicidal or self-harming behaviours
- Feelings of emptiness
- Emotional instability
- Intense and inappropriate anger
- Transient, stress-related dissociative states or paranoia

Significantly more females than males are diagnosed with BPD, the DSM-IV reporting a prevalence rate of 75% of patients diagnosed with BPD being female. There are higher prevalence rates among women for other personality disorders, such as histrionic personality disorder and dependent personality disorder. Men are more likely to be diagnosed with antisocial personality disorder and narcissistic personality disorder. This raises the question of whether BPD, and other personality disorders, is a gendered diagnosis.

Potter (2009) observes how the borderline patient has come to be commonly pictured as being the "manipulative, demanding, aggressive, and angry woman" (p. 6). Potter (2009) provides an analysis of the diagnosis as underpinned by assumptions of acceptable behaviour and social roles, which are often gendered in its evaluation. For example, one of the possible symptoms of BPD is "inappropriate anger", which may result in more women being diagnosed as having inappropriate anger as a result of historically gendered constructions of women's emotions as out-of-control and irrational. Thus a woman, who is angry, may be perceived as being irrationally and thus inappropriately angry, whereas men, who are historically perceived as emotionally rationale, will be seen to express angry rationally and appropriately. Insecurity and difficulties with trusting in the context of relationships may also be shaped by gendered expectations and assumptions about relationships and the role of men and women in such (heterosexual) relationships. Think, for example, of commonly experienced differences in how romance is expressed in relationships. Or who in the relationship takes most of the responsibility for household chores, despite both partners working full-time, and the conflicts that this at times may cause. Such perceived unfairness in who does what within the relationship may lead to differential levels of unhappiness in the quality of the relationship (Potter, 2009).

Another gendered symptom discussed by Potter is that of impulsivity, which is often seen as taking the form of impulsivity in sex (such as promiscuity and casual sex). It is well established how in many societies there are gendered differences in what is regarded as an acceptable number of sexual relationships. As Potter points out, "what is considered sexual prowess and normal sex drives for males is considered promiscuous for females" (p. 77). Gender norms have been changing, and there has been increasing gender equality in many societies, but differences in such perceptions remain ingrained. How often are men called "slag" and "slut"? Brown (1992) argues that male gender-role behaviour was and often continues to be perceived as the normative behaviour for healthy psychological functioning, while female gender-role behaviour is perceived as potentially pathological by comparison (p. 212).

The diagnosis of BPD is also strongly associated with a history of early trauma and abuse. Herman and colleagues (1989) found the following childhood history in BPD patients:

- 71% had been physically abused
- 68% had been sexually abused
- 62% had witnessed domestic violence

These are also gendered experiences, where significantly more women than men are victims of abuse and domestic violence. However, the effects of trauma become pathologized as a disorder of the individual, where the individual is diagnosed as having a mental 'illness', rather than considering distress as an appropriate response to trauma and abuse in the relational environment. Similar criticisms can be made for the diagnosis of PTSD following an incidence of rape. Brown (1992) argues that a feminist analysis of mental disorders such as BPD would need to "take into account the lifetime learning experience of living in a sexist, racist, homophobic, ageist, and otherwise oppressive cultural context" (p. 220).

While taking such a perspective on the gendered constructions of diagnostic criteria is useful in understanding the higher prevalence of BPD in women, it is important not to dismiss the reality of distress (Ussher, 2010) in women (and men) diagnosed with BPD. BPD is associated with very chaotic and distressing emotional and behavioural experiences, and with self-harming behaviour which may be disturbing and potentially dangerous for the individual.

The current proposals for the DSM-V are to collapse the various types of personality disorder into one diagnostic category of personality disorder, which is assessed along a continuum of level of functioning and dimensions of personality traits, with a limited set of personality types included in diagnostic criteria (see www.dsm5.org). The stated intention for these new criteria is for the personality characteristic of the psychiatric patients to be described, whether this represents a personality disorder or not. The five personality types included (antisocial/psychopathic, avoidant, borderline, obsessive-compulsive, and schizotypal) are described in a narrative format with a dimensional rating of degree to which the patient fits the description, rather than corresponding to a list of symptom criteria. This offers some flexibility and captures a continuum of personality difficulties.

GENDER AND DISABILITY

6.6

While much attention has been given to the oppression of women and the oppression of people with disabilities in society, less attention has been given to the particular concerns of women with disabilities, who have argued that they have been largely excluded from the disability rights movements as well as women's rights movements (Lloyd, 2001). Sheldon (2004) points out that one key area of concern for disabled women is around issues of sexuality, reproduction and motherhood. For many years, a eugenic way of thinking advocated the widespread sterilization of disabled women (Hubbard, 1997). The sexuality of young women (and men) with disabilities is an arena of considerable anxiety, with many ethical and moral dilemmas regarding sexual and human rights, and protection (Rogers, 2010).

Women with disabilities may continue to experience attitudinal barriers to accessing sexual health care. For example, in a study conducted in the USA (Nosek, Howland, Rintala, Young, & Chanpong, 2001), it was found that women with physical disabilities generally do not receive the same quality of gynaecological health care as do women without disabilities. The study found that 31% of the women with physical disabilities taking part in the study reported having experienced being refused a consultation with a physician because of their disability. Similarly, Becker and colleagues (1997), in a study of women with physical disabilities in the USA, reported that they were often treated as if they were asexual by health care providers, and how at times staff at clinics appeared shocked at the woman's request for contraception. The women in this study also reported feeling that health care providers were unaware of and insensitive to disability and sexuality issues, and they felt that health care providers were reluctant to discuss sexual issues and family planning with them. In South Africa, a woman with a disability, writing about her experience of accessing family planning services, similarly states how she is treated as if asexual by clinic staff, and questioned as to her presence in the clinic, leaving her feeling as if her presence at the clinic is a problem (Mgwili & Watermeyer, 2006). Tilley (1998) makes the following observation about the treatment of women with physical disabilities and women with learning disabilities:

> Women with physical disabilities are stereotypically characterised as 'asexual', so commonly they are instructed/presumed to be unable to manage pregnancy, birth and motherhood and are implored to 'rationally' forgo these possibilities. In contrast, women with intellectual disabilities are commonly constructed as hyper- and inappropriately sexual and unable to 'control' their sexual selves. It is these women who are often deemed unable to decide for themselves and for whom sterilisation is promoted. (pp. 96–97)

With regards participation in society, women with disabilities are in general more disadvantaged than men with disabilities in terms of education, employment, income and social assistance (Emmett, 2006; Emmett & Alant, 2006). Women with disability have been described as experiencing a "double disadvantage" (Emmett & Alant, 2006: 447) in terms of their gender and their disability. Research has shown that women with disabilities may be particularly excluded from employment and receiving an adequate income. This may reflect the greater devaluing of women with disabilities than men with disabilities. For example, in the USA, Hanna and Rogovsky (1991) found that women with disabilities were more likely to be unemployed or have a lower monthly income than disabled men. There is a well-known gender gap in income between men and women generally, and women with disabilities may be at an added disadvantage, earning less than women without disabilities (Emmett, 2006; Emmett & Alant, 2006). With regards education, girls with disabilities are more likely to be excluded from education than men (Emmett & Alant, 2006). In developed countries, women with disabilities have been found to receive less social and welfare support than men with disabilities (Emmett & Alant, 2006). As a result, more women with disabilities than men with disabilities live in poverty. Women with disabilities in low-income, developing countries may be especially disadvantaged. Epidemiological statistics indicate that while slightly more women than men are disabled in developed countries, there are more men than women with disabilities in developing countries. Some have suggested that this may be attributed to a higher mortality rate for women with disabilities as a result of inadequate health care and support (Emmett & Alant, 2006).

Some of these issues of disadvantage and social exclusion are explored in a qualitative study among women with disabilities in Cameroon (Kiani, 2009), where it was found that women experienced multiple barriers to participation in society. These included physical barriers, such as food markets that were too far and difficult to access, with the result that these women bought their food at local shops at much higher prices. Attitudinal barriers included the reluctance, even antagonism, of others who found their presence irritating and annoying, for example requiring additional time or special requirements to get on public transport. The women also spoke of the challenges faced in forming lasting relationships, with many reporting abandonment or maltreatment from male partners. For example, one women was quoted as saying:

> A boy look at you, tell you he loves you. We are together, our relationship is going well. I ask him: 'Please would you like to get married to me?' He says: 'I can't get married to you; your responsibility is too much. I cannot carry your responsibility. First, you will not know how to cook. If I am sick, you cannot take care of me'. They will complain, so many complaints that he will start to make you go mad. (Kiani, 2009: 524)

This quote points to the gendered roles and expectations of women in relationships, where women with disabilities are non-normative and are perceived as unable to fulfil their gendered social roles. This results in women with disabilities not being considered as valuable spouses (Hanass-Hancock, 2009). This is also reflected in research which suggests that women with disabilities are anxious about proving 'normality' by becoming pregnant, thus showing to others that they are 'normal' women (e.g. Rohleder, 2010). Although I have focused here on women with disabilities, this is also pertinent to men with disabilities, who are considered as a non-normative masculinity. However, the experiences of men with disabilities have remained relatively under-represented (Robertson, 2004).

As we saw in Chapter 5, poverty may lead some women to turn to prostitution and transactional sex as a means of survival. This is the case for women with disabilities too. McCarthy (1993) highlights the practice of transactional sex among women with learning disabilities in institutional settings in the UK. Women were found to engage in sex with men with learning disabilities in exchange for money and other material goods. This places women with disabilities at risk for sexually transmitted disease, including HIV (see Chapter 7 for a more detailed discussion of this). Collins and colleagues (2001) observe how women with mental health disabilities, many of whom are unemployed, may be financially and materially dependent on men, and thus may not have "the freedom to prioritize their safety in sexual relationships above material needs" (p. 163). In addition to this, women with disabilities may be especially vulnerable to sexual abuse and exploitation (Hannass-Hancock, 2009). The sexual abuse of people with disabilities is explored further in Chapter 7.

SUMMARY

6.7 This chapter has explored some of the gender differences that have been found in physical and mental ill-health and disability. A medical model would suggest that such differences exist as a result of biological and physical factors. But we have seen in this chapter how constructions of masculinity and femininity and gender roles may offer important explanations and understanding of these gender health differences. Many women across the world may be at increased risk for illness, disability and mental health problems as a result of oppressive, gendered social practices and structures. Men may be represented as dominant and powerful, which in turn places them at risk for health risks. These are generalizations, and may leave us thinking of all women as victims and men as perpetrators and brutes. We have also seen how changes in social roles and social constructions of gender may be associated with changes in health issues. Research often tends to focus on women, and so this chapter has also explored emerging research into masculinities and health. As with all other social factors, gender intersects with culture, race, socio-economic status, age, sexual orientation and so on, so this chapter should be read bearing in mind that gender disparities are compounded by the social issues explored in the other chapters.

FURTHER READINGS

Fine, C. (2010). *Delusions of gender: The real science behind sex differences*. London: Icon Books. Although this book is not about health, it provides an interesting challenge to the scientific research that states that men and women are biologically different in their behaviour and capabilities. It is written in an accessible style, as a popular read.

Gough, B., & Robertson, S. (Eds.) (2010). *Men, masculinities and health: Critical perspectives*. Basingstoke: Palgrave Macmillan. This edited book provides different chapters which take a critical perspective on constructions of masculinity and how this affects men's health, health risk and health-seeking behaviours. It explores psychological and sociological factors that impact on men's health.

Ussher, J. (Ed.) (2000b). *Women's health: Contemporary international perspectives*. Leicester: BPS books. This edited book presents a number of chapters by leading writers in the field of women's health, taking a critical approach to understanding gender issues in health, looking at both physical health and mental health. The chapters cover issues of women's health across the lifespan.

SEXUALITY

7

INTRODUCTION

7.1 Issues of sex and sexuality can often provoke strong opinion, anxiety and moral judgement. Many are embarrassed or ashamed about sex. Others consider their sex life to be central to their experience of life. Many societies have strong moral and religious mores about sex, for example no sex before marriage. There are opinions and assumptions, even laws that dictate who shall have sex, how and with whom.

Sexuality refers to the way in which people express themselves as sexual beings. The World Health Organization has utilized a working definition of sexuality as:

> a central aspect of being human throughout life and encompasses sex, gender identities and roles, sexual orientation, eroticism, pleasure, intimacy and reproduction. Sexuality is experienced and expressed in thoughts, fantasies, desires, beliefs, attitudes, values, behaviours, practices, roles and relationships. While sexuality can include all of these dimensions, not all of them are always experienced or expressed. (WHO, Gender and Human Rights, www.who.int/reproductivehealth/topics/gender_rights/sexual_health/en/) [accessed 8 January 2011]

One of the areas of sexuality that has perhaps provoked the most judgement and controversy is that of homosexuality. I recall a 'joke' in the 1980s that said something along the lines of: "What does gay stand for? Got Aids Yet?" There are many other 'gay jokes'. Homosexuality is also often constructed as abnormal and deviant. In some countries, homosexuality is accepted as a normal variant of sexuality. In others, homosexuality is illegal and a punishable offence.

This chapter shall explore sexuality and health, specifically mental health and sexual health. The chapter will start of by exploring the mental health professions' relationship with homosexuality, where homosexuality was historically understood to be a mental 'illness', which could be 'treated'. With this history as a backdrop, this chapter will also look at the mental health needs of gay, lesbian, bisexual and transgendered (LGBT) individuals.

But, as the working definition quoted above outlines, sexuality is not only about sexual orientation. This chapter will also focus on how constructions of the sexuality and sexual lives of particular groups of people are pathologized, and the relationship that this has with sexual health. This shall first be explored with reference to the HIV epidemic and the metaphors of sexual deviance that are associated with HIV/AIDS, looking in particular at constructions of 'gay sexuality' and 'African sexuality' as explanations for the disease. Another collection of people for whom sexuality has been problematized is persons with disabilities. The final part of the chapter will explore constructions of 'disabled sexuality' and the implications that this has had for sexual health.

HOMOSEXUALITY AND THE MENTAL HEALTH PROFESSIONS

7.2 In Chapter 2 we read how, in psychiatry, mental disorders are diagnosed using medical classification systems, such as the ICD and the DSM, which claims the universality of disorders, founded on empirical evidence. For example, the DSM-IV-TR claims to review the empirical evidence with the aim of providing "comprehensive and unbiased information and to ensure that DSM-IV reflects the best available clinical and research literature" (APA, 2000: p. xxvii). In this sense, the DSM and ICD aim to be value-free and objective. However, the notion of such diagnostic classification systems being objective and value-free has been frequently contested. As we have seen in Chapter 4, the DSM has been critiqued for upholding a western bias to mental ill-health. That the DSM is also a product of cultural norms, values and morals is perhaps well illustrated with the history of homosexuality as viewed by psychiatry, psychoanalysis and psychology.

There is a long history of religious condemnation (which still continues) of homosexuality as an abomination and sin. Homosexuality was and still is viewed in some religious perspectives, as being against the laws of nature, and thus to be condemned. Homosexual acts were considered unnatural, an evil sin and to be punished. People caught engaging in homosexual acts could be severely punished, even put to death. Oscar Wilde is a famous example in the United Kingdom; an Irish writer and poet who in 1895 was sentenced to two years of hard labour for sodomy and gross indecency.

What was regarded as sin was translated into psychopathology in psychiatry (Bayer, 1987). In 1952, The American Psychiatric Association included homosexuality as a personality disorder in the first edition of the DSM. The publication of the Kinsey report in 1948 began a move to consider homosexuality as a normal variant of sexuality. The Kinsey reports (the *Sexual behaviour in the human male* in 1948 and the *Sexual behaviour in the human female* in 1953) reported findings of a large-scale survey study led by Dr Alfred Kinsey, investigating the sexual behaviours of men and women in the USA. The report was one of the first pieces of research that investigated male homosexuality (as part of a survey on sexual behaviours) in a 'normal' non-patient population. The report found that homosexual behaviours among American men were far more prevalent than previously thought. It was clear that a large number of men had homosexual tendencies and maintained normal psychological functioning. This

led to a development in rethinking homosexuality among the psychiatric profession. The psychoanalytic profession, however, remained largely "unaffected"
by the report (Lewes, 1995: 110). More research began to be conducted on
'normal' functioning among homosexual men, and there was a gradual accu-
mulation of evidence that contested the notion that homosexuality was psycho-
pathological. There was an increase in momentum in the early 1970s, with a
growing gay human rights movement. Bayer (1987) documents American psychiatry's reconsideration of homosexuality during this time, and points out
how some of the homosexual members of the APA, who had kept their sexual
orientation a secret from the peers, gradually began to speak against the stance
of viewing homosexuality as pathological.

Homosexuality was eventually removed from the DSM in 1973, after a considerable public and internal political debate (Bayer, 1987). Bayer documents
the controversial debates in the early 1970s about the 'value-laden' notion of
homosexuality as a mental 'illness'; that the diagnosis of homosexuality as mental 'illness' was founded on moral values which viewed heterosexuality as
healthy and optimal, and any deviation from that as unhealthy and abnormal.
The claim that the diagnosis rested on empirical evidence was countered by evidence which demonstrated healthy adjustment and relationships in people who
were homosexual. The 'evidence' of homosexuality as pathological relied on
homosexual patients who were experiencing distress, where what was labelled
as pathological was homosexuality rather than the experience of distress, which
might be caused by social homophobia. After much discussion, and under pressure from gay activist groups, homosexuality was officially removed from the
official nomenclature of the APA in December 1973. This was a major step forward in the gay liberation struggle which began to gain momentum at about this
time, as the APA could then argue against the legal and social discrimination
against homosexuality. However, the resolution to remove homosexuality as a
mental disorder was criticized by many in the APA, and divisions still remained
within the APA. A call was made to investigate the resolution. Groups of psychiatrists also advocated for the possibility of 'treatment' for homosexuality for
patients who sought a cure. The diagnosis of 'ego-dystonic homosexuality' was
proposed as a diagnosis to replace homosexuality as a mental disorder. Thus
individuals who were unhappy and distressed about being homosexual, and who
wanted to be heterosexual, could be diagnosed as having a mental disorder and
receive treatment to change their sexual orientation. However, this was criticized for continuing to focus on and pathologize homosexuality, in that a person
could be treated for being distressed about being homosexual, rather than
helped in developing a more affirming view of their own sexuality. The argument was made that if homosexuality was not officially considered abnormal,
then people distressed about being heterosexual could be similarly treated to
become homosexual. The diagnosis of ego-dystonic homosexuality was eventually removed from the DSM-III-R in 1987.

The World Health Organization followed suit, but only in 1992 was homosexuality removed from the *International Classification of Diseases*, with the
publication of ICD-10. However, the diagnosis of 'ego-dystonic sexual orientation'

still remains in the ICD-10. The ICD-10 describes ego-dystonic sexual orientation as being indicated when a person's "gender identity or sexual preference is not in doubt but the individual wishes it were different because of associated psychological and behavioural disorders and may seek treatment in order to change it" (WHO, 1992: 173). King (2003) critiques the conflation of gender identity with sexual orientation as inaccurate and creating confusion, suggesting that sexual orientation can be treated. King goes on to point out that it can be assumed that it would be perceived as acceptable that gay men and lesbian women would seek to be changed, whereas heterosexual men and women seeking to become gay or lesbian would be perceived as being illogical. Thus, homosexual people unhappy about experiencing homosexual desires and who wish to be heterosexual can be treated, with the aim of converting their sexual orientation to that of heterosexuality. This is known as conversion therapy (discussed further below). A heterosexual man or women unhappy about their heterosexuality and seeking to be changed to gay or lesbian may, in all likelihood, be considered delusional or psychotic.

Psychoanalysis has been slower to change its views on homosexuality. The psychoanalytic community was most opposed to the APA decision to remove homosexuality from the DSM (Bayer, 1987). There have been a range of psychoanalytic theories to account for the development of homosexuality, most of which generally argue that homosexuality was a developmental fixation to a pre-Oedipal stage of development (Lewes, 1995). This refers to Sigmund Freud's concept of the Oedipus complex, which forms part of the third stage of psychosexual development (see Chapter 2). In psychoanalytic theory, the resolution of the Oedipus complex results in heterosexuality. Thus homosexuality was understood as a fixation in 'normal' development to pre-Oedipal stage. This fixation could be as a result of an environment which was perceived as threatening to 'normal' heterosexual development. Homosexuality was thus seen as a paranoid or phobic defence against heterosexuality. Homosexuals were considered to have not successfully resolved the Oedipus complex, and were thus neurotic and pathological. This was not always the view of homosexuality. In his *Three essays on the theory of sexuality* (1905), Freud argued that homosexuality could be seen in well-adjusted individuals who exhibited no significant deviations in behaviour and functioning, and thus homosexuality in itself could not be considered degenerate. Freud argued that we are innately bisexual, and that homosexuality is a variant of the resolution of the Oedipus complex and love-object choice. This is evident in a letter that Freud wrote to a mother who was concerned about her son's sexuality, in which Freud wrote:

> Homosexuality is assuredly no advantage, but it is nothing to be ashamed of, no vice, no degradation, it cannot be classified as an illness; we consider it to be a variation of the sexual function produced by a certain arrest of sexual development. Many highly respectable individuals of ancient and modern times have been homosexuals, several of the greatest men among them (Plato, Michelangelo, Leonardo da Vinci, etc.). It is a great injustice to persecute homosexuality as a crime, and cruelty too. ... (Freud, 1935, reprinted in the *American Journal of Psychiatry*, 1951, 107, 786–787)

Since the views of Freud, many psychoanalysts have developed theories of homosexuality which view heterosexuality as normative and homosexuality as pathological (Lewes, 1995), and illustrating a "deep level of antihomosexal bias" (Twomey, 2003: 9). There has been a gradual change in psychoanalytic theorizing about homosexuality since the 1980s, but there remained very anti-homosexual stances among the psychoanalytic community, and these continue to remain, although to a lesser extent (Twomey, 2003). For example, Twomey quotes Hildebrand (1992), a British psychoanalyst, who published a criticism of voluntary organizations and hospices who cared for people (homosexuals) with AIDS, stating that:

> the difference between the psychoanalytic approach and the approach of the caring organizations which I have described is that we do not allow for a collusion that they are living a sanctified life in the way in which the hospice group do and we would, in fact, insist very strongly on the profound aggression towards the object which seems central to their psychopathology. (Hildebrand, 1992: 459)

As a result of the anti-homosexual bias of psychoanalysis, homosexuals were, until only recently, not admitted into psychoanalytic training. Only in 1999 did the International Psychoanalytic Association pass a final resolution condemning discrimination of any kind, including sexual orientation (Roughton, 2003).

Clinical psychology has been influenced by psychiatry, and the classification systems of the DSM and the ICD. Clinical psychology has to a lesser extent been influenced by psychoanalysis in recent decades, particularly with the rise of behaviourism and cognitive psychology in the twentieth century. Since 2000, the British Psychological Society (BPS) has had a gay, lesbian and bisexual special section. However, clinical psychology has played a part in the administering of behavioural and cognitive therapy techniques to 'treat' homosexuality.

7.2.1 CONVERSION THERAPY

King and Bartlett (1999) give a brief review of the response of psychiatry and psychology to homosexuality. They cite some studies where behavioural therapy was used in order to change gay men's sexual orientation to become heterosexual. King and Bartlett (1999) cite only one study that uses behavioural techniques to change the sexual orientation of lesbian women. Conversion therapy used aversion techniques which today would be considered unethical. For example, gay men would be administered low levels of electric shock while being shown images of naked men, and rewarded when shown images of naked women. Other forms of aversion techniques involved apomorphine, a potent emetic that induces severe nausea and vomiting. Gay men would be injected with apormorphine to induce nausea while being shown images of naked men. The aim was to condition a negative reaction to homosexual stimuli. In a study of gay men in Britain who had undergone conversion therapy since the 1950s (Smith, Bartlett, & King, 2004), it was found that most participants sought conversion therapy as a result of hostile family and social attitudes. Many were referred for conversion therapy by their GPs in their late adolescence. None of the participants in the study felt that the treatment they had received had had any benefits, and in fact many felt that the treatment had had long-term negative effects, as it had added to their confusion, shame and emotional isolation. In a complimentary study of professionals' experiences, King and colleagues (2004), found that aversion therapy with electric shock was the most commonly used treatment. Many professionals in hindsight felt that their treatments were based on little evidence, and driven rather by social and legal pressures.

Despite the reported damaging effects such therapy had on patients, therapists maintained that such therapy was beneficial to homosexual men and women. King and Bartlett (1999) argue that changes in psychiatry and other mental health professions have followed from societal attitude changes to homosexuality, but point out how professionals who were adherents for conversion therapy and the treatment of homosexuality have remained unreflective of their past unethical practices, and in fact many continue to occupy senior positions. King and Bartlett (1999) conclude:

> Few other psychiatric labels have led to such pain and disarray. This peculiar history has exposed the conservative social bias inherent in psychiatry and psychology, damaged the lives of gay men and lesbians, and provided grounds for discrimination. It has contributed to the fact that gays and lesbians in Britain still lack many basic human rights enjoyed by the majority and continues to provide grounds for discrimination by the conservative press. (p. 111)

Conversion therapy is still being practised today, and efficacy studies continue to be published, despite homosexuality no longer being classified as an 'illness' requiring treatment. Cramer and colleagues (2008) conducted a review of conversion therapy studies, critiquing their arguments of efficacy, presenting published evidence as to its harmful effects, and so concluding that the practice of conversion therapy is ethically questionable and irresponsible. Critiques of conversion therapy (e.g. Drescher, 1998; Haldeman, 1994) have observed how conversion therapy is promoted by professionals who have often adopted religious orientations to homosexuality, and who have never accepted the removal of homosexuality from the DSM. What has instead been advocated for is affirmative therapeutic approaches (Langdridge, 2007), where gay, lesbian and bisexual men and women are helped to overcome feelings of shame and self-denigration as a result of homophobia and heterosexism.

HOMOSEXUALITY, ILL-HEALTH AND HEALTH CARE

7.3
The history of oppression and pathologizing of homosexuality, and the continuing social stigmatization of gay, lesbian, bisexual and transgendered individuals, has significant implications for mental health and general health. Young people who are openly gay are at risk of being bullied and harassed (King et al., 2003), and this can lead to tragic

outcomes. There was considerable media outcry in the USA during October 2010 when it came to light that four young men over a period of a month had committed suicide as a result of gay-related bullying (McKinley, 2010). Many gay, lesbian and bisexual older adults also report experiences of victimization and physical attack during their lifetimes (D'Augelli & Grossman, 2001). In a recent review of the research literature on the mental health of gay, lesbian and bisexual people (King et al., 2008), it was found that homosexual and bisexual men and women were at higher risk for depression and anxiety. They were also at higher risk for substance abuse, self-harm and suicide ideation. The review further found that lesbian and bisexual women were more at risk for substance abuse, while gay and bisexual men were more at risk for suicide. Higher prevalence of mental health problems among homosexual and bisexual participant groups compared to a heterosexual participant group have been found in studies in various countries, for example in the UK (King et al., 2003), the USA (Cochran, Sullivan, & Mays, 2003) and Australia (Jorm, Korten, Rodgers, Jacomb, & Christensen, 2002). Ethnic minority gay men and lesbian women may bear added levels of disadvantage and discrimination, adding to vulnerability for developing mental health difficulties (Greene, 1994).

Furthermore, gay men and lesbian women who may seek treatment for psychological problems will often tend to be treated by heterosexual psychologists, psychotherapists and psychiatrists, who may have received a theoretical training that may have an overt or covert anti-homosexuality bias (Bartlett, King, & Phillips, 2001). Bartlett and colleagues (2001) found that 64% of a sample of psychotherapists believed that their homosexual client's "sexual orientation was central to their difficulties" (p. 547). They go on to conclude that a homosexual man or women seeking psychotherapy "may encounter overt or covert bias, including the pathologisation of homosexuality *per se*" (p. 545). Negative attitudes of gay men and lesbian women may be held by medical and health professionals (Bhugra & King, 1989; Evans, Bingham, Pratt, & Carne, 1993), and gay, lesbian and bisexual people using mental health care services may face equivalent levels of prejudice from the health service as they do in the wider society (King & McKeown, 2003; McFarlane, 1997). In a more recent study from the UK, Bartlett and colleagues (2009) conducted a survey study with a respondent sample of 1,328 registered psychiatrists (from the Royal College of Psychiatrists), psychologists (from the British Psychological Society (BPS)) and psychotherapists (from the United Kingdom Council of Psychotherapy (UKCP)). Of the 1,328 respondents, 4% reported that they would attempt to help a client change his or her homosexual orientation to heterosexuality. Seventeen per cent reported having previously assisted a client reduce or even change his or her sexual orientation. These respondents were more likely to be older, male and registered with the BPS or UKCP (21% of the sample of BPS-registered psychologists reported this). Ninety-two per cent of these had helped a client who was referred to them after 1980. Most respondents cited clients' conflicts with religious, cultural and social values as reasons for assisting in changing sexual orientation. Only a small number of respondents made overtly negative comments. The authors quote a comment from a registered psychologist as an example:

> Although homosexual feelings are usual in people, their physical expression, and being a person's only way of having sexual relations is problematic. The physical act for male homosexuals is physically damaging and is the main reason in this country for AIDS/HIV. It is also perverse ... (Bartlett et al., 2009: 6)

Although the view of homosexuality as pathological has changed in western mental health professions, and continues to change, it is well known that disparities continue to exist with regards how homosexuality is perceived and treated worldwide. For example, there are significant differences regarding age of consent to sex (Worldwide Ages of Consent, www.avert.org/age-of-consent. htm, accessed 11 September 2010). In the UK, the age of consent for both heterosexual and homosexual sex is 16. Homosexuality in the UK was only decriminalized in 1967. In Ireland, the age of consent is 17, for both homosexuality and heterosexuality. The age of consent varies between countries in Europe, and between states in the USA. Homosexuality is illegal in 60 countries, most of which are African countries and Islamic states. In some countries, male–male sex is illegal whereas female–female sex is legal. This has implications for working in multicultural society, with clients and health care practitioners who, coming from different cultural backgrounds, have differing understanding of homosexuality and 'normality' to their adopted country.

7.3.1 HOMOSEXUALITY, HIV AND SEXUAL HEALTH CARE

The gay, lesbian and bisexual community had made a gain towards liberation with the removal of homosexuality from the DSM in 1973. The pathologizing of homosexuality was on its way out. However, the constructions of homosexuality as sin, immoral, pathological and dangerous flared once again with the eruption of the HIV epidemic in the USA in 1981. It was feared that the gains made in the 1970s would reverse, as conflict and controversy arose about the nature of HIV and its prevention. Shilts (1987) gives a detailed factual account of the first few years of the HIV epidemic in the USA. He gives a timeline account of the slow response by the USA authorities to addressing the HIV epidemic at a public health level. The first years were mired with conflict, suspicion, blame and accusation as the disease was perceived to be a disease of the gay community. In these early years HIV was referred to as the 'gay cancer', and HIV and AIDS was commonly regarded as a plague associated with sin and punishment (Sontag, 1991). A more concerted public health response to the emerging epidemic followed the death of actor Rock Hudson from an AIDS-related illness in 1985. Up until then, 12,000 American men and women had died of AIDS-related illnesses. Shilts (1987) argues that a more concerted public health response may have done much to curtail the resulting AIDS epidemic. In these first years, HIV was considered a concern for the gay community, and prevention was seen to be an issue for gays rather than a concern for the general population. There were splits within the gay community as to responding to HIV, with many of the gay community regarding HIV prevention and safe sex messages with suspicion. In the early 1980s, prevention messages to the gay community in the USA of calling for abstinence from anal sex, multiple partners, using condoms and shutting down bath houses, was met with a backlash from a large section of the gay community, who regarded such messages as an oppression of their freedom of sexual expression, and as a moral judgement on their sexuality by heterosexual society (Shilts, 1987). In addition, because of the link that was made with HIV/AIDS and gay men as a particular risk group, the resulting stigma of gay identities was destructive in work aiming to educate on HIV prevention.

As in the USA, there were similar debates in the UK as to the concern of HIV for the general populations. In an analysis of British press media reporting on HIV and AIDS in the early years of the epidemic, Beharrell (1993) details the public debates that took place in the media on whether there was a risk of HIV for the heterosexual population. Much of the press reports challenged the risk to those who engage in 'straight' sex or 'normal' sex as a myth, emphasizing the construction of HIV as a gay disease.

In an effort to destigmatize HIV and AIDS among the gay population, the phrase 'men who have sex with men' (MSM) began to be used, emphasizing HIV risk in terms of behaviours rather than identity. Caution has been raised as to the blanket use of the term MSM in HIV prevention research, as potentially undermining self-determined identities and obscuring specific sexual behaviours that are important in sexual health promotion (Young & Meyer, 2005). Thus, the term MSM becomes a sort of blanket, non-stigmatizing term for risk behaviours that are presumed, such as anal sex for example.

HIV continues to be a significant health problem for gay men and men who have sex with men. Despite considerable education and knowledge about HIV transmission and prevention, there continues to be new diagnoses of HIV among men who have sex with men in several countries. Some research has attempted to explore why it is that some gay men continue to practise unprotected sex, despite the known seriousness of the HIV epidemic. Shilts (1987) documents how there was a resistance among gay men in San Francisco and other major cities in the USA against sex with a condom, as this was seen as an attack against sexual freedom. More recently, in the UK, Crossley (2004) has argued that this resistance against anal sex with a condom remains a feature of the 'psyche' of many gay men, and forms part of a so-called gay 'cultural psyche'. Her analysis was met with considerable criticism for, among other things, making generalizations from selective, and arguably inappropriate, data sources (autobiographies), and for constructing unprotected anal sex (in this case what is referred to in some sub-sectors of the gay community as 'barebacking') as a feature of 'gay culture', without fully considering that unprotected anal sex also occurs in heterosexual relationships (Barker, Hagger-Johnson, Hegarty, Hutchison, & Riggs, 2007). Flowers and colleagues (1997) review quantitative studies on gay men and condom use, which have consistently shown that gay men are less likely to use condoms with primary regular sexual partners, and are more likely to use condoms with casual sexual partners, suggesting a relationship between being in a romantic relationship and engaging in unprotected sex. They went on to conduct a qualitative study to explore gay men's understanding of unprotected anal sex and relationships. Their findings confirmed previous research findings on difference in condom use between casual and romantic relationships. In the case of romantic relationships, the (eventual) practice of unprotected anal sex was considered to be an important sign of commitment. This study provides a good example of the way that research can be used to explore nuances of a critical issue, exploring the specificity of a phenomenon (see Box 7.1).

BOX 7.1

A Spotlight on Research: Understanding unprotected sex in gay relationships

Flowers, P., Smith, J.A., Sheeran, P., & Beail, N. (1997). Health and romance: Understanding unprotected sex in relationships with gay men. *British Journal of Health Psychology, 2,* 73–86.

Aims: Given previous research findings that suggest that gay men tend to practise unprotected anal sex with regular sexual partners, and use condoms with casual sexual partners, this study aimed to explore how individual gay men understood and conceptualized the connections between unprotected anal sex and relationships. The researchers did not want to be led by their preconceived assumptions about the connection, but rather attempted to explore how gay men themselves make sense of it.

Methods: As a means of exploring participants' subjective experiences and views, the researchers adopted qualitative methods for collecting and analysing data. The authors adopted the method of Interpretative Phenomenological Analysis, which allows for the perspective of the participants to be explored in-depth (see Chapter 8). Data were collected by means of individual interviews with 20 gay men from a town in England. Interviews were non-directive and lasted between one and four hours. This ensured that participants were able to freely articulate and expand on their views and experiences. The interviews were recorded and transcribed, and transcripts were analysed to identify themes that reflected shared understandings.

Results: The analysis indicated that there was a consistent difference in the manner in which casual partners and romantic partners were described. Sex with casual partners was described with a sense of detachment, whereas sex with romantic partners was described with a sense of involvement of the self. Anal sex was more likely to be part of the sexual act within relationships than with casual partners. Penetrative (anal) sex was seen as a milestone on the development of a serious relationship, and men spoke about there being a "right time" for penetrative sex to become part of the sexual repertoire. With the threat of HIV, penetrative sex without a condom has, for the men interviewed, come to represent a powerful symbol, not only of trust, but also of love. In this sense, it represents a final milestone in the development of a serious committed relationship.

Conclusion: The authors conclude that sexual activity is understood not as an end result of a sexual decision-making process, but rather as a means of achieving other aims and goals, in this case romantic relationships. Sexual activity in this sense involves calculated choice and is communicative of the nature of the relationship (casual or romantic). Condoms become a final barrier between a detached sexual relationship and a fully involved romantic sexual relationship. The researchers go on to discuss how this has implications for health promotion programmes, which are generally informed by the health behaviour models outlined in Chapter 2. Such models view condom use as a decision based on 'health-rationality', whereas this study shows that gay men may make decisions about condom used based on 'romantic-rationality'. Thus decisions are largely determined by the social (relationship) context rather than being determined by health and disease prevention. This highlights the importance of considering the social contexts in which decisions are made.

Discussions about sexual health and the treatment of sexual health problems involve communicating issues of sexuality between patient and practitioner. As noted above in relation to mental health care professionals, general health care professionals will often be heterosexual. Gay, lesbian, bisexual and transgendered patients may have to negotiate fears of heterosexism and homophobia in their interaction with health care. Research does suggest that this can result in uncomfortable encounters. General practitioners in the UK have reportedly found it uncomfortable and embarrassing to talk about sexual health with patients who are lesbian or gay (Hinchliff, Gott, & Galena, 2005). Some GPs expressed concerns about being ignorant of lesbian and gay lifestyles and sexual health issues, and were anxious about coming across inappropriately. A minority of participants expressed what the researchers considered to be homophobic attitudes. This has some similarity to health care professionals anxieties around cultural sensitivity (see Chapter 4), and, as with the case of cultural differences, can act as a barrier for general practitioners when talking with their gay and lesbian patients about sexual health. In a review of qualitative research on gay men and lesbian women experiences of accessing health care in the UK (Pennant, Bayliss, & Meads, 2009), it was found that communication barriers were frequently reported, arising out of service users' concerns about perceived or actual homophobia and heterosexism on the part of the health care service. Many studies that were reviewed further reported that gay and lesbian service users felt that GPs would not understand or have knowledge of particular sexual practices, and that the interaction between patient and professional would be uncomfortable. Similar findings have been reported on gay men and lesbian women's perception of health care services in the USA (Beehler, 2001; Eliason & Schope, 2001). Research in the UK suggests that many gay men and lesbian women do not mention their sexual orientation to their GP (Carr, Scoular, Elliott, Ilett, & Meager, 1999; Fitzpatrick, Dawson, Boulton, McLean, Hart, & Brookes, 1994). Gay men and lesbian women who do not mention their sexual orientation to GPs have reported not doing so for fear of possible negative reaction or negative impact on treatment, or concern that their sexual orientation will not be kept confidential and will be 'leaked out' into the community (Cant, 2002; Carr et al., 1999).

The focus of the chapter up till now has been on homosexuality. I shall now turn to constructions of sexuality and identities which have at times been pathologized and constructed as deviant and problematic. I will explore this with reference to 'African sexuality' and the sexuality of persons with disabilities.

'AFRICAN SEXUALITY' AND HIV/AIDS

7.4 The HIV epidemic has grown to become the most destructive disease in modern history. Sub-Saharan Africa has over the years become the most affected region in the world. As the reported epidemic in Africa, particularly sub-Saharan Africa, began to worsen, HIV began to be gradually decoupled from homosexuality and rather coupled to Africa and race. There has from the start been a link between Africa and HIV/AIDS with regard to the origins of HIV, which has, controversially, been understood as originating in Africa (Bancroft, 2001). One early link was made that HIV was transmitted from Africa to Haiti and on to North America, resulting in accusations and complaints of racism (Farmer, 2006). Countries in sub-Saharan Africa have been worst affected by the growing global HIV/AIDS epidemic. Statistics published by the Joint United Nations Programme on HIV/AIDS (UNAIDS, 2010) report that 68% of adults and children living with HIV in the world live in sub-Saharan Africa; an estimated total of 22.5 million individuals living with HIV. This is a region in a serious health crisis, and as a result much focus has been on HIV/AIDS in sub-Saharan Africa, and factors contributing to this high prevalence.

In an effort to try to find the explanation for this significantly higher prevalence, much research focused on the sexual behaviours and sexual relations of African men and women, and the construction of an 'African sexuality'. For example, two frequently cited articles on discussions of an 'African sexuality' are that of Caldwell and Caldwell (1987) and Caldwell and colleagues (1989), who argue that there exists a distinct African sexual system that differs from the sexual system in western countries, that contributes to the significant heterosexual HIV epidemic in Africa. Caldwell and colleagues (1989) state on a few occasions in their article that African society can be thought of as "an alternative civilization", with patterns of sexual behaviour that are different from those seen in western countries. Their work has been criticized by some for being methodologically flawed (LeBlanc, Meintel, & Piché, 1991; Stillwaggon, 2003), and for constructing a generalized and overarching 'African sexuality' (Reid & Walker, 2005; Stillwaggon, 2003), which is seen to differ from the sexuality of those people living in other parts of the world.

Early ethnographic studies often tended to describe 'African sexuality' as different and "wild, animal-like, exotic, irrational and immoral" (Gausset, 2001: 510), and with the identification of AIDS, the focus of study once again became the sexuality of Africans as potentially unhealthy and immoral (Gausset, 2001). This has the potential to echo and reinforce what may be racist beliefs about African sexuality as 'other' – a construction of "hypersexualized Africans" (Stillwaggon, 2003: 821).

Similarly, as with the gay community in the USA in the 1980s, messages of HIV prevention and safe sex was met with suspicion and scepticism by many black African men and women. For example, in South Africa there was considerable suspicion among black South Africans about HIV and HIV prevention. This was in light of the history of the apartheid government's attempts to find ways to reduce the black South African population (Crewe, 1992). The promotion of safe sex and condom use was initially seen as yet another method for attempting to prevent pregnancies, and thus prevent an increase in the black population. Caldwell and colleagues (1992) have also reported that HIV was viewed as a myth by many people in sub-Saharan Africa. HIV and the campaign of safe sex was viewed as a campaign by westerners to restrict the pleasures and sexual moralities of people's sexual lives, attempting to "make Africans conform to Western norms" (p. 1171). In South Africa, until recently, there has been a continued racialized politics related to HIV, with the South African government under president Thabo Mbeki advocating for an 'African' solution to HIV treatment, rather than 'foreign' solutions. This was also fuelled by assumptions of race and sexuality. For example, the then president Thabo Mbeki argued against the severity of the HIV epidemic, stating that discourses about HIV and HIV treatment rested on racist assumptions about African sexuality. Posel (2002) quotes from a speech given by Thabo Mbeki where he stated:

> thus does it happen that others who consider themselves our leaders take to the streets carrying their placards, to demand that because we are germ carriers, and human beings of a lower order that cannot subject its [sic] passion to reason, we must perforce adopt strange opinions, to save a depraved and diseased people from perishing from self-inflicted disease [...] Convinced that we are but natural-born, promiscuous carriers of germs, unique in the world, they proclaim that our continent is doomed to an inevitable mortal end because of our unconquerable devotion to the sin of lust. (Quoted in Posel, 2002: 19)

Much has been written in the UK about the increase in HIV prevalence among the African population. By the end of 2008 in the UK, an estimated 83,000 people were living with HIV (Health Protection Agency, 2009). Since 2000, there has been a significant increase in the prevalence of HIV among heterosexual adults, who are now the dominant transmission 'group' in the UK (The UK Collaborative Group for HIV and STI Surveillance, 2007). The increase in prevalence among the heterosexual population has been partly attributed to the increase in prevalence among black African-born men and women living in the UK, who have either arrived in the country already diagnosed HIV-positive, or who have been diagnosed here after their arrival. By the end of 2008, the prevalence rate of HIV among the black African population in England was 3.7%, compared to 0.4% among the black Caribbean population and 0.09% among the white population (Health Protection Agency, 2008). Research suggests that the majority of HIV infections acquired through heterosexual sex were probably acquired in African countries, particularly the high-prevalence countries of Zimbabwe, Uganda and South Africa (Sinka, Mortimer, Evans, & Morgan, 2003). The inclusion of race and ethnicity in sexual health statistics is controversial (Fenton, Johnson, & Nicoll, 1997), and could lead to easy stereotyping.

For example, there is a growing anti-immigration sentiment in the UK, particularly with regards migrants from countries outside Europe. Migrants, and particularly asylum seekers from Africa, have been constructed as an HIV threat, fuelling anti-immigration lobbying and discussion about HIV screening at immigration (Power, 2004). This is a prevailing discourse around 'health tourism' and 'health migrants', with immigrants being perceived as coming to the UK for the purpose of accessing free NHS health care. In the context of HIV, migrants who are HIV-positive are perceived as arriving in the UK knowing of their HIV status, and having the intention of accessing free HIV health care. The 'health migrant' is seen as abusing the British health care system. While this may happen in some cases, the 'reality' of 'health tourism' is not supported by data. For example, research data on HIV-positive African migrants in the UK suggests that the majority of migrants only learnt of their HIV status some time after arriving in the UK (National AIDS Trust, 2008).

With growing concerns about African migrants and HIV, the sexual health and sexual behaviours of African men and women have become a focus of study. Research suggests that HIV-positive African migrants living in the UK present later for HIV diagnosis than non-African men and women (Burns, Fakoya, Copas, & French, 2001; Del Amo et al., 1996) and so present with more advanced stages of the disease. Delay in presentation may be due to low perceived levels of risk for infection as well as general issues around access to health care. In Chapter 5 we explored how access to health care and the quality of health care is related to socio-economic status. Ethnic minorities in the UK are more likely to live in poorer neighbourhoods than the ethnic majority population. Dixon-Woods and colleagues (2005) have indicated that access to NHS health care for ethnic minorities is generally an issue. Delay in presentation of HIV-positive migrants in the UK may also be related to immigration status. Delay in presentation could be partly due to inadequate or expensive testing and health care facilities in the countries of origin. Once in the UK, factors that may influence an individual's decision or ability to access care, may include uncertain immigration status, particularly for asylum seekers (Erwin & Peters, 1999) and the logistics involved in settling to life in a new country (for recent immigrants), and low levels of perceived HIV risk (Dodds et al., 2008; Erwin, Morgan, Britten, Gray, & Peters, 2002). Delay in presentation may also be affected by related issues of race and racism, and the links made and suspicions associated with AIDS and race. For example, Erwin and Peters (1999), in a study involving African migrants in the UK and their perceptions of health care received, found that there were some important levels of mistrust about the provision of health care by the NHS. For example, some participants in the study felt that the antiretroviral drugs being used in the NHS to treat AIDS were potentially harmful for black African patients, as these were drugs that were researched using white patients. Some participants also spoke about African patients not being properly cared for in hospital and it was at times believed that some doctors actually quicken the death of African patients. In Chapter 4 we explored perceived and actual discrimination or discrepant NHS treatment in relation to ethnicity and race in the UK. Some of the perceptions of differences in HIV treatment related to HIV may indeed reflect realities. For example, Malanda and colleagues (2001) found that HIV-positive patients classed as black African were almost three times less likely to be referred to mental health care services than patients who were not classed as black African.

Recent UK national guidelines for HIV testing (British HIV Association, 2008) stipulate that HIV testing should be routinely offered to individuals coming from a country with a high HIV prevalence or individuals who have reported sexual contact with individuals from such countries. This would be relevant to many Africans in the UK. Given the history of colonialism, racism and constructions of 'African sexuality', there is a danger here of problematizing the sexuality of African men and women in the contexts of health care. This needs to be considered in the current discourses about 'health migrants' and asylum seekers as a potential health threat. Dixon-Woods and colleagues (2005) point out how people from ethnic minorities may feel alienated from a health care organization that treats them in an insensitive and stereotypical manner. Thus the potential to stereotype around notions of African sexuality may be alienating. In my discussions with relevant HIV-related organizations (e.g. the National AIDS Trust and the Terence Higgins Trust) about the issue of HIV and African migrants, anecdotal reports were given of health care workers feeling anxious about raising the suggestion of an HIV test, for fear of being seen as racist. These are similar anxieties reported by participants in the study by Kai and colleagues (2007) in relation to providing culturally sensitive health care to ethnic minorities in the UK. These issues of cultural sensitivity in health care were explored more in depth in Chapter 4.

SEXUALITY AND PEOPLE WITH DISABILITIES

7.5 Persons with disabilities are often perceived as being asexual because they are considered to have diminished or absent sexual needs, or lack the capacity to engage in relationships (Craft, 1987; Milligan & Neufeldt, 2001). For example, people with learning disabilities are often perceived as "forever children" (Craft, 1987) and thus asexual. Alternatively, people with learning disabilities might be perceived to be behaviourally and sexually disinhibited. People with physical disabilities may be viewed as unable to have sex and thus as being asexual. This, however, is a myth; people with disabilities are as sexually active as people who are not disabled, as shown by a number of research studies which indicate this (for example, Blum, Kelly, & Ireland, 2001; Cheng & Udry, 2002; Peinkofer, 1994). There is increasing recognition of the rights of people with disabilities to lead fully sexual lives, but this still raises some anxiety for parents and people without disabilities (see Box 7.2.)

BOX 7.2

Video Clip: Disability and sexuality

The Sex Education Show on Channel 4 in the UK is an educational series exploring aspects of sexuality and sexual health. Series 3 is subtitled "Am I Normal?" and explores primarily concerns about sex, sexuality and the body among teenagers. Included in this series is a look at sexuality for people with disabilities. In episode 2, the presenter meets with people with physical disabilities and learns more about their experiences of dating and sexuality. In episode 4, the presenter meets young people with learning disabilities and their parents and explores issues of relationships and sexuality. In this episode we also meet a married couple, both with learning disabilities, who have had a happy married life and sex life.

You can see the clips online on the Channel 4 website: www.channel4.com/programmes/the-sex-education-show/episode-guide/series-3. Clips are also available on *YouTube*.

Disability is a stigmatized experience, with people with disabilities often the recipients of stigmatizing attitudes and assumptions from non-disabled persons. This has significant effects on a person's self-esteem. Stigma and assumptions about sexuality and disability may leave people with disabilities feeling rejected and socially isolated as a sexual human being. The perception from others is understandably often an important issue for people with disabilities. For example, in a study of men (White, Rintala, Hart, Young, & Fuhrer, 1992) and women (White, Rintala, Hart, & Fuhrer, 1993) with physical disabilities following spinal cord injury, some of the most mentioned concerns of respondents were:

- concerns about finding a partner (43% of men and 26% of women);
- feeling sexually unattractive (49% of men and 51% of women);
- concerns about other people viewing them as sexually unattractive (47% of men and 51% of women).

De Klerk and Ampousah (2003), conducting research on the sense of self of women with physical disabilities in South Africa, use a framework of understanding that includes various aspects of the self – the private self, the public self, the material self and the physical self. The authors concluded that the women in their study generally had a positive sense of their private self. However, their public self was more negatively influenced by the opinions of others. If we look more closely at the comments made by the women in the study, there is some indication of a sense of self that is compromised by internalized stigma. For example, one woman comments that she likes "to compare myself with *normal* people" (p. 1137; italics inserted here for emphasis). Another states: "Sometimes I feel shy because I want to be like able people" (p. 1136). In such comments, their sense of self is negatively influenced in comparison to others, but rather than being negatively influenced by the opinions of others, they are negatively influenced by the notion of themselves as different and 'abnormal' in comparison to 'normal' and 'able' people.

There is a long history of oppression with regards sexuality and people with disabilities. In the past, people with disabilities, particularly with learning disabilities, were regularly sterilized, as the assumption was that they would have babies who were disabled or they were incapable of parenting. Sterilization still occurs, particularly for people with severe disabilities. There is a historical and continuing experience of stigma and social exclusion around sexuality and disability, with the result that sexuality is a topic that is painful. As Tom Shakespeare (2000) so movingly states:

> Sexuality, for disabled people, has been an area of distress, and exclusion, and self-doubt for so long, that it was sometimes easier not to consider it, than to engage with everything from which so many were excluded. Talking about sex and love relates to acceptance on a very basic level – both acceptance of oneself, and acceptance by significant others – and forces people to confront things which are threatening, given the abuse and isolated lives of many disabled people. (p. 160)

As we have seen in Chapter 6, gender is a critical factor for disparities in health and mental health, and likewise women with disabilities may be more affected by stigma and social isolation than men are. This is suggested by Groce (2003), who states that being female as well as disabled is "often referred to as being doubly disabled" (p. 9). For example, women with disabilities have been found to be more likely to be unmarried, separated or divorced than men with disabilities, and non-disabled men and women (Hanna & Rogovsky, 1991). Low self-esteem has implications for mental health as well as sexual health. For example, youths with disabilities are more likely to have attempted suicide that their non-disabled peers (Blum et al., 2001).

People with disabilities with low self-esteem may become sexually promiscuous and appreciative of any sexual attention received (Becker, Stuifbergen, & Tinkle, 1997). Low self-esteem may also affect confidence about negotiating safe sex (Yousafzai & Edwards, 2004). Becker and colleagues (1997) also argue that low self-esteem may result in women with disabilities putting up with some levels of abuse from their partners "because they feel they are lucky to have anyone who wants them" (Becker, et al. 1997: S-30). We should be careful here of victim-blaming, however. Sexual abuse of people with disabilities is a serious concern.

7.5.1 DISABILITY AND SEXUAL ABUSE

In an epidemiological study in the USA (Sullivan & Knutson, 2000), it was found that children with disabilities were 3.4 times more likely to experience maltreatment, abuse and neglect than children with no disabilities. Children with behavioural disorders and learning disabilities had the highest prevalence rate of maltreatment. Neglect was the most prevalent form of maltreatment, followed by sexual abuse. Furthermore, the study also found that children with disabilities were most likely to experience multiple forms of abuse and more episodes of abuse than children with no disabilities. The increased prevalence of abuse of people with disabilities is consistently found in numerous studies investigating abuse of people with varying disabilities. Studies have also indicated gender differences in the prevalence of maltreatment (Sobsey, Randall, & Parilla, 1997; Sullivan & Knutson, 2000). Female children with disabilities experience more sexual abuse than male children with disabilities and children with no disabilities. Male children with disabilities experience more physical abuse and neglect than female children with disabilities. Male children with disabilities experiences more abuse of all types (physical, sexual, emotional abuse and neglect) than male children with no disabilities. Such abuse takes place both at home and in institutions.

One of the possible reasons why children (and adults) with disabilities may be at increased risk for abuse is that they may be more dependent on others for care. Depending on the nature of the disability, children with disabilities may be more dependent on varying care workers, not only parents, to assist with daily functioning. For example, some children with physical disabilities may require assistance with dressing and toileting, both at home and outside the home if spending a day at a particular care organization. This places them in a vulnerable, intimate interaction with a number of adults. There may also be a reduced capacity for self-defence and physical helplessness. Sobsey and Doe (1991) investigated reported cases of sexual abuse of people with disabilities in the USA, and found that in 37% of cases of abuse of people with disabilities, the abuse took place in "environments that the victim encountered as a result of being disabled" (p. 249), such as hospitals, institutions, and in specialized transport vehicles. Similar patterns are found in the UK. In a study involving an analysis of reported cases of abuse from a database of protected adults in the UK (Beadle-Brown, Mansell, Cambridge, Milne, & Whelton, 2010), adults with learning disabilities in particular were found to be at increased risk of abuse, and that such abuse was more likely to have occurred in care homes and by staff and service users. Physical abuse was the most common type of abuse, and people with learning disabilities were most likely to be sexually abused than any other client group. As can be deduced from this, in many cases the perpetrator is thus known to the victim. People with disabilities are also made vulnerable by the assumption on the part of the perpetrator that they would 'get away with it' as the child with disability will not be believed or cannot accurately identify the perpetrator.

Consideration also needs to be given to the use of terminology in describing acts of abuse. I have been using the term 'sexual abuse' to describe a type of violence. This is the term often used in the literature. Marks (1999) points to the importance of considering what is being constructed in the use of this term. She argues that there is a diminished value given to people with disabilities, with the seriousness of sexual and assault crimes committed against people with disabilities often being diminished by referring to it as 'abuse' rather than rape. She quotes Williams, who states: "Women with learning disabilities are 'sexually abused' – other women are raped. Men with learning disabilities are 'physically abused' – other men are assaulted" (Williams, 1995, cited in Marks 1999: 41). Perpetrators of such crimes committed against people with disabilities are then referred to as 'abusers' rather than 'criminals' or 'rapists'.

Perhaps related to this is a consideration of how we might educate people with disabilities about abuse and rape. I recall taking part as a co-facilitator in a sex education programme for young adult males with learning disabilities in South Africa. When the programme focused on issues of safety and vulnerability for abuse, frequently used phrases, as I think is often the case, is 'bad touch' or 'good touch' and so on. We may not be explicit enough in educating the concept of rape. This may result in the victim being unable to fully express the seriousness of the crime, with the result that the incident is not taken as seriously as it should. For example, in a study in Australia, McCabe and colleagues (1994) compared the knowledge and experience of sexual abuse among people with mild learning disabilities and non-disabled students. They found that people with learning disabilities were less likely to understand and know the meaning of 'rape' and 'incest' than the non-disabled peers. They went on to find that once people with learning disabilities were educated about the meaning of the term 'rape', the reported prevalence rate of rape was three times higher for people with learning disabilities than for people with no disabilities. In the UK, Oosterhoorn and Kendrick (2001) interviewed staff members at schools with students with learning disabilities and highlighted the difficulties around disabled children's ability to communicate and understand concepts of abuse. While staff felt that discovery of abuse might be made through physical signs and symptoms, far more difficult was communication with students about it. Staff were unsure as to how best to educate appropriate vocabulary and concepts to aid such communication.

7.5.2 DISABILITY AND SEXUAL HEALTH

As a result of the social construction of disabled people as asexual, people with disabilities have been historically excluded from sexuality education and sexual health care, and in many cases continue to be excluded (Milligan & Neufeldt, 2001). With the construction of asexuality, sex education is regarded as unnecessary and irrelevant. In the case of learning disabilities (and also psychiatric disabilities), there also exists the construction of disabled people being 'oversexed' and disinhibited, and thus sex education is regarded as problematic, even potentially dangerous, as it would encourage sexual expression. For example, in a study by Heyman and Huckle (1995) of informal carers of young adults with learning disabilities, the carers regarded the sexuality of the people they cared for as a source of danger. The carers felt that the adults with learning disabilities would be unable to understand the physical and emotional issues involved in sexuality, and that they would not understand the social mores around this, thus leading to inappropriate and uninhibited sexual activity. The carers also felt that sexuality would lead to a vulnerability to unplanned pregnancy and sexual abuse. Heyman and Huckle went on to find that the informal carers were resistant to providing sex education, and attempted to control the sexuality of the adults with learning disabilities that they cared for. For example, they would prevent opportunities for men and women with learning disabilities to be alone together. The authors argued that displays of 'inappropriate sexual behaviours' (such as public sexual displays) may be a result of the restrictions placed by carers as well as a result of lack of understanding and cognitive ability. Sex education with children and adolescents raises anxiety in most parents.

Talking about sex is not an easy thing to do. Remember what it was like when your own parents tried (or they may not have) to talk to you about sex. If you are a parent and have talked to your child about sex, what has it been like for you? Many parents leave it to the teachers to do most of the sex education. When it comes to teaching a child with a disability about sex, anxieties may be amplified, as they may be intertwined with uncomfortable feelings associated with vulnerability and notions of 'damage' that disability evoke in us (Marks, 1999). Teachers may also have these anxieties, coupled with concern for parents' views and opinions. Research has shown that while teachers and carers might agree to providing sex education for people with disabilities, they lacked the confidence and felt inadequately trained to do so (Bratlinger, 1992; Christian, Stinson, & Dotson, 2001; Howard-Barr, Rienzo, Pigg, & James, 2005). For example, Bratlinger (1992) found that not only did teachers feel inadequately trained, but they were anxious about possible adverse reactions from students with learning disabilities and their parents. Bratlinger quotes a teacher as saying "I had a sense of foreboding about it – like thinking that it would get out of hand" (Bratlinger, 1992: 37). This often relates to the constructions of people with learning disabilities as oversexed and disinhibited. Providing sex education would, in such a case, be seen as potentially destructive and a loss of control. In Box 7.3 an example is provided from my own work in this area which explores educators' experiences and views of providing sex education for young people with learning disabilities in South Africa.

BOX 7.3

A Spotlight on Research: Educators' views on providing sex education for young people with learning disabilities

Rohleder, P., & Swartz, L. (2009). Providing sex education to persons with learning disabilities in the era of HIV/AIDS: Tensions between discourses of human rights and restriction. *Journal of Health Psychology*, 14(4), 601–610.

Aims: In the context of a massive HIV epidemic in South Africa, and literature that suggests that people with disabilities may be at increased risk for HIV infection, this study aimed to explore the challenges and concerns expressed by teachers who provide sex education for young people with learning disabilities.

Methods: Data were collected from interviews with staff affiliated to an organization that serviced and supported a number of schools and organizations for people with learning disabilities. Data were collected from four individual interviews with staff affiliated to this organization, and one group interview with three teachers from two associated schools. Interviews were semi-structured but attempted to allow participants to freely narrate their experiences and views. The interview transcripts were analysed by means of discourse analysis (see Chapter 8), which aimed to identify how participants spoke about providing sex education for people with learning disabilities and what constructions were made of people with learning disabilities, paying close attention to any variations in participants' attitudes and views.

Results: The results of the analysis revealed a tension in the participants' talk between a discourse of human rights and a more restrictive discourse. While on the one hand participants recognized the right of young people with learning disabilities to lead fully sexual lives, and to thus receive sex education, their talk also constructed this as problematic in relation to the young people's sexuality. Particular tensions arose around morality and sexuality, with sex before marriage and homosexuality being constructed as particularly problematic. Fears were expressed that sex education may promote these behaviours, as well as encouraging sexual relations. People with disabilities were in some cases constructed as oversexed or disinhibited, and thus sex education was seen as potentially encouraging sexualized behaviour. Some of the teachers' talk suggested that sex education was provided in a way that attempted to discourage people with learning disabilities from having sex, as sex was constructed as potentially dangerous.

Conclusion: The authors highlight a dilemma for teachers, who are concerned with the vulnerability of people with learning disabilities for sexual abuse and exploitation, while at the same time ensuring their rights to lead fully sexual lives. This was influenced by the teachers' own concerns and anxieties related to constructions of the sexuality of people with learning disabilities as potentially problematic. The researchers suggest that sex education may be done in a way that demonizes sex, by emphasizing sexual abuse and sexually transmitted diseases, as a way to discourage people with learning disabilities from having sex.

The usefulness of using qualitative methods in this study is that it elicits the tensions experienced by teachers in providing sex education for people with learning disabilities. I am sure that were teachers requested to complete a questionnaire, that their acknowledgement of the sexual rights of people with learning disabilities would be predominantly expressed in their answers, while the tensions and complexities of their views may not be captured.

As a result of constructions as to the sexuality of people with disabilities, and their resulting exclusion from sex education, as well as vulnerability to sexual abuse and other risk factors, people with disabilities may be at increased risk for sexually transmitted diseases, including HIV. This is a concern in many of the poorer countries in the world, where a larger number of people with disabilities in the world live (Groce, 2003; see also Chapter 5). These are also often the countries with high rates of HIV prevalence, for example countries in sub-Saharan Africa.

It is suggested that people with disabilities may be at increased risk for HIV infection (Groce, 2003; Rohleder, Braathen, Swartz, & Eide, 2009), due to increased risk factors, including poverty and unemployment, vulnerability to sexual abuse, low levels of education, lack of knowledge about HIV and safe sex, unsafe sexual behaviours and other risk behaviours such as substance abuse. As with the general population, people with disabilities also have sex and may also have unprotected sex. However, people with disabilities have, until only recently, been generally excluded from general HIV prevention programmes. As with knowledge about sex generally, studies have shown that people with disabilities have low levels of HIV-related knowledge, and lower levels than the general population (Bat-Chava, Martin, & Kosciw, 2005; Philander & Swartz, 2006; Wazakili, Mpofu, & Devlieger, 2006; Yousafzai, Dlamini, Groce, & Wirz, 2004). Lower levels of knowledge result in misconceptions about HIV risk and protection. For example, in a study involving women with learning disabilities in Britain (McCarthy, 1998), some participants believed that keeping their bodies clean prevented infections, including HIV. The equal risk for HIV among people with disabilities, as with people without disabilities, is now being recognized, but few HIV prevention campaigns explicitly include people with disabilities (see Figure 7.1).

FIGURE 7.1   "AIDS does not discriminate"

© Inter-American Institute on Disability and Inclusive Development (IIDI), in partnership with Central-America Integration System, Central-America Social Inclusion System, World Bank (reproduced here with permission from the IIDI)

In 2009, the Inter-American Institute on Disability and Inclusive Development (IIDI) carried out an outdoor poster campaign in cities within six Central American countries, which aimed to raise awareness about the exclusion of people with disabilities from HIV prevention efforts. The poster states: "AIDS does not discriminate. All of us have a role in its prevention", and includes silhouette figures of people with different types of disability.

People with disabilities may face numerous barriers to accessing general HIV prevention information: for example, information that is not available in Braille formats, or verbal information that cannot be given with the aid of sign language interpretation, or information that is in a language that is too complex for people with learning disabilities. In poorer countries, such as in sub-Saharan African countries, physically disabled people living in rural areas may find it difficult to access health clinics that may be too far or inaccessible to wheelchair users. However, this is not an issue only for poorer countries. In any country, people with disabilities may be disadvantaged in terms of access to health care facilities. It is beyond the scope of this chapter to explore this issue more fully, but it is worth having a brief look at access to sexual health services. People with disabilities may face both environmental as well as attitudinal barriers to accessing sexual health services. Environmental barriers, for example, include health care services that are inaccessible to wheelchair users, or that are difficult to navigate for people who are blind. Access for wheelchair users is often the area where adjustments are made, but barriers remain for people with other types of disability. For example, in a study of family planning services in Northern Ireland (Anderson & Kitchin, 2000), it was found that in all facilities there was not full access to all people with disabilities. They found that people using wheelchairs had better access to services, whereas people with sensory disabilities did not. Only two facilities out of the 34 studied responded as being accessible for deaf people, for example. Typically, family planning information was not accessible for people with sensory disabilities. The authors argue that this lack of physical access and access to information is as a result of assumptions and expectations that people with disabilities do not need to use family planning services. This relates to constructions of people with disabilities as asexual, and may be shown in attitudinal barriers to accessing sexual health care (discussed in Chapter 6).

Although we have come a long way in recognizing the rights for people with disabilities, particularly learning disabilities, to lead fully sexual lives, there still remain considerable barriers to accessing education, support and health care that would make this possible. The issues are complex, and it in many cases involves issues of vulnerability, 'damage' and sex, topics which evoke considerable anxiety.

SUMMARY

7.6 In this chapter, we first explored the history of how the mental health professions have understood homosexuality. This provides us with a clear example of how value-laden some mental 'disorders' can be. This challenges a biomedical understanding of mental 'disorders' as expressions of underlying physical pathology. In the remainder of the chapter we have explored social constructions of sexuality, with particular reference to 'African sexuality' and the sexuality of persons with disabilities. What I perhaps have hoped to do in this chapter is demonstrate that issues of sexuality are often laden with preconceived assumptions about what is 'normal' and 'abnormal', what is 'moral' and 'immoral', and what is 'acceptable' and 'unacceptable'. These broader social factors impact on the individual in the same way that other broader concepts, such as gender and race, do, and have implications for, and determine, both physical (in this chapter we have only looked at sexual health) and mental health. Also highlighted in this chapter is how such assumptions may act as attitudinal barriers in health care, where service users may be excluded from appropriate services or may perceive the service to be judgemental and unwelcoming.

FURTHER READINGS

Bayer, R. (1987). *Homosexuality and American psychiatry: The politics of diagnosis*. Princeton, NJ: Princeton University Press. This book gives a detailed account of the controversy and debates surrounding the removal of homosexuality from the APA nomenclature.

Shakespeare, T., Gillespie-Sells, K., & Davies, D. (1996). *The sexual politics of disability: Untold desires*. London and New York: Cassell. This book explores the sexual politics of disability and the sexual rights of people with disability. The book draws on accounts of disabled people themselves to explore the emotional and sexual experiences of disabled people.

Shilts, R. (1987). *And the band played on*. New York: St Martin's Press. This book gives a fascinating account of the first years of the HIV epidemic in the USA, and the response on the part of the public health sector, the political sector and the gay community.

RESEARCH METHODS FOR A CRITICAL APPROACH TO CLINICAL AND HEALTH PSYCHOLOGY

8

INTRODUCTION

8.1 Mainstream psychology adopts a scientific approach to understanding human behaviour. This approach has as its basic assumptions that the world is a reality that exists out there, which can be accurately observed and measured in a way that reflects that reality. Thus knowledge about reality can be discovered. In contrast, critical research approaches in psychology seek to challenge the positivism and rationalism of mainstream psychology (Stainton-Rogers, 2009). It often draws on social constructionist theory (see Burr, 1995; and Gergen, 1985), which argues that reality is not a fact that exists out there to be observed, but rather is created, or constructed, by us. Knowledge, from this perspective, is seen as "a human product"; knowledge is made, not discovered (Stainton-Rogers, 2009: 338). Thus a social constructionist approach is critical of the idea that our observations and experience of the world are accurate and realistic and that traditional scientific knowledge, including psychology, is based on objective and unbiased observations of the world. In everyday life we generally assume that we are dealing with a *real* world – a world of events and objects that exists out there and that exists as separate to our thoughts and interpretations of it. However, our views of the world depend on the perspective from which we are coming. We have seen in the previous chapters that there are varying perspectives on how health and illness experiences are understood and interpreted. This is a more relativist stance rather than a positivist one. Willig (2008) uses a simple analogy to illustrate the idea of knowledge being relative: a glass which contains water half-way. Some people view this glass as half full; others view it as half empty. One perspective and experience of the glass is more negative, while the other is more positive. People experience and think about this same object in different ways. Our knowledge and understanding of the world, however, are shared in that we share similar views with other people. Coming back to the simple analogy, any number of people will see the glass as half full; while a different number of people will see the glass as half empty. Our shared constructions of the world, then, give our understandings of the world a 'reality status'. As Burr (1995) explains: "It is through the daily interactions between people in the course of social life that our versions of knowledge become fabricated" (p. 4).

Social constructionism also argues that knowledge we have about the world is an artefact of culture and history. There is variation in notions of reality that change as a product of the particular social, cultural and historical context. Take homosexuality as an example. Our notions about homosexuality have changed over the years (see Chapter 7). Up until the 1970s, homosexuality was regarded as abnormal and included as a mental illness in the DSM. Today, in western societies, homosexuality is no longer understood as a mental 'illness'. However, variation still exists as to our understanding of homosexuality, depending on belief systems such as religious views. Homosexuality is also understood differently in different countries, with it being accepted and legal in countries like the United Kingdom, The Netherlands and South Africa, and unaccepted and illegal in other countries, such as Libya, Saudi Arabia and Sudan. These represent different understandings of a phenomenon, which is situated within specific social and cultural contexts, and there is thus no one factual observable 'truth', as a positivist approach would claim.

Social constructionism, then, is concerned with the various ways in which we understand and make sense of the world. Language, and how we use it to describe our experience of the world, is fundamental to this approach. Reality and what we know as being 'true' about the world is created through our shared discourses and language (Burr, 1995; Gergen, 1985). This has resulted in what has become known as 'the turn to language' in psychological research, and the rise of research methods that aim to capture a social constructionist stance to understanding and exploring human behaviour. Qualitative research methods have arisen as methods for exploring social complexities, exploring relativist understandings of phenomena. Not all qualitative research is conducted within a social constructionist paradigm, but the nature of the data is non-numerical, primarily language, rather than numbers. This qualitative research is predominantly concerned with meaning, and aims to describe, understand and explain phenomena. Qualitative research methods, then, are often considered as the preferred method for more critical approaches in psychology.

Clinical psychology and health psychology have traditionally aligned themselves to positivist science and biomedical models of health and mental health. A lot of the research in health and medicine is epidemiological, and many of the studies cited in this book have been epidemiological. These have been important in establishing patterns in the incidence and prevalence of illnesses and diseases, and for measuring the degree of differences between various population groups (see Box 8.1 for a brief description of epidemiology).

BOX 8.1

Epidemiology

According to the World Health Organization (WHO) (Bonita, Beaglehole, & Kjellström, 2006), epidemiology is the fundamental scientific research method of public health. Epidemiology is concerned with mortality as well as incidence and prevalence of illnesses and disability, as well as states of positive health. *Incidence* refers to the number of new cases of a given disease or health state in a given period within a specific population, whereas *prevalence* refers to the frequency of total cases in a specific population in a given period. Epidemiology also investigates the various causal factors of illnesses or diseases in a given population. Thus epidemiological studies aim to study variations in the levels of morbidity (illness) and mortality in populations and to compare populations, and their causal factors. An aim of epidemiology is to inform public health prevention and intervention efforts. Epidemiology adopts quantitative research methods to analyse such patterns of health states and events in human populations. It is thus concerned with the generalizability and standardization of data across various variables, such as age, gender, socio-economic status (SES) and race. Moon and colleagues (2000) differentiate between three overarching types of epidemiology: clinical epidemiology, which is concerned with studies of clinical, medical cases focusing on biomedical or physical functioning; social epidemiology, which is concerned with studying the various social determinants of health illness, such as SES, employment status, and education; critical epidemiology, which is concerned with social and power relations, and with action at a broader population level.

There has been an increased diversity in the discipline of health psychology, with an increase in the use of diverse research methods, including qualitative research methods to explore issues of health and ill-health (Chamberlain & Murray, 2008). Qualitative methods have been found useful to explore and understand peoples' experiences of illness and health, capturing the complexity of that experience and the complexities related to health care and promotion. Qualitative research methods have also been found to be a useful tool for advocating social change related to health and illness. Qualitative research methods have been less used in clinical psychology. Research in clinical psychology has been influenced by a medical approach, where randomized controlled trials and other quantitative research has been the preferred method for informing evidence-based practice. However, there has been a gradual increase in qualitative research in clinical psychology, particularly in the UK (as compared to the USA) (Harper, 2008). Qualitative methods have been found to be useful in understanding phenomena such as service user experiences, which traditionally was only taken into account when collecting a case history and investigating accounts of symptoms and their history. Increasingly, the experience of what it means and feels like to have mental health difficulties, or the experience of interactions with mental health services, has become an important focus of research.

There are a number of qualitative research methods that are used in the social sciences and in psychology, and it is beyond the scope of this chapter to explore all or most of these in depth. Several books are available that detail the different methods used in qualitative research. Some recommended texts are listed at the end of this chapter. Here, I shall briefly outline some of the more commonly used methods used in health and clinical psychology, which are useful in taking a more critical approach to understanding issues in health and ill-health.

DIFFERENT METHODS IN QUALITATIVE RESEARCH

8.2
A brief description of some of these methods and examples of their use in clinical and health psychology now follows. I have presented them, more or less, in terms of their historical inclusion in clinical and health psychology.

8.2.1 PARTICIPATORY ACTION RESEARCH

Participatory action research is more a research approach than a specific method. It is normally included as a qualitative research method, in that it is concerned with capturing multiple perspectives and experience, as per the principles of social constructionism. Participatory action research aims to generate knowledge and practical solutions to problems affecting individuals and communities, through a process of participation and reflection with multiple partners (Kagan, Burton, & Siddiquee, 2008). The people who would typically be considered the 'subjects' of research actively participate in the generation of knowledge and seeking of practical solutions. The aim is to bring about social change, thus bringing together both the theoretical and the practical, and focuses on the individual as well as the social (be it, for example, the group, the community or the organization). In this sense, action research has as its primary purpose the production of "practical knowledge that is useful to people in the everyday conduct of their lives" (Reason & Bradbury, 2008: 4).

Action research emerged in social psychology in the 1940s in the USA as an approach to research to investigate intergroup relations in real-life contexts (i.e. outside the laboratory and in the community setting). Collier (1945) argued for research that could generate understanding and bring about changed improvements in American Indian Affairs. Collier observes how research can be used as "a tool of action" (Collier, 1945: 275). Similarly, Lewin (1946) introduced the notion of action research as an approach for generating knowledge and understanding about a social system, while simultaneously seeking to change that system. In the UK, action research developed primarily from the Tavistock Institute for Human Relations, as a means of addressing post-Second World War social and health problems, such as the treatment of war trauma, and the rehabilitation of war casualties and prisoners of war (Rapoport, 1970). Action research also emerged in Latin America around the same time, and was particularly influenced by the work of Paulo Freire (1972), a Brazilian educationist who encouraged the view of inclusion of participants as active members in a process of inquiry, and argued for the need for participatory dialogue as a process of learning. While early action research in the UK and USA developed out of a need to respond to immediate social problems, action research began to be applied to organizational and workplace problems (Elden & Chisholm, 1993). Action research declined in use in social psychology, until the 1970s, when critiques of the dominant positivistic and reductionist research in social psychology led to the development of new paradigms. Action research re-emerged as a useful critical approach to social psychology research. In more recent years, action research has a central use in community psychology and in critical psychology. Community psychology as a sub-discipline of psychology is growing worldwide as an applied psychological approach which is critical in orientation and aims to bring about social change and social justice at the community and structural level (Hanlin et al., 2008). In the UK, community psychology was incorporated as a special section of the British Psychological Society in late 2010. Community health psychology has taken on the principles of social justice and community empowerment to focus on bringing about health change within the community context (see Chapter 3).

Lewin (1946) describes action research as a cyclical process of inquiry that involves the initial exploration and conceptualization of the problem situation, planning and implementing action steps, and evaluation of the outcomes of action taken. This evaluation of outcomes in turn leads to renewed diagnosis of the problem situation, taking into consideration what has been previously learnt. Action research uses scientific knowledge to solve practical problems, in collaboration with those who are experiencing the problem situation, in order to generate new knowledge. Data are collected by utilizing a variety of methods, involving observational, visual, textual and spoken data. Ideas and issues are explored collaboratively with all partners (both researchers and 'participants'). During this process, areas that need to be changed or researched further are identified, and plans made for action. Evaluation of actions taken similarly involves the collection of evaluative data utilizing a variety of methods (see Kagan, Burton, & Siddiquee, 2008, for a detailed discussion of the research process).

Action research, and its emphasis on social change, is a popular research approach in critical health psychology and community psychology. It is an important and useful research approach when the aim is to bring about community-level changes to social and health problems (see Chapter 3 for a discussion of community-level and structural-level perspectives on health, and a good example of a participatory action research project involving a community in Cambodia in Box 3.1). With its emphasis on participation and involvement, it is a good tool for including people who may be otherwise marginalized or whose views are often not considered important. A good example is the Sonagachi Project in the red light district of Kolkata. This is a multi-level community participation HIV prevention project led by female sex-workers in India. It has been a very successful project, and has run for over 15 years (see Jana, Basu, Rotheram-Borus, & Newman, 2004, for details of the project; and also Cornish & Ghosh, 2007, for an examination of the community involvement in the project).

Participatory action research in its true sense has been less utilized in clinical psychology. However, there has been an increased recognition of the importance of considering and involving mental health service-users' views and experiences when researching, evaluating and planning mental health care. In the UK, the *National Service Framework for Mental Health* (Department of Health, 1999) explicitly states that service users' views should be taken into account in planning and delivering mental health services. However, in many cases there is merely a token involvement of service users in this way. There has also been a call to ensure that service users are involved at all stages of a research process, including identifying research priorities (Appleby, 2004). Service users' views can add an important perspective that differs from what professionals think is important. New and innovative ways of caring can be developed by listening to the views of service users and what coping strategies and resources they themselves have found useful. For example, the user-led *Strategies for Living* project involved five mental health service users who were employed by the National Centre for Social Research and trained in research skills. The five co-researchers collected data by interviewing 71 mental health service users throughout the UK about the coping strategies used by service users to help them manage their mental health difficulties, analysed the data and produced a report on the project and its findings (Faulkner & Layzell, 2000).

Participatory action research is also important with regards to studies involving people with disabilities. One of the key slogans of the disability movement is "Nothing About Us Without Us", which emphasizes that policy affecting people with disabilities should not be implemented without the knowledge and participation of disabled people themselves in the drawing up of such policies. Regarding research, this extends to participating in research, not merely as subjects of research, but as active participants in the design and implementation of research. The emphasis is placed on conducting research *with* people with disabilities, rather than *on* people with disabilities.

8.2.2 GROUNDED THEORY

Grounded theory was originally developed in the discipline of sociology (Glaser & Strauss, 1967), but has since also become very popular as a qualitative research method in psychology. Grounded theory was developed as a method for analysing data through inductive enquiry rather than deductively. This is analysis that is data-driven, working from the data towards the development of theory, rather than analysing or testing the data from theory-driven hypotheses. It was developed as a critique of research that is centred around hypothesis-testing, where existing theories are tested against new data, which makes it difficult for new theories to be developed. Grounded theory was developed as a method for generating new theories which would be 'grounded' to the data that are collected within a specific context.

Willig (2008) outlines three areas of ongoing debate and tension in grounded theory, with debates centring around the role of induction, whether the process of analysis is one of discovery versus construction, and whether grounded theory is focused on outlining social processes or exploring individual experiences. First, there is much debate as to whether grounded theory can be considered as data-driven, as there is some imposition of pre-existing assumptions and ideas on the part of the researcher. Furthermore, thorough guidelines were produced detailing step by step the method of analysis and the coding of data, which was argued to add a deductive element to analysis. As a result, some grounded theory adopts more flexible approaches, adapted to what is needed from the data, while others adopt a more prescribed method for approaching the data. Secondly, Glaser and Strauss (1967) described grounded theory as a method of discovering new theory from the data. This suggests a positivist view of a social reality that exists and can be objectively observed. As Willig (2008: 44) states: "The use of the term 'discovery' suggests that the researcher uncovers something that is already there". Later developments of grounded theory regarded it as a social constructionist approach, where meanings in the data are *constructed* by the researcher, rather than *discovered* in the data (Charmaz, 1990; Charmaz & Henwood, 2008). Thirdly, grounded theory was originally intended to be used as a method for mapping out social processes, such as the management of illness. Grounded theory is a useful method for answering research questions related to processes or actions, rather than merely experiences. For example, questions like "*How* do people manage the stigma of HIV?" rather than "*What* are HIV-positive people's experiences of stigma?" The first lends itself to understanding the management processes that people adopt and go through so that theories of stigma management can be identified. The second question lends itself to the phenomenological exploration of people's lived experiences (see below for interpretative phenomenological analysis as an appropriate method for such research questions). However, more recently, researchers have adopted the coding procedures (see below) of grounded theory for analysing participants' understanding of a phenomenon or their experiences. Rather than using grounded theory as a cyclical approach to 'discovering' and mapping out social processes, the procedure of coding has been used as a method for analysing and managing data, by identifying "categories of meaning and experience" (Willig, 2008: 45). Such an approach is more akin to thematic analysis (Braun & Clarke, 2006). Although, as you will see later in this chapter, interpretative phenomenological analysis is concerned with the analysis of participants' experiences, this method is bound theoretically to phenomenology, whereas grounded theory used to analyse participants' experiences is not theoretically bound; rather, it aims to generate or develop theory (Braun & Clarke, 2006).

Data are collected by means of a variety of possible techniques, such as interviews, focus group interviews, observation and documents. The process of data collection and analysis is explicitly cyclical. Data are collected and analysed with the aim of identifying *"categories of meaning"* (Willig, 2008: 35) in the data. The data are analysed by means of coding, which involves identifying emerging meaning categories or themes. Codes are developed as a categorical name for themes, and data are selected and identified according to these codes. These codes are used to identify and label similar categories and themes in the remaining data. Themes or categories of meaning are then integrated by identifying links and relationships between categories. The end purpose is to provide an explanatory theory for the phenomenon being studied. As an emerging data-driven theory is developed, further data are collected and analysed in relation to theoretical ideas which have emerged from the earlier stages of data analysis. Samples are purposively used to test out or challenge these emerging ideas. This is known as theoretical sampling. This allows for the emerging theory to be checked against the phenomenon being studied. This process continues until no new categories of meaning can be identified. This is referred to as 'theoretical saturation'.

Grounded theory has been a popular choice of qualitative research in both clinical psychology and health psychology, as it lends itself to research which considers patients' and clients' concerns and the development of appropriate services, interventions and treatments (Charmaz & Henwood, 2008). For example, grounded theory methods have been used to explore the experiences and the processes of treatment of patients having soma surgery for the treatment of cancer (McVey, Madill, & Fielding, 2001). Hussain and Cochrane (2003) used grounded theory to outline the various coping strategies of South Asian women living with depression. An example of a study using grounded theory from a social constructionist framework is described in Chapter 5, Box 5.2.

8.2.3 CONVERSATION ANALYSIS

Conversation analysis was first developed in the late 1960s and early 1970s by Harvey Sacks, in his investigation of callers' accounts to a suicide telephone counselling centre (Silverman, 1998). Sacks observed that talk was a form of action, in that when people converse, they engage in social action through processes such as turn-taking, questions, initiating and closing topics for conversations, making requests, agreeing and disagreeing, and so on. Thus talk-in-interaction is a form of social action rather than just a medium for communicating information, and so the management of the activity of conversations can be the focus of investigation (Drew, 2008). Naturally occurring conversations are used as data for analysis. Conversations are recorded and observed as they naturally occur, rather than research-generated interviews. Naturally occurring conversations that are often used as data are ordinary conversations and institutional talk (Wilkinson & Kitzinger, 2008). Ordinary conversations provide researchers with a 'snap shot' of everyday life and everyday talk of people, as opposed to the retrospective stance of a research interview. Institutional talk involves more specialized forms of talk, such as giving diagnostic news, typical of health care settings, for example. Conversations can be captured through auditory or visual recording. These conversation recordings are then transcribed in detail, with indications made of the details of verbal and non-verbal aspects of talk, for example length of pauses, tone and inflection, pace of talk and interruptions. The transcripts are then analysed with the focus on the intersubjective nature of turn-taking in talk; how people understand what is being said and how they respond to one another, and the performances, sequences and actions of a conversation. Attention is also paid to any recurring patterns in conversations. Conversation analysis is thus interested in the constructive nature of talk. As stated by Drew (2008: 136):

> The objective of CA's methodological approach is to attempt to document and explicate how participants arrived at understandings of one another's actions during the back-and-forth interaction between them, and how they construct their turns so as to be suitably responsive to prior turns.

Conversation analysis also takes into account the context in which such conversations take place. Doctor–patient communication is an important topic in health psychology. Thus conversation analysis can be useful for exploring interactions between professionals and services users in health or mental health settings. For example, Rapley (2004) points out how people with learning disabilities are often understood as being acquiescent, and thus incompetent to report on their own subjective experience. He demonstrates, by means of conversation analysis of assessment interviews between a professional and a person with disability, how an acquiescent response may be the product of the interview process, where the professional might ignore certain responses as 'incorrect' replies to questions that the professional assumes a certain answer for. Questions are repeated and rephrased until the interviewee eventually says "yes". Similarly, Pilnick and colleagues (2010) analyse review meetings between professionals and service users and their parents in which transitions from child to adult services are discussed. They show how attempts to invite the participation of service users can be quickly blocked, thus undermining the service user's choice and control over the agenda of the review meeting.

8.2.4 DISCOURSE ANALYSIS

Particular forms of discourse analysis have been used in linguistics and sociology, prior to its development as a method in psychology, particularly social psychology.

Discursive approaches in psychology were highly influenced by the work of social psychologists Potter and Wetherell (1987), who developed a discourse analysis approach to understanding and investigating social attitudes. They critiqued the traditional, experimental approach in social psychology as an inadequate way to investigate 'real world' issues, as it involves methods of collecting data which are artificial (in the laboratory rather than in the real world) and reduces social phenomena to individual behaviours. Discursive approaches in psychology have as their primary focus how we construct our social world and ourselves through language and communication. It critiques traditional notions of language as a neutral transmission of information from one person to another (see further below). A discursive approach in psychology views language not merely as describing and representing phenomena, but as actively constructing understanding and meaning. A social discursive approach argues that when we talk, we do not merely describe things, but rather we construct a version of events and when we talk, we act upon the social world (Potter & Wetherell, 1987). Thus talk has an *action orientation*. For example, when we talk to someone about an event, we are actively trying to put forward and convince others of *our* particular version of events.

Discourse analysis is a qualitative research method of analysing spoken and written text. Generally, this is naturally occurring talk and text. This may include recordings of naturally occurring discussions and conversations (for example, in relation to clinical and health psychology, this may include case conferences or doctor–patient consultations). However, because of the ethical complexity of using recording and using such data, many researchers use semi-structured interviews or focus group interviews as sources of data. Written text would include, for example, published texts, public interview transcripts, advertisements, and so on. In discourse analysis, attention is paid to "the structure and organization of discourse" (Marshall, 1994: 91), and the possible consequences of using particular discursive constructions in the text. Discourse analysis also involves investigating the various constructions and meanings given to phenomena and events in the social world, which people draw on to make sense of their world. The text is examined with the aim of identifying "interpretive repertoires" (Potter & Wetherell, 1987), which are recurrent patterns of words, terms and phrases which cluster together to construct a particular discourse. Attention is paid to variations in the text, in order to indentify various repertoires that may be used, and how they are used by the subject in the text. Of interest here is any use of contradictory repertoires, which may indicate dilemmas or ambivalence in people's attitudes. For example, Rohleder and Swartz (2009) identified tensions between discourses of human rights and discourses of control or restriction when educators talked about the sexuality of persons with learning disabilities (see Chapter 7, Box 7.2). Attention is also given for the possible consequences of using the various discourses. Thus discourse analysis pays attention to *what* is being said and *how* it is being said. This process requires interpretation on the part of the researcher and so the researcher is actively involved in reconstructing the discourses of the research subjects (Banister, Burman, Parker, Taylor, & Tindall, 1994).

There are two different versions of doing discourse analysis in psychology, discursive psychology and Foucauldian discourse analysis. Foucauldian discourse analysis draws upon the work of French philosopher Michel Foucault. The two versions aim to answer different research questions. Willig (2008: 96) differentiates between the two:

> Discursive psychology asks how participants use language in order to negotiate and manage social interactions so as to achieve interpersonal objectives (e.g. disclaim an undesirable social identity, justify an action, attribute blame). Foucauldian discourse analysis seeks to describe and critique the discursive worlds people inhabit and to explore their implications for subjectivity and experience (e.g. what is it like to be positioned as 'asylum seeker' and what kind of actions and experiences are compatible with such a positioning?).

Both are interested in how language is used to construct social phenomenon. However, discursive psychology is more interested in how people make use of language to act upon the social world, while Foucaulidan discourse analysis is more interested in what versions of social phenomenon are being constructed and the implications this has for subjects. Foucauldian discourse analysis is more concerned with issues of power in social relationships and how people are positioned in relation to power.

Discourse analysis in psychology was developed as a critique of the cognitive paradigm in social psychology, which reduced social behaviour to individual cognitive processes. Since then it has gained in popularity in psychology and is now also used in health psychology and clinical psychology. An example of a study that utilizes discourse analysis is described in Chapter 6, Box 6.1.

8.2.5 NARRATIVE RESEARCH

Narrative psychology is a fairly new approach in psychology, influenced largely by the work of Sarbin (1986) and colleagues. Narrative psychology draws on the theoretical principles of phenomenology (discussed further below) to focus on the way in which people make sense of and organize their experiences. When people talk about their lives, they make connections between previous events and memories in a manner that creates a sense of coherence. People attempt to create order to their everyday life experiences. Thus when people talk about their lives they do so as though they are telling a coherent story. As articulated by Hiles and Čermák (2008: 149):

> Narrative plays a crucial role in almost every human activity. Narratives dominate human discourse, and are fundamental to the cultural processes that organize and structure human action and experience. They offer a sense-making process that is fundamental to understanding human reality.

Narrative research, therefore, is interested in the ways in which people construct stories about their lives. Narrative research adopts a 'narrative oriented inquiry' (Hiles & Čermák, 2008). Data are collected by means of a narrative interview, which can be either very open-ended or semi-structured. Rather than being structured like a question-and-answer interview, a narrative interview aims to elicit a natural dialogue and story about the participant's experiences.

The participant is given the opportunity to give a detailed account of his or her experience. The narrative which is created is considered as a whole, with a beginning, a middle and an end, much like a story has. The life story narrative is an obvious example of this. Attention is paid to the representation of events in the story, the strategies used to construct stories that give it a sense of coherence, as well as to the content of the story. It is also important to consider that the story or narrative is not only about the events being experienced, but is also about the identity of the person. The subject, when telling a story, is also constructing an identity of themselves in relation to that story – a narrative identity (Murray, 2008). The story or narrative told is also influenced by the context in which it is told; the social and cultural context. Thus it is useful to also account for the social cultural context in which the experience has taken place.

An example of narrative research in health psychology is the work of Corinne Squire with people living with HIV in South Africa (Squire, 2007). Squire uses interviews with 37 people living with HIV, exploring the participants' experiences of living with HIV in depth and how they have managed and made sense of their illness. The analysis of the interviews follows a temporal scheme, observing how the participants talk about the meaning of their illness as moving from one of stigmatization, exclusion and othering, to a point where they have come to accept their HIV status and found ways of positively managing their status, for example by adopting a more political and activist identity. This is a progressive narrative, which has a positive and optimistic tone, rather than a regressive narrative which has a negative and pessimistic tone (Murray, 2008). These narratives are considered in the context of an epidemic in South Africa that has developed into a massive social and health problem, is highly stigmatized and has sparked controversial political conflict and debate. In this context, a tone of hope and optimism in such a negative context is important.

Recently, researchers wanting to integrate a psychoanalytic framework to their studies have adopted a free association narrative interview (Hollway & Jefferson, 2000), which aims to elicit unconscious material in the interview. A free association narrative interview is open-ended in structure, where the agenda of the interview is fluid and open to change. It is proposed that the narrative or story follows the unconscious logic of the narrator as well as the interviewer. Interview questions are asked as a way to elicit the stories of the participants, following not only on what they have said, but also what has been left unsaid. The interviewer pays attention to the emotional nuances of the interview, and uses the feelings that are evoked in the interviewer (what in psychoanalysis is referred to as the countertransference) as additional sources of data, which may inform where to probe with further questions. In this way the story is co-constructed by the narrator and the interviewer. This method has generated some interest in psychosocial studies and social psychology in relation to identity and subjectivity. However, given the various emotions that health and ill-health evoke, it does lend itself to research in health psychology and clinical psychology. For example, in exploring educators' experiences of providing sex education to people with learning disabilities, I incorporated a psychoanalytic framework for considering how participants managed the anxiety that their work evoked in them (Rohleder, 2010). Educators recognized the need for sexuality education and the rights of people with learning disabilities to lead full sexual lives where possible. However, they had some anxiety of possible damaging consequences, such as encouraging sexual disinhibition and promiscuity, or encouraging what they considered to be immoral sexual behaviour. The educators first attributed these anxieties to others, to which they had to respond or consider when providing sexuality education. One of the ways in which some educators could manage this anxiety was to provide sex education in a way that portrayed sex as potentially dangerous, and thus encouraging the disabled people they taught to rather have relationships that were not necessarily sexual.

8.2.6 INTERPRETATIVE PHENOMENOLOGICAL ANALYSIS

Interpretative phenomenological analysis (IPA) is a method of analysing qualitative data developed by Jonathan Smith (1996). It is informed by the philosophical principles of phenomenology and hermeneutics. Phenomenology, as developed by Husserl and Heidegger, is concerned with the individual's personal, lived experience of the social world. Husserl called for experience to be examined as it occurs and is subjectively experienced by the person. In phenomenology, the object of a phenomenon cannot be removed from the subject experiencing it. In this way, a phenomenological approach recognizes that different people experience a phenomenon in different ways, as they have different subjective experiences of it. Research following a phenomenological approach attempts to tap into that subjective, unique experience. In investigating human experience, Husserl argued that one should bracket off one's prior assumptions about that phenomenon, to cast aside what he referred to as our natural attitude, and to examine the phenomenon anew, as it occurs. A key method in phenomenological research is that, in order to capture a person's subjective experience and be true to that experience, the researcher has to bracket off their own assumptions about the experience being studied. The phenomenological method is concerned not with attempting to establish some objective measure of a phenomenon, but rather in exploring and describing in detail the personal, subjective experience that a person has of a phenomenon.

Heidegger developed these ideas further to develop a hermeneutic version of phenomenology. Hermeneutics is concerned with interpretation. Heidegger argued that any experience of a phenomenon cannot occur outside an interpretative stance, thus a person does not only have an experience of a phenomenon, but also interprets that experience so that the phenomenon acquires a meaning for the subject. In such a phenomenological approach, meaning, rather than just perceptual and sensory experience, is then of primary importance.

Interpretative phenomenological analysis draws on these two philosophical principles in that it is a method in which, rather than merely just describing or summarizing a person's experience, there is a process of interpretation of the data. The aim is not merely to describe, but also to understand. The aim of IPA is to understand personal meaning, which is achieved through a process of "reflective engagement" (Smith, Flowers, & Larkin, 2009: 80) with the data. The analysis aims to explore the participant's perspective on the world, representing that perspective as closely as possible, but which is constructed by the researcher through the process of interpreting that experience. IPA is concerned with an in-depth analysis of a person's experience and meaning. Thus IPA is idiographic, concerned with the unique rather than with generalizations. Thus IPA often works at a case study level, using small sample sizes. Smith, Flowers, and Larkin (2009) recommend a sample of between three and six for undergraduate and postgraduate students, and sample sizes of between four and ten for PhD students. Smith and colleagues (2009) argue that successful analysis using IPA requires time and a process of reflection, which can be achieved with better quality with smaller sample sizes rather than larger ones. They therefore stress that "it is more problematic to try to meet IPA's commitments with a sample which is 'too large', than with one that is 'too small'" (Smith et al., 2009: 51).

IPA typically works with transcripts of interviews as data for analysis. Interviews are usually semi-structured, using an interview schedule to guide discussion around a topic. Questions should be open-ended and non-directive. This guide functions as a loose agenda, with the aim being that the interview functions as more of an in-depth discussion of the topic, on the part of the participant. Good interviews should explore participants' experiences in depth, so participants should be allowed the opportunity to talk at length and with as much detail as possible. The interviewer should use probes to explore issues further. An interview that generates short answers, lacking in description, becomes too 'thin' for good IPA analysis to occur.

IPA has been particularly popular in health psychology. For example, it has been frequently used as a method of capturing patients' lived experiences of illness. For example, Bramley and Eatough (2005) explored experiences of living with Parkinson's disease; Smith and Osborn (2007) explored experiences of living with chronic lower back pain. Smith (2004) observes how many IPA studies focus on significant life-threatening or life-transforming events, with identity being a key construct. It has been less used in clinical psychology, but is increasing in popularity as it similarly allows for the capturing of personal experience and meaning in mental ill-health. For example, Knight and colleagues (2003) explored the experience of stigma in patients diagnosed with schizophrenia (Knight, Wykes, & Hayward, 2003); Shinebourne and Smith (2009) explored people's experiences of alcohol addiction and its impact on self identity. The method lends itself to a critical approach in health and clinical psychology as it allows for investigating people's experiences and the meaning of that experience for them, particularly people who might have been otherwise marginalized or whose voice and experience is seldom heard. It is concerned with the unique, rather than with universals. An example of a study using IPA to explore gay men's understandings of unprotected sex is detailed in Chapter 7, Box 7.1.

So far I have briefly outlined six different approaches in qualitative research. There are other qualitative approaches, but these six are perhaps the most widely used or increasingly used qualitative methods in health and clinical psychology. In the boxes in previous chapters, various qualitative studies have been described in more detail, many of which make use of one of these methods. These methods are summarized in Table 8.1 as an easy reference, and some example research papers have been provided for each method.

TABLE 8.1 A summary of some key qualitative research methods in clinical and health psychology

Method	Description	Sources of data	Some examples
Participatory action research	More a research approach than a specific method. It aims to generate knowledge and practical solutions to problems affecting individuals and communities through a process of participation and reflection with multiple partners.	For example: observation, interviews, focus groups, documentation and visual material.	• Jana, S., Basu, I., Rotheram-Borus, M.J., & Newman, P.A. (2004). The Sonagachi project: A sustainable community intervention program. *AIDS Education and Prevention, 16*(5), 405–414. • Ramon, S., Castillo, H., & Morant, N. (2001). Experiencing personality disorder: A participative research project. *International Journal of Social Psychiatry, 47*(4), 1–15
Grounded theory	A method for analysing data through inductive enquiry rather than deductively. This is analysis that is data-driven, working from the data towards the development of theory, rather than analysing or testing the data from a theory-driven hypothesis.	For example: interviews, focus groups, observation and documentation.	• Dilks, S., Tasker, F., & Wren, B. (2010). Managing the impact of psychosis: A grounded theory exploration of recovery processes in psychosis. *British Journal of Clinical Psychology, 49*(1), 87–107. • Patel, S., Peacock, S.M., Mckinley, R.K., Clark-Carter, D., & Watson, P.J. (2008). GPs' experiences of managing chronic pain in a South Asian community: A qualitative study of the consultation process. *Family Practice, 25,* 71–77.
Conversation analysis	The analysis of talk-in-interaction as a form of social action in naturally occurring conversations. It is a method for analysing the structure, pattern and order of conversations.	Recorded or published conversations between two or more people.	• Finlay, W.M., Antaki, C., & Walton, C. (2008). Saying no to the staff: An analysis of refusals in a home for people with severe communication difficulties. *Sociology of Health & Illness, 30*(1), 55–75. • Pilnick, A., Clegg, J., Murphy, E., & Almack, K. (2010). Questioning the answer: Questioning style, choice and self-determination in interactions with young people with intellectual disabilities. *Sociology of Health & Illness, 32*(3), 415–436.

(Continued)

TABLE 8.1 (Continued)

Method	Description	Sources of data	Some examples
Discourse analysis	The analysis of spoken and written text, with the primary aim of analysing how we construct our social world and identity through language and communication.	For example: interviews, focus groups, naturally occurring conversations, and written texts.	• Gough, B. (2006). Try to be healthy, but don't forgo your masculinity: Deconstructing men's health discourse in the media. *Social Science & Medicine, 63*, 2476–2488. • Malson, H., Finn, D.M., Treasure, J., Clarke, S., & Anderson, G. (2004). Constructing 'the eating disordered patient': A discourse analysis of accounts of treatment experiences. *Journal of Community and Applied Social Psychology, 14*, 473–489.
Narrative analysis	The analysis of the ways in which people construct stories about their lives.	For example: interviews, published autobiographies.	• Gray, R.E., Fergus, K.D., & Fitch, M.I. (2005). Two black men with prostate cancer: A narrative approach. *British Journal of Health Psychology, 10*, 71–84. • Stern, S., Doolan, M., Staples, E., Szmukler, G.L., & Eisler, I. (1999). Disruption and reconstruction: Narrative insights into the experience of family members caring for a relative diagnosed with serious mental illness. *Family Process, 38*(3), 353–369.
Interpretative phenomenological analysis	A method of analysing an individual's personal, lived experience of the social world. It aims to explore and represent the individual's subjective perspective of the world.	Typically interviews, and sometimes focus groups.	• Perry, B.M., Taylor, D., & Shaw, S.K. (2007). 'You've got to have a positive state of mind': An interpretative phenomenological analysis of hope and first episode psychosis. *Journal of Mental Health, 16*(6), 781–793. • Senior, V., Smith, J.A., Michie, S., & Marteau, T.M. (2002). Making sense of risk: An interpretative phenomenological analysis of vulnerability to heart disease. *Journal of Health Psychology, 7*(2), 157–168.

MIXED METHODS

8.3 Very often critical approaches in psychology, for example critical health psychology, adopt a position of being in opposition to statistics and quantitative research methods. A radical position may be to view statistics and quantitative research as telling us little about the social world and about people's lived experiences. In some cases, a critical health psychology or critical clinical psychology becomes all about merely criticizing biomedical science, epidemiology and its statistics. Quantitative studies do adopt a particular way of describing the world in which numbers are privileged, but this does not mean that they do not provide important, useful and helpful knowledge, and should certainly not be ignored. Statistics, for example epidemiological statistics related to illness, help us to understand the existence and prevalence of certain illness. Statistical studies also allow us to establish clear causal relationships between factors that *may* affect illness experiences. Many epidemiological studies cited in previous chapters have allowed us to observe how health and health care have different impacts for different population groups. Taking a critical approach is not just to criticize such statistical findings, but rather to critically consider what they mean. It is also incorrect to assume that all researchers working with statistical studies are not critical in their thinking about what the findings might imply. Great pains are often taken to think about what epidemiological findings may mean about how illness may be variously (or unequally) experienced. Quantitative research can be used as a very important tool for highlighting discrimination and inequality and advocating social change (Fox, Prilleltensky, & Austin, 2009). Quantitative data can be used to bring causal patterns to our attention, which we can then think about critically. I will use HIV as an example.

Quantitative and epidemiological studies have given us a large source of reliable and valid evidence of a number of aspects about the HIV epidemic. For example:

1   HIV causes AIDS.
2   HIV is transmitted from one person to another through infected blood.
3   Various risk factors contribute to the risk of HIV infection – e.g. unprotected sex with an infected partner; the use of contaminated needles.
4   The prevalence of HIV and AIDS is higher in certain parts of the world than in other parts of the world.
5   Sub-Saharan Africa is the region most affected by HIV/AIDS.

There are many more examples of HIV knowledge generated by statistical data. A multitude of well-designed studies combine to give us a good understanding of the epidemic. A critical stance would be to question and explore some of these 'facts' in terms of what they mean. For example, with reference to point 3 above: Why do individuals practise unsafe sex and how can we help them to change their risk behaviours? In Chapter 3 we saw how a traditional cognitive-behavioural approach would be to look at factors at the level of the individual, for example level of knowledge. A critical approach would be to consider what social, cultural and political factors facilitate risk behaviours, for example structural factors that contribute to the subordination of women which places them at increased risk of unsafe sex. Or with reference to point 5 above, the epidemiological evidence that shows the highest prevalence of HIV/AIDS being in sub-Saharan Africa. Quantitative data have highlighted this disparity in the global HIV epidemic, and the ways in which people from poorer regions of the world are at increased risk for HIV infection. A critical approach may seek to understand and explore some of the broader structural and political factors that contribute to broader global health inequalities.

In terms of research, then, investigating health and illness from multiple perspectives and approaches allow for a greater depth of understanding of health issues. Mixed methods approaches, combining quantitative and qualitative methods, could thus be particularly valuable. Quantitative methods would allow for the establishment of causal relationships between factors, and the use of complementary qualitative methods would allow us to explore in depth some of the factors and causal relationships. The use of combined quantitative and qualitative methods helps compensate for some of the weaknesses of individual quantitative and qualitative methods (Connidis, 1983; Steckler, McLeroy, Goodman, Bird, & McCormick, 1992). This allows for a more in-depth investigation of complex health-related phenomena. As Steckler and colleagues (1992) have argued, health education and promotion programmes, for example, "are complex phenomena which require the application of multiple methodologies in order to properly understand or evaluate them" (Steckler et al., 1992: 4).

Steckler and colleagues (1992) outline four possible approaches to integrating quantitative and qualitative methods:

1   Qualitative methods are often first used in order to initially explore a phenomenon in order to help develop and construct quantitative research measures. For example, conducting focus group interviews in order to identify relevant issues related to barriers to accessing health care among ethnic minorities so as to construct a questionnaire to measure barriers to health care.

2   Quantitative methods can be used to support some of the findings of a qualitative study. For example, administering standardized measures of mental health to participants in a qualitative study exploring the psychological and emotional experiences of people living with depression and anxiety.

3   Qualitative methods can be used to support and help in understanding a predominantly quantitative research study. For example, conducting individual interviews with HIV-positive men to further understand the statistical association between alcohol use and unsafe sex as measured in a questionnaire-based study.

4   Both quantitative and qualitative methods are used equally and in parallel to one another. Results from both methods are compared and evaluated against each other. For example, one sub-study measuring the level of knowledge about sex among a group of learning disabled young adults. A second complimentary sub-study might involve interviewing the parents of the young adults to explore their views on sex education for young people with learning disabilities.

It is often the case that researchers include a couple of open-ended questionnaires as a way of 'including' qualitative methods into their research design. This may end up just being a token addition of qualitative methods and not the most useful or valuable way of mixing methods. And in this case, it is not making full and effective (or proper) use of qualitative methods, of which one of the strengths is to elicit in-depth accounts of participants' experiences. The same may be the case where a basic quantitative measure is added to a predominantly qualitative design. Steckler and colleagues (1992) warn against a tendency to reduce quantitative and qualitative methods in one design to merely elementary forms. While the strengths of each approach can be used in conjunction to enrich a research project, there are some challenges and problems to consider in using mixed methods. Yardley and Bishop (2008) point out that using a combination of quantitative and qualitative studies in one research project requires decisions about which study (or which approach) takes priority and how the combined approaches should be managed and planned in terms of the project time-frame. If one approach is to be conducted first in order to inform the second approach, delays in the first will result in delays in the second. For example, if focus group interviews are to be used to identify possible items for a to-be-developed questionnaire measure, the focus group study (data collection, transcription of interviews and analysis of data) needs to be completed before the second phase can begin. This can make the process a lengthy one. Another challenge may be that the different findings that are elicited from mixed quantitative and qualitative methods may appear to be incompatible and thus difficult to analyse as a whole (Yardley & Bishop, 2008). However, as Yardley and Bishop point out, such apparently incompatible findings may be used to generate a further hypothesis to be studied.

QUALITY IN QUALITATIVE RESEARCH

8.4 Qualitative research methods are often critiqued as having unclear minimal requirements for method and quality. Qualitative research involves interpretation on the part of the researcher, and as Henwood and Pidgeon (1992: 105) observe, "there are no methodological criteria capable of guaranteeing the *absolute* accuracy of qualitative research". An often-made critique of qualitative research is that it is unscientific and lacks rigour. However, there is a growing body of literature, with guidelines for good practice, which can be used to evaluate qualitative research and help ensure reliability and validity. These criteria for judging the quality of qualitative research include:

1 *Findings should relate closely to the data.* Qualitative data analysis should involve more than just mere description of what participants have said, with good qualitative research requiring interpretation of the data that provides insight into participants' experiences (Chamberlain, 2000). However, this does not mean that 'anything goes', as interpretation should fit the data well. Details should be given for why data have been analysed and interpreted in a certain way, with evidence provided in the form of verbatim quotes that illustrate such an interpretation. Findings should be presented in a coherent manner, with a clear argument presented (Parker, 2004).

2 *Proper use of theory.* Qualitative research data should be properly theorized, whether it be grounded in existing theory, or whether the meaning of the findings should be adequately theorized (Chamberlain, 2000). This includes grounding the work in existing research (Parker, 2004).

3 *Reflexivity.* As discussed earlier, qualitative research often (but not always) draws on social constructionist understanding of knowledge, which argues against the notion of science being neutral and objective. Qualitative research recognizes that research is subjective, with the researcher having a subjective involvement. A lot of the methods used in analysing qualitative data involve some form of interpretation of the data, involving researcher subjectivity. There are methods of analysing qualitative data which are more aligned to a positivist approach. For example, content analysis may involve the counting of the number of instances in which a certain word is used or a phenomenon is referred to during an interview. Good qualitative research thus should make explicit the role of the researcher in the research process. Thus the researcher is required to be reflexive of his or her role, the attitudes and values that they bring into the research process and the analytic perspective taken, and should acknowledge any possible alternative views. Elliott and colleagues (1999: 221) refer to this as "owning one's perspective".

4 *Detailed documentation.* In order to aid reflexivity in qualitative research, good documentation of the research process should be conducted, detailing what has been done, how and why (Henwood & Pidgeon, 1992). Researchers can document their actions and reflections in a research diary. Such documents can thus be available to peers for scrutiny of the manner in which the research was conducted.

5 *Triangulation.* This involves investigating the phenomenon from different perspectives, by comparing perspectives that may differ from

emerging findings or negative case analysis (Henwood & Pidgeon, 1992). Triangulation of results can also be achieved through comparison of data collected by other methods, such as quantitative data (Elliott, Fischer, & Rennie, 1999). Validity of findings is enhanced if similar themes emerge from different perspectives on the same issue.

6 *Transferability*. Because qualitative research is typically concerned with the specificity of a phenomenon, findings cannot be said to be generalizable. However, qualitative researchers may be able to talk about the transferability of findings from the context under study to similar contexts (Henwood & Pidgeon, 1992). This also involves providing details of the sample of participants used and their context, so that the reader may assess the applicability and relevance of the findings for other, similar contexts (Elliott et al., 1999). Furthermore, any theoretical insights gained or theoretical developments made may be transferable, adding to the knowledge base of a particular subject area.

Other methods for ensuring quality in qualitative research may include respondent validation, where emerging findings of the analysis are communicated to the research participants who may then respond as to the accuracy of the analysis (Henwood & Pidgeon, 1992). This is complicated when the analysis may involve theoretical interpretation of participants' actions that may be outside their conscious awareness. Elliott and colleagues (1999) includes respondent validation as one of several "credibility checks" (p. 222), which may also include verification of accuracy of analysis by peers, or triangulation (mentioned above).

8.4.1 LANGUAGE AND RESEARCH – USING TRANSLATION AND INTERPRETATION

We are living in an increasingly globalized society, and with increased migration most societies in the world are now multicultural and multilingual. The issue of language becomes important when considering research that involves cross-cultures. This can be within one's own country – the UK, for example, is a multicultural society where it may be the case that one interacts with someone who speaks another language and may have limited use of English. Language becomes a particular issue when conducting research in other countries where other languages are spoken. It is often the case that research (and clinical work) needs to involve the use of translation and interpretation. This presents various challenges and difficulties, particularly if we view language from a social constructionist perspective. We have discussed the use of translation and interpretation in research in a previous publication (Swartz & Rohleder, 2008). I will draw from this and expand on it here.

A traditional, empiricist approach to language would view language as labels that are used to represent phenomena that exist in reality (both internal and external reality). This approach views language as a neutral process of transmitting ideas from one person to another. Thus different languages will have different words that are used to label objects and realities that exist universally –the small furry animal with whiskers that we know as '*cat*' will be labelled '*gato*' in Spanish or '*kat*' in Dutch (I use these three languages because I have some familiarity with them!). A translator or interpreter would then have to find and use the label (word) that represents the phenomenon being spoken about. If we think about this in relation to issues of health, the experience which we refer to as '*headache*' in English is labelled '*dolor de cabeza*' in Spanish and '*hoofdpijn*' in Dutch.

However, a social constructionist approach (which is a philosophical foundation for a critical approach in psychology and for many qualitative research methods), understands language as the means through which social reality and meaning is created, including the experience of self (Bruner, 1991; Burr, 1995). Thus a social constructionist approach does not view language as merely a neutral process of communication, but rather as a complex process whereby nuanced meaning and individual and social experience is constructed. If we view language from such a perspective, translation and interpretation become a complex activity. An example here would be the use of terms such as '*feeling down*' or '*feeling blue*' to convey the experience of feelings of sadness. These words may not have the same equivalences in some other languages, leading to such an experience being translated or interpreted as '*depressed*' (in other languages). In clinical terms, '*depressed*' and '*feeling blue*' are not the same thing! From a social constructionist perspective, language not only is used to convey neutral information, but also personal experience and values, and beliefs about the social world. Experience is thus conveyed in the act of communication between two (or more) people as the speaker and listener make sense of what is being communicated. Thus as Swartz (1998) suggests, we need to consider "the extent to which the act of translation implies the construction of a particular reality" (Swartz, 1998: 29).

Translation

Research in clinical and health psychology (as with psychological research generally), very often make use of questionnaires or written texts as data for analysis. When conducting research in other cultures and languages, it may be necessary to then translate these into different languages. Not only may questionnaires need to be translated into other languages (which has implications for construct validity), but the responses to questionnaires and the written texts need to be translated in order to be analysed. The act of translation may be difficult when trying to accurately translate the meaning of questions or what is being communicated in written responses or written texts, particularly when there are more than one possible translation for a particular word. Swartz (1998) gives the example from South Africa of the Xhosa word *ukukhathazekile* which means to 'feel bad inside', and may mean either 'depressed' or 'anxious' depending on the context in which it is used.

Brislin (1986) suggests some methods that help to ensure best possible results in translations. These include using bilingual translation and back-translation to allow for comparisons of the accuracy of translated texts. In compiling questionnaires, for example, a person who is bilingual can be asked to complete both the original and translated versions of the questionnaire, and responses are then compared to ensure the accuracy of the questions (bilingual translation). In back-translation, one translator translates a written text (or interview transcript) from the original language to the target language (for example, from Spanish to English). This translated text is then translated back to the original language by a second translator (in this case, the English translation back to Spanish). The back-translation can then be compared to the original text for accuracy and equivalence. This process can be enhanced by the use of translation committees, where aspects of the translated texts can be discussed.

Interpretation

When conducting qualitative research in clinical and health psychology, interviews may need to be conducted with participants who speak a different language from that of the interviewer. Such interviews require the use of an interpreter. This presents a number of challenges and difficulties in terms of ethics as well as validity of results.

First, the use of an interpreter introduces a third person into the interview situation and so needs to be discussed with participants when gaining informed consent for their participation. Furthermore, the participation of an interpreter has implications for the confidentiality of the interviews. The addition of an interpreter may influence what the interviewee feels comfortable sharing in the interview as he or she considers the presence of two people listening to what they have to say. This is not only an issue for research practice, but also obviously for clinical practice, where practitioners may require the use of an interpreter to communicate with a patient. It may be the case that the interpreters used are trained, but often in hospital settings in lower income countries staff members are commonly called on to interpret interviews that are conducted when they may not be specifically trained as interpreters. Lack of training and the unclear role of staff stepping in as *ad hoc* interpreters may contribute in errors and failures in interpreted interviews (Drennan, 1996, 1999; Elderkin-Thompson, Silver, & Waitzkin, 2001). Confidentiality and interpretation are also issues in the use of sign language interpretation when interviewing individuals who are deaf or hard of hearing. For example, in a study exploring organizational responses to the HIV epidemic as it affects persons with disabilities in South Africa (Rohleder, Swartz, Schneider, Groce, & Eide, 2010), the use of sign language interpretation was highlighted as a barrier to HIV testing as it created problems around confidentiality. Often family members were called on to provide the sign language interpretation in consultations between deaf persons and health care professionals.

Secondly, the use of interpreters needs to be considered with regards to the accuracy of what is being translated, and the implications this has for the validity and reliability of results. Unlike the translation of a written text, interpretation requires translation in the moment. This can result in many errors being made. Vasquez and Javier (1991) outline some common errors that are made by interpreters. These are:

1 *Omission.* This happens when an interpreter leaves out sections of what a person (interviewer and/or interviewee) says in an interview. This is most common when a large amount is being said.
2 *Condensation.* This is when an interpreter gives a summary of what is being said, which is further influenced by what the interpreter regards as being most important in a message. This may differ from the views of the interviewer or interviewee and what they may regard as most important in a message.
3 *Substitution.* This happens when an interpreter replaces something that is said with something that was not said, as a result of assumptions that may arise within the interaction.
4 *Addition.* As opposed to omission, this is where an interviewer adds to what has been said. This may be as a result of the interpreter wishing to make the message clearer or simply being polite.
5 *Role exchange.* This is when the interpreter starts to take over the role of interviewer and may start to ask their own questions or may substitute the interviewer's questions with their own.

It is clear, then, the implication this has for the accuracy of the data and the validity thereof in relation to the research question. Interpreted interviews are difficult and need to be planned for and conducted carefully. Swartz (1998) and Swartz and Rohleder (2008) provide some suggestions for improving the success of interpreted interviews:

1 *Planning.* It is important to prepare in advance how the interpretation will work. The interviewer and interpreter need to discuss and understand clearly what the aims of the interview are and what each other's role is during the interview. There must be a plan for how the interview is to be structured and managed, and how any problems that may arise will be dealt with. The interviewer/researcher will have a clear idea of how the interview and interpretation should happen. However, it is also useful to engage with the interpreter to explore any ideas or suggestions that they may have.
2 *Starting the interview.* Prior to starting the interview, it is important to discuss with the person being interviewed the use of interpretation during the interview. The use of interpreters has obvious implications for confidentiality, and these have to be adequately considered by the person being interviewed in giving their consent. The person being

interviewed needs to be fully informed as to the aim and purpose of the interview, how the interview will be structured, and what the roles are of the people taking part in the interview – interviewer, interviewee(s) and interpreter. In order to facilitate improved accuracy of interpretation, it is a good idea to suggest to the person being interviewed that they deliver their responses in a manner that allows for periodic interpretation of what is said, rather than long, continuous dialogue. Prior to proceeding, interviewees should be invited to ask questions and raise any concerns.

3 *Conducting the interview.* The interview should be conducted in a manner that is considerate of the interviewee's feelings and comfort. It is useful to pause at intervals to enquire how the interviewee feels the process is working. In addition, interpreted interviews generally take longer that non-interpreted interviews, so they can be tiring and frustrating as different people take their turns to talk. Interviewees may feel that a break would be useful.

4 *Discussions after the interview.* As with any other interview, it is important to debrief with the person being interviewed about how the interview was experienced. Any concerns that interviewees may have can be raised and discussed. With interpreted interviews it is also important for the interviewer and interpreter to spend some time reflecting on the interview and discussing what happened. Any unclear points or questions which arose during the interview can be discussed and clarified. The impressions of the behaviour of the person being interviewed can also be shared and discussed. This may provide useful additional data or points of clarity. Research interviews in clinical and health psychology may focus on sensitive issues as a topic (e.g. health, illness, risk behaviour, the body, mental health), which may elicit uncomfortable feelings in the interpreter. This should be talked about and addressed afterwards. I recall once using an interpreter in an interview with an HIV-positive South African woman who spoke one of the traditional African languages, Xhosa. The interpreter was a Xhosa woman who spoke fluent English. The focus of the study (and thus the interview) was on the experiences of HIV-related stigma. The interpreter was herself HIV-positive, and worked as an HIV activist, so was open about her diagnosis. During this interview, the interviewee recalled and gave an account of past experiences of discrimination, experiences which were traumatic and upsetting for the interviewee. Once the interview was over, when reflecting on the interview with the interpreter, the interpreter talked about how she had felt saddened about what the interviewee had said as it resonated with some of her own past experiences. It is an ethical requirement to consider any potential harm to participants resulting from their involvement in research. This should extend to interpreters too.

The discussion here has focused on interpretation in the context of research, but the same issues are involved in interpretation in health care interactions. Many such interactions involve professionals and patients from different cultural groups, where language barriers may be an issue.

SUMMARY

8.5 This chapter has primarily explored some often-used qualitative methods in research, methods that are popular in critical approaches in health and clinical psychology. The chapter has described only six such approaches: participatory action research; grounded theory; conversation analysis; discourse analysis; narrative analysis; and interpretative phenomenological analysis. These are summarized in Table 8.1. There are other qualitative methods which have not been covered, but these provide an introduction to some of the more popular methods used in health psychology and clinical psychology. Qualitative research methods are popular in that they are useful for exploring complex phenomena, capturing subjective, lived experiences, and for developing theoretical insights. They are useful for aiding some of the aims of critical approaches in psychology (see Chapter 2). For example, discourse analysis may be useful in the analysis of power in terms of how certain discourses are privileged over others. Participatory action research is often concerned with issues of social justice, and has been a useful method for empowering communities in bringing about social change. IPA has been useful in exploring service users' lived experiences, which can be considered in relation to the structures of the health care system, and are useful for identifying changes that can be made in service delivery.

Qualitative and quantitative research methods are often placed in opposition to one another. They are sometimes bitter rivals, and mirror the rivalry between science and social science. This chapter has focused on qualitative research, as this is a method most favoured by critical psychologists. However, this is not to say that quantitative methods, with their focus on statistics, are not important, useful and helpful, or that they cannot be critical. Much of the work cited in this book has been quantitative, particularly the epidemiological studies. Increasingly, the usefulness of adopting mixed methods in multi-disciplinary research projects has been recognized. Qualitative research has also been critiqued as lacking rigour, as being unscientific, and just anecdotal. This chapter has outlined some of the emerging criteria for judging quality in qualitative research. This has included guidelines for reliability and validity in translation. This book has included issues of difference – e.g. culture, ethnicity and religion. Together with this diversity is diversity in language. If we wish to investigate differences in experience across cultures or in a multicultural society, effective communication across language barriers is increasingly important. Some further readings are listed below, for readers who want to learn more about different qualitative research methods.

FURTHER READINGS

Marks, D.F., & Yardley, L. (Eds.) (2004). *Research methods for clinical and health psychology*. London: Sage. This book provides detailed explanations of both quantitative and qualitative research methods used in clinical and health psychology.

Smith, J.A. (Ed.) (2008). *Qualitative psychology: A practical guide to research methods* (2nd edition). London: Sage. This is an edited text that provides chapters on different qualitative methods which include details of how to do the practical aspects of the various methods (data collecting, data analysis and writing up).

Willig, C. (2008). *Introducing qualitative research in psychology* (2nd edition). Maidenhead: Open University Press. This book provides an accessible general introduction to qualitative research methods in psychology.

Willig, C., & Stainton-Rogers, W. (Eds.) (2008). *The Sage handbook of qualitative research in psychology*. London: Sage. This is a comprehensive edited text on qualitative research in psychology, and includes separate chapters on qualitative research in various sub-disciplines of psychology, including in health psychology and clinical psychology.

REFERENCES

Abberley, P. (1987). The concept of oppression and the development of a social theory of disability. *Disability, Handicap & Society, 2*(1), 5–19.

Abberley, P. (1998). The spectre at the feast: Disabled people and social theory. In T. Shakespeare (Ed.), *The disability reader: Social science perspectives* (pp. 79–93). New York: Continuum.

Abraham, C., Sheeran, P., Spears, R., & Adams, D. (1992). Health beliefs and promotion of HIV-preventive intentions among teenagers: A Scottish perspective. *Health Psychology, 11*(6), 363–370.

Adler, N.E., & Matthews, K. (1994). Health psychology: Why do some people get sick and some stay well? *Annual Review of Psychology, 45*, 229–259.

Adler, N.E., & Snibbe, A.C. (2003). The role of psychosocial processes in explaining the gradient between socioeconomic status and health. *Current Directions in Psychological Science, 12*(4), 119–123.

Agliata, D., & Tantleff-Dunn, S. (2004). The impact of media exposure on males' body image. *Journal of Social and Clinical Psychology, 23*(1), 7–22.

Ahern, A.L., Bennett, K.M., Kelly, M., & Hetherington, M.M. (2011). A qualitative exploration of young women's attitudes towards the thin ideal. *Journal of Health Psychology, 16*(1), 70–79.

Ahlström, S.K., & Österberg, E.L. (2004/2005). International perspectives on adolescent and young adult drinking. *Alcohol Research and Health, 28*, 258–268.

Aikins, A.D., & Marks, D.F. (2007). Health, disease and healthcare in Africa. *Journal of Health Psychology, 12*(3), 387–402.

Ajzen, I. (1991). The theory of planned behaviour. *Organizational Behavior and Human Decision Processes, 50*, 179–211.

Ajzen I., & Fishbein, M. (1980). *Understanding attitudes and predicting social behaviour.* Englewood Cliffs, NJ: Prentice-Hall.

Albarracín, D., Johnson, B.T., Fishbein, M., & Muellerleile, P.A. (2001). Theories of reasoned action and planned behavior as models of condom use: A meta-analysis. *Psychological Bulletin, 127*(1), 142–161.

Ali, N.S. (2002). Prediction of coronary heart disease preventive behaviors in women: A test of the health belief model. *Women & Health, 35*(1), 83–96.

Allamani, A., Voller, F., Kubicka, L., & Bloomfield, K. (2000). Drinking cultures and the position of women in nine European countries. *Substance Abuse, 21*(4), 231–247.

American Psychiatric Association (APA) (2000). *DSM-IV-TR: Diagnostic and statistical manual of mental disorders.* Washington, DC: American Psychiatric Press Inc.

Anderson, P., & Kitchin, R. (2000). Disability, space and sexuality: Access to family planning services. *Social Science & Medicine, 51*(8), 1163–1173.

Annandale, E., & Hunt, K. (2000). Gender inequalities in health: Research at the crossroads. In E. Allandale & K. Hunt (Eds.), *Gender inequalities in health* (pp. 1–35). Buckingham: Open University Press.

Appleby, L. (2004). *The national service framework for mental health – five years on.* London: Department of Health. Retrieved December 12, 2010, from www.dh.gov.uk/en/Publicationsandstatistics/Publications/PublicationsPolicyAndGuidance/DH_4099120

Archer, M., Bhaskar, R., Collier, A., Lawson, T., & Norrie, A. (Eds.) (1998). *Critical realism: Essential readings.* London: Routledge.

Armitage, C.J. (2005). Can the theory of planned behavior predict the maintenance of physical activity? *Health Psychology, 24*(3), 235–245.

Armitage, C.J., & Conner, M. (2001). Efficacy of the theory of planned behaviour: A meta-analytic review. *British Journal of Social Psychology, 40*, 471–499.

Armstrong, D. (1987). Theoretical tensions in bio-psychosocial medicine. *Social Science and Medicine, 25*, 469–485.

Arney, W.R., & Bergen, B.J. (1983). The anomaly, the chronic patient and the play of medical power. *Sociology of Health and Illness, 5*(1), 1–24.

Baker, C., Lund, P., Nyathi, R., & Taylor, J. (2010). The myths surrounding people with albinism in South Africa and Zimbabwe. *Journal of African Cultural Studies, 22*(2), 169–181.

Bancroft, A. (2001). Globalisation and HIV/AIDS: Inequality and the boundaries of a symbolic epidemic. *Health, Risk & Society, 3*(1), 89–98.

Bancroft, J. (2002). The medicalization of female sexual dysfunction: The need for caution. *Archives of Sexual Behavior, 31*(5), 451–455.

Banister, P., Burman, E., Parker, I., Taylor, M., & Tindall, C. (1994). *Qualitative methods in psychology: A research guide*. Buckingham: Open University Press.

Barker, M., Hagger-Johnson, G., Hegarty, P., Hutchison, C., & Riggs, D.W. (2007). Responses from the Lesbian & Gay Psychology Section to Crossley's 'Making sense of "barebacking"'. *British Journal of Social Psychology, 46*(3), pp. 667–677.

Barnes, C., & Oliver, M. (1993). *Disability: A sociological phenomenon ignored by sociologists*. Retrieved March 21, 2006, from http://leeds. ac.uk/disability-studies/archiveuk/titles.html

Bartlett, A., King, M., & Phillips, P. (2001). Straight talking – an investigation of the attitudes and practice of psychoanalysts and psychotherapists in relation to gays and lesbians. *British Journal of Psychiatry, 179*, 545–549.

Bartlett, A., Smith, G., & King, M. (2009). The response of mental health professionals to clients seeking help to change or redirect same-sex sexual orientation. *BMC Psychiatry, 9*(11), doi: 10.1186/1471-244X-9-11.

Barton, L. (1998). Sociology, disability studies and education: Some observations. In T. Shakespeare (Ed.), *The disability reader: Social science perspectives* (pp. 53–64). New York: Continuum.

Bat-Chava, Y., Martin, D., & Kosciw, J.G. (2005). Barriers to HIV/AIDS knowledge and prevention among deaf and hard of hearing people. *AIDS Care, 17*(5), 623–634.

Bayer, R. (1987). *Homosexuality and American psychiatry: The politics of diagnosis*. Princeton, NJ: Princeton University Press.

Beadle-Brown, J., Mansell, J., Cambridge, P., Milne, A., & Whelton, B. (2010). Adult protection of people with intellectual disabilities: Incidence, nature and responses. *Journal of Applied Research in Intellectual Disabilities, 23*(6), 573–584.

Beck, A.T. (1989). *Cognitive therapy and the emotional disorders*. London: Penguin Books.

Becker, A.E., Burwell, R.A., Gilman, S.E., Herzog, D.B., & Hamburg, P. (2002). Eating behaviors and attitudes following prolonged exposure to television among ethnic Fijian adolescent girls. *British Journal of Psychiatry, 180*(6), 509–514.

Becker, H., Stuifbergen, A., & Tinkle, M. (1997). Reproductive health care experiences of women with physical disabilities: A qualitative study. *Archive of Physical Medicine and Rehabilitation, 78*(Suppl. 5), S26–S33.

Becker, H.M., & Maiman, L.A. (1975). Sociobehavioral determinants of compliance with health and medical care recommendations. *Medical Care, 13*(1), 10–24.

Beehlar, G.P. (2001). Confronting the culture of medicine: Gay men's experiences with primary care physicians. *Journal of the Gay and Lesbian Medical Association, 5*(4), 135–141.

Beharrell, P. (1993). AIDS and the British press. In J. Eldridge (Ed.) *Getting the message: News, truth and power*. London: Routledge.

Belloc, N.B., & Breslow, L. (1972). Relationship of physical health status and health practices. *Preventive Medicine, 1*, 409–421.

Bennett, J. (2003). *Review of school feeding projects*. London: Department for International Development.

Bentall, R.P. (2003). *Madness explained: Psychosis and human nature*. London: Penguin.

Bentler, P.M., & Speckart, G. (1979). Models of attitude–behavior relations. *Psychological Review, 86*(5), 452–464.

Benzeval, M., & Judge, K. (2001). Income and health: The time dimension. *Social Science & Medicine, 52*(9), 1371–1390.

Betancourt, J. (2004). Cultural competence – marginal or mainstream movement? *New England Journal of Medicine, 351*, 953–954.

Bhugra, D., & Bhui, K. (2003). Eating disorders in teenagers in east London: A survey. *European Eating Disorders Review, 11*(1), 46–57.

Bhugra, D., & King, M.B. (1989). Controlled comparison of attitudes of psychiatrists, general practitioners, homosexual doctors and homosexual men to male homosexuality. *Journal of the Royal Society of Medicine, 82*, 603–605.

Bhui, K. (Ed.) (2002). *Racism and mental health: Prejudice and suffering*. London: Jessica Kingsley Publishers.

Blankenship, K.M., Friedman, S.R., Dworkin, S., & Mantel, J.E. (2006). Structural interventions: Challenges and opportunities for research. *Journal of Urban Health: Bulletin of the New York Academy of Medicine, 83*, 59–72.

Blaxter, M. (1997). Whose fault is it? People's own conceptions of the reasons for health inequalities. *Social Science & Medicine, 44*(6), 747–756.

Blum, R.W., Kelly, A., & Ireland, M. (2001). Health-risk behaviors and protective factors among adolescents with mobility impairments and learning and emotional disabilities. *Journal of Adolescent Health, 28*(6), 481–490.

Boesten, J., & Poku, N.K. (Eds.) (2009). *Gender and HIV/AIDS: Critical perspectives from the developing world*. Farnham: Ashgate.

Bond, M.H. (1991). Chinese values and health: A cultural-level examination. *Psychology & Health, 5*, 137–152.

Bonita, R., Beaglehole, R., & Kjellström, T. (2006). *Basic epidemiology* (2nd edition). Geneva: World Health Organization.

Braathen, S.H., & Ingstad, B. (2006). Albinism in Malawi: Knowledge and beliefs from an African setting. *Disability & Society, 21*(6), 599–611.

Brach, C., & Fraser, I. (2000). Can cultural competency reduce racial and ethnic health disparities? A review and conceptual model. *Medical Care Research & Review, 57*, 181–217.

Bramley, N., & Eatough, V. (2005). The experience of living with Parkinson's disease: An interpretative phenomenological analysis case study. *Psychology and Health, 20*(2), 223–235.

Bratlinger, E. (1992). Sexuality education in the secondary special education curriculum: Teachers' perceptions and concerns. *Teacher Education and Special Education, 15*(1), 32–40.

Braun, V., & Clarke, V. (2006). Using thematic analysis in psychology. *Qualitative Research in Psychology, 3*, 77–101.

Breslow, L., & Enstrom, J.E. (1980). Persistence of health habits and their relationship to mortality. *Preventive Medicine, 9*, 469–483.

Bresnahan, M., Begg, M.D., Brown, A., Schaefer, C., Sohler, N., Insel, B., Vella, L., & Susser, E. (2007). Race and risk of schizophrenia in a US birth cohort: Another example of health disparity? *International Journal of Epidemiology, 36*, 751–758.

Brislin, R.W. (1986). The wording and translation of research instruments. In W.J. Lonner & J.W. Berry (Eds.), *Field-methods in cross-cultural research* (pp. 137–164). Berkeley, CA: Sage.

British HIV Association (2008). *UK national guidelines for HIV testing 2008*. London: British HIV Association.

Bronfenbrenner, U. (1972). *Influences on human development*. Fort Worth, TX: Dryden Press.

Brofenbrenner, U. (1977). Toward an experimental ecology of human development. *American Psychologist, 32*(7), 513–531.

Brown, L.S. (1992). A feminist critique of the personality disorders. In L.S. Brown & M. Ballou (Eds.), *Personality and psychopathology: Feminist reappraisals* (pp. 206–228). New York: The Guilford Press.

Bruner, J. (1991). The narrative construction of reality. *Critical Inquiry, 18*, 1–21.

Bundy, D. (2005). School health and nutrition: Policy and programs. *Food and Nutrition Bulletin, 26*(Suppl. 2), S186–S192.

Burns, F., Fakoya, A.O., Copas, A.J., & French, P.D. (2001). Africans in London continue to present with advanced HIV disease in the era of highly active antiretroviral therapy. *AIDS, 15*(18), 2453–2455.

Burr, V. (1995). *An introduction to social constructionism*. London: Routledge.

Butler, J. (2006). *Gender trouble*. New York: Routledge.

Caldwell, J.C., & Caldwell, P. (1987). The cultural context of high fertility in sub-Saharan Africa. *Population and Development Review, 13*(3), 409–437.

Caldwell, J.C., Caldwell, P., & Quiggin, P. (1989). The social context of AIDS in sub-Saharan Africa. *Population and Development Review, 15*(2), 185–234.

Caldwell, J.C., Orubuloye, I.O., & Caldwell, P. (1992). Underreaction to AIDS in sub-Saharan Africa. *Social Science and Medicine, 34*, 1169–1182.

Cameron, D., & Kulick, D. (1993). *Language and sexuality*. Cambridge: Cambridge University Press.

Cameron, E., & Bernardes, J. (1998). Gender and disadvantage in health: Men's health for a change. *Sociology of Health & Illness, 20*(5), 673–693.

Campbell, C. (2001). Social capital and health: Contextualising health promotion within local community networks. In S. Baron, J. Field, & T. Schuller (Eds.), *Social capital: Critical perspectives* (pp. 182–196). Oxford: Oxford University Press.

Campbell, C. (2003). *'Letting them die': Why HIV/ AIDS intervention programs fail*. Bloomington, IN: Indiana University Press.

Campbell, C. (2004). Health psychology and community action. In M. Murray (Ed.), *Critical health psychology* (pp. 203–221). Basingstoke: Palgrave Macmillan.

Campbell, C., & Gibbs, A. (2009). Stigma, gender and HIV: Case studies of inter-sectionality. In J. Boesten & N.K. Poku (Eds.), *Gender and HIV/ AIDS: Critical perspectives from the developing world* (pp. 29–46). Farnham: Ashgate.

Campbell, C., & Murray, M. (2004). Community health psychology: Promoting analysis and action for social change. *Journal of Health Psychology, 9*(2), 187–195.

Campbell, C., Nair, Y., Maimane, S., & Gibbs, A. (2009). Strengthening community responses to AIDS: Possibilities and challenges. In P. Rohleder, L. Swartz, S. Kalichman, & L. Simbayi (Eds.), *HIV/AIDS in South Africa 25 years on: Psychosocial perspectives* (pp. 221–235). New York: Springer.

Campbell, C., Wood, R., & Kelly, M. (1999). *Social capital and health*. London: Health Education Authority.

Cant, B. (2002). An exploration of the views of gay and bisexual men in one London borough of both their primary care needs and the practice of primary care practitioners. *Primary Health Care Research and Development, 3*, 124–130.

Carr, A., & O'Reilly, G. (2007). Diagnosis, classification and epidemiology. In A. Carr, G. O'Reilly, P.N. Walsh, & J. McEvoy (Eds.), *The handbook of intellectual disability and clinical psychology practice* (pp. 3–49). London: Routledge.

Carr, S.V., Scoular, A., Elliott, L., Ilett, R., & Meager, M. (1999). A community-based lesbian sexual health service: Clinically justified or politically correct? *British Journal of Family Planning, 25*(3), 93–95.

Carroll, D., & Smith, G.D. (1997). Health and socio-economic position: A commentary. *Journal of Health Psychology, 2*(3), 275–282.

Cartwright, S.A. (1981 [1851]). Report on the diseases and physical peculiarities of the Negro race. *New Orleans Medical and Surgical Journal*, May, 691–715 (reprinted in A.C. Caplan, H.T. Englehart, & J.J. McCartney (Eds.), *Concepts of health and disease*. Reading, MA: Addison-Wesley).

Chamberlain, K. (1997). Socio-economic health differentials: From structure to experience. *Journal of Health Psychology, 2*(3), 399–411.

Chamberlain, K. (2000). Methodolatry and qualitative health research. *Journal of Health Psychology, 5*(3), 285–296.

Chamberlain, K., & Murray, M. (2008). Health psychology. In C. Willig & W. Stainton-Rogers (Eds.), *Handbook of qualitative research methods in psychology* (pp. 390–406). London: Sage.

Chamberlain, K., & Murray, M. (2009). Critical health psychology. In D. Fox, I. Prilleltensky, & S. Austin (Eds.), *Critical psychology: An introduction* (2nd edition) (pp. 144–158). London: Sage.

Chang, D.F., Myers, H.F., Yeung, A., Zhang, Y., Zhao, J., & Yu, S. (2005). Shenjing Shuairuo and the DSM-IV: Diagnosis, distress, and disability in a Chinese primary care setting. *Transcultural Psychiatry, 42*(2), 204–218.

Chang, J. (2009). Chronic pain: Cultural sensitivity to pain. In S. Eshun & R.A.R. Gurung (Eds.), *Culture and mental health: Sociocultural influences, theory and practice* (pp. 71–89).Chichester: Wiley-Blackwell.

Charmaz, K. (1990). 'Discovering' chronic illness: Using grounded theory. *Social Science & Medicine, 30*(11), 1161–1172.

Charmaz, K., & Henwood, K. (2008). Grounded theory. In C. Willig & W. Stainton-Rogers (Eds.), *Handbook of qualitative research methods in psychology* (pp. 240–259). London: Sage.

Cheng, M.M., & Udry, J.R. (2002). Sexual behaviors of physically disabled adolescents in the United States. *Journal of Adolescent Health, 31*(1), 48–58.

Cheshire, K., & Pilgrim, D. (2004). *A short introduction to clinical psychology*. London: Sage.

Christian, L., Stinson, J., & Dotson, L.A. (2001). Staff values regarding the sexual expression of women with developmental disabilities. *Sexuality and Disability, 19*(4), 283–291.

Church, K. (1997). *Using the economy to develop the community: Psychiatric survivors in Ontario*. Ottawa: Caledon Institute of Social Policy. Retrieved March 27, 2011, from: www.caledon-inst.org/Publications/PDF/240ENG.pdf

Clarke, V., & Braun, V. (2009). Gender. In D. Fox, I. Prilleltensky, & S. Austin (Eds.), *Critical psychology: An introduction* (2nd edition) (pp. 232–249). London: Sage.

Coburn, D. (2000). Income inequality, social cohesion and the health status of populations: The role of neo-liberalism. *Social Science & Medicine, 51*, 135–146.

Coburn, D. (2004). Beyond the income inequality hypothesis: Class, neo-liberalism, and health inequalities. *Social Science & Medicine, 58*, 41–56.

Cochran, S.D., Sullivan, J.G., & Mays, V.M. (2003). Prevalence of mental disorders, psychological distress, and mental health services use among lesbian, gay, and bisexual adults in the United Sates. *Journal of Consulting and Clinical Psychology, 71*(1), 53–61.

Cockerham, W.C. (2011). *The sociology of mental disorders* (8th edition). Boston, MA: Pearson Education.

Cohen, D.A., Scribner, R.A., & Farley, T.A. (2000). A structural model of health behaviour: A pragmatic approach to explain and influence health behaviours at the population level. *Preventive Medicine, 30*, 146–154.

Collier, J. (1945). United States Indian Administration as a laboratory of ethnic relations. *Social Research, 12*, 275–286.

Collins, P.Y., Geller, P.A., Miller, S., Toro, P., & Susser, E.S. (2001). Ourselves, our bodies, our realities: An HIV prevention intervention for women with severe mental illness. *Journal of Urban Health, 78*(1), 162–175.

Colombo, M., & Senatore, A. (2005). The discursive construction of community identity. *Journal of Community and Applied Social Psychology, 15*, 48–62.

Connell, R. (2009). *Gender* (2nd edition). Cambridge: Polity Press.

Conner, M., & Armitage, C.J. (1998). Extending the theory of planned behavior: A review and avenues for further research. *Journal of Applied Social Psychology, 28*(15), 1429–1464.

Conner, M., Johnson, C., & Grogan, S. (2004). Gender, sexuality, body image and eating behaviours. *Journal of Health Psychology, 9*(4), 505–515.

Conner, M., Norman, P., & Bell, R. (2002). The theory of planned behavior and healthy eating. *Health Psychology, 21*(2), 194–201.

Connidis, I. (1983). Integrating qualitative and quantitative methods in survey research on ageing: An assessment. *Qualitative Sociology, 6*(4), 334–352.

Cooke, D., Newman, S., Sacker, A., DeVellis, B., Bebbington, P., & Meltzer, H. (2007). The impact of physical illnesses on non-psychotic psychiatric morbidity: Data from the household survey of psychiatric morbidity in Great Britain. *British Journal of Health Psychology, 12*(3), 463–471.

Cornish, F. (2004). Making 'context' concrete: A dialogical approach to the society-health relation. *Journal of Health Psychology, 9*(2), 281–294.

Cornish, F., & Ghosh, R. (2007). The necessary contradictions of 'community-led' health promotion: A case study of HIV prevention in an Indian red light district. *Social Science & Medicine, 64*, 496–507.

Cosgrove, L. (2000). Crying out loud: Understanding women's emotional distress as both lived experience and social construction. *Feminism & Psychology, 10*(2), 247–267.

Costello, E.J., Compton, S.N., Keeler, G., & Angold, A. (2003). Relationships between poverty and psychopathology: A natural experiment. *Journal of the American Medical Association, 290*, 2023–2029.

Cougnard, A., Grolleau, S., Lamarque, F., Beitz, C., Brugère, S., & Verdoux, H. (2006). Psychotic disorders among homeless subjects attending a psychiatric emergency service. *Social Psychiatry and Psychiatric Epidemiology, 41*(11), 904–910.

Courtenay, W.H. (2000). Constructions of masculinity and their influence on men's well-being: A theory of gender and health. *Social Science & Medicine, 50*, 1385–1401.

Craft, A. (1987). Mental handicap and sexuality: Issues for individuals with a mental handicap, their parents and professionals. In A. Craft (Ed.), *Mental handicap and sexuality: Issues and perspectives* (pp.13–33). Tunbridge Wells, Kent: Costello.

Crago, M., Shisslak, C.M., & Estes, L.S. (1996). Eating disturbances among African American minority groups: A review. *International Journal of Eating Disorders, 19*(3), 239–248.

Cramer, R.J., Golom, F.D., LoPresto, C.T., & Kirkley, S.M. (2008). Weighing the evidence: Empirical assessment and ethical implications of conversion therapy. *Ethics & Behavior, 18*(1), 93–114.

Crawford, R. (1994). The boundaries of the self and the unhealthy other. *Social Science & Medicine, 38*(10), 1347–1365.

Crawford, R. (2006). Health as a meaningful practice. *Health: An Interdisciplinary Journal for the Social Study of Health, Illness and Medicine, 10*(4), 401–420.

Crewe, M. (1992). *AIDS in South Africa: The myth and the reality*. Johannesburg: Penguin Books.

Crisp, A.H., Gelder, M.G., Rix, S., Meltzer, H.I., & Rowlands, O.J. (2000). The stigmatisation of people with mental illness. *The British Journal of Psychiatry, 177*, 4–7.

Crossley, M.L. (2004). Making sense of 'barebacking': Gay men's narratives, unsafe sex and the 'resistance habitus'. *British Journal of Social Psychology, 43*, 225–244.

Darker, C.D., & French, D.P. (2009). What sense do people make of a theory of planned behaviour questionnaire?: A think-aloud study. *Journal of Health Psychology, 14*(7), 861–871.

D'Augelli, A.R., & Grossman, A.H. (2001). Disclosure of sexual orientation, victimization, and mental health among lesbian, gay, and bisexual older adults. *Journal of Interpersonal Violence, 16*(10), 1008–1027.

Davies, D., & Bhugra, D. (2004). *Models of psychopathology*. Maidenhead: Open University Press.

Davison, C., & Davey Smith, G. (1995). The baby and the bath water: Examining socio-cultural and free-market critiques of health promotion. In R. Bunton, S. Nettleton, & R. Burrows (Eds.), *The sociology of health promotion: Critical analysis of consumption, lifestyle and risk* (pp. 91–99). London and New York: Routledge.

Day, K., Gough, B., & McFadden, M. (2004). 'Warning! Alcohol can seriously damage your feminine health': A discourse analysis of recent British newspaper coverage of women and drinking. *Feminist Media Studies, 4*, 165–183.

Daykin, N., & Naidoo, J. (1995). Feminist critiques of health promotion. In R. Bunton, S. Nettleton, & R. Burrows (Eds.), *The sociology of health promotion: Critical analysis of consumption, lifestyle and risk* (pp. 59–69). London and New York: Routledge.

Dein, S. (2004). Explanatory models of and attitudes towards cancer in different cultures. *Lancet Oncology, 5*, 119–124.

De Klerk, H.M., & Ampousah, L. (2003). The physically disabled woman's experience of self. *Disability and Rehabilitation, 25*(19), 1132–1139.

Del Amo, J., Petruckevitch, A., Phillips, A.N., Johnson, A.M., Stephenson, J.M., Desmond, N., Hanscheid, T., Low, N., Newell, A., Obasi, A., Paine, K., Pym, A., Theodore, C.M., & De Cock, K.M. (1996). Spectrum of disease in Africans with AIDS in London, *AIDS, 10*(13), 1563–1569.

Demyttenaere, K., Bruffaerts, R., Posada-Villa, J., Gasquet, I., Kovess, V., Lepine, J.P., et al. (2004). Prevalence, severity, and unmet need for treatment of mental disorders in the World Health Organization world mental health surveys. *Journal of the American Medical Association, 291*(21), 2581–2590.

Department for International Development (DFID) (2000). *Disability, poverty and development.* London: DFID.

Department of Health (1999). *National service framework for mental health: modern standards and service models.* London: Department of Health.

Desjarlais, R., Eisenberg, L., Good, B., & Kleinman, A. (1995). *World mental health: Problems and priorities in low-income countries.* New York and Oxford: Oxford University Press.

De Visser, R.O., & Smith, J.A. (2007). Alcohol consumption and masculine identity among young men. *Psychology and Health, 22*(5), 595–614.

DiClemente, R.J., Crittenden, C.P., Rose, E., Sales, J.M., Wingood, G.M., Crosby, R.A., & Salazar, L.F. (2008). Psychosocial predictors of HIV-associated sexual behaviours and the efficacy of prevention interventions in adolescents at-risk for HIV infection: What works and what doesn't work? *Psychosomatic Medicine, 70,* 598–605.

Dilks, S., Tasker, F., & Wren, B. (2010). Managing the impact of psychosis: A grounded theory exploration of recovery processes in psychosis. *British Journal of Clinical Psychology, 49*(1), 87–107.

Dittmar, H., Lloyd, B., Dugan, S., Halliwell, E., Jacobs, N., & Cramer, H. (2000). The 'body beautiful': English adolescents' images of ideal bodies. *Sex Roles, 42*(9–10), 887–915.

Dixon-Woods, M., Annandale, E., Arthur, A., Harvey, J., Hsu, R., Katbamna, S., Olsen, R., Riley, R., & Smith, L. (2005). *Vulnerable groups and access to health care: A critical interpretive review.* Report for the National Co-ordinating Centre for NHS Service Delivery and Organisation R & D (NCCSDO). Retrieved April 18, 2010, from www.sdo.nihr.ac.uk/projdetails.php?ref= 08-1210-025

Dodd, R., & Munck, L. (2002). *Dying for change: Poor people's experience of health and ill-health.* Geneva: World Health Organization and World Bank.

Dodds, C., Hickson, F., Weatherburn, P., Reid, D., Hammond, G., Jessup, K., & Adegbite, G. (2008). *BASS Line 2007 Survey: Assessing the sexual HIV prevention needs of African people in England.* London: Sigma Research.

Doyal, L. (1998). *Gender and health: A technical document.* Geneva: World Health Organization.

Doyal, L. (2000). Gender equity in health: debates and dilemmas. *Social Science & Medicine, 51,* 931–939.

Doyal, L. (2001). Sex, gender, and health: the need for a new approach. *British Medical Journal, 323,* 1061–1063.

Draguns, J.G. (1997). Abnormal behaviour patterns across cultures: Implications for counselling and psychotherapy. *International Journal of Intercultural Relations, 21*(2), 213–248.

Drennan, G. (1996). Counting the cost of language services in psychiatry. *South African Medical Journal, 86,* 343–345.

Drennan, G. (1999). Psychiatry, post-apartheid integration and the neglected role of language in South African institutional contexts. *Transcultural Psychiatry, 36*(1), 5–22.

Drescher, J. (1998). I'm your handyman: A history of reparative therapies. *Journal of Homosexuality, 36,* 19–42.

Drew, P. (2008).Conversation analysis. In J.A. Smith (Ed.), *Qualitative psychology: A practical guide to research methods* (2nd edition) (pp. 133–159). London: Sage.

Drimie, S. (2006). *Junior farmer field and life schools in Swaziland: Lessons learned assessment.* United Nations Joint Programme, Swaziland, Mbabane.

Drummond, M. (2010). Understanding masculinities within the context of men, body image and eating disorders. In B. Gough & S. Robertson (Eds.), *Men, masculinities and health: Critical perspectives* (pp. 198–215). Basingstoke: Palgrave Macmillan.

Dyer, O. (2004). Bush accused of blocking access to cheap AIDS drugs. *British Medical Journal, 328,* 783.

Eagly, A.H., & Chaiken, S. (1993). *The psychology of attitudes.* Fort Worth, TX: Harcourt Brace & Company.

Edwards, S.D. (1997). Dismantling the disability/ handicap distinction. *The Journal of Medicine and Philosophy, 22,* 589–606.

Elderkin-Thompson, V., Silver, R.C., & Waitzkin, H. (2001). When nurses double as interpreters: A study of Spanish-speaking patients in a US primary care setting. *Social Science & Medicine, 52,* 1343–1358.

Eldin, M., & Chisholm, R.F. (1993). Emerging varieties of action research: Introduction to the special issue. *Human Relations, 46*(2), 121–142.

Eliason, M.J., & Schope, R. (2001). Does 'don't ask don't tell' apply to health care? Lesbian, gay, and bisexual people's disclosure to health care providers. *Journal of the Gay and Lesbian Medical Association, 5*(4), 125–134.

Elliott, R., Fischer, C.T., & Rennie, D. (1999). Evolving guidelines for publication of qualitative research studies in psychology and related fields. *British Journal of Clinical Psychology, 38*(3): 215–230.

Elwan, A. (1999). *Poverty and disability: A survey of the literature.* Washington, DC: World Bank, Social Protection Unit. Retrieved February 24, 2006, from http://siteresources.worldbank.org/DISABILITY/Resources/Poverty/Poverty_and_Disability_A_Survey_of_the_Literature.pdf

Emmett, T. (2006). Disability, poverty, gender and race. In B. Watermeyer, L. Swartz, T. Lorenzo, M. Schneider, & M. Priestley (Eds.), *Disability and social change: A South African agenda* (pp. 207–233). Cape Town: HSRC Press.

Emmett, T., & Alant, E. (2006). Women and disability: Exploring the interface of multiple disadvantage. *Development Southern Africa, 23*(4), 445–460.

Emslie, C., & Hunt, K. (2008). The weaker sex? Exploring lay understandings of gender differences in life expectancy: A qualitative study. *Social Science & Medicine, 67,* 808–816.

Emslie, C., Ridge, D., Ziebland, S., & Hunt, K. (2006). Men's accounts of depression: Reconstructing or resisting hegemonic masculinity? *Social Science & Medicine, 62*(9), 2246–2257.

Engel, G.L. (1977). The need for a new medical model: A challenge for biomedicine. *Science, 196,* 129–136.

Engel, G.L. (1980). The clinical application of the biopsychosocial model. *American Journal of Psychiatry, 137,* 535–544.

Erwin, J., Morgan, M., Britten, N., Gray, K., & Peters, B. (2002). Pathways to HIV testing and care by black African and white patients in London. *Sexually Transmitted Infections, 78*(1), 37–39.

Erwin, J., & Peters, B. (1999). Treatment issues for HIV + Africans in London. *Social Science & Medicine, 49,* 1519–1528.

Eshun, S., & Caldwell-Colbert, T. (2009). Culture and mood disorders. In S. Eshun & R.A.R. Gurung (Eds.), *Culture and mental health: Sociocultural influences, theory and practice* (pp. 181–195). Chichester: Wiley-Blackwell.

Eshun, S., & Gurung, R.A.R. (2009). Introduction to culture and psychopathology. In S. Eshun & R.A.R. Gurung (Eds.), *Culture and mental health: Sociocultural influences, theory and practice* (pp. 3–17).Chichester: Wiley-Blackwell.

Evans, J.K., Bingham, J.S., Pratt, K., & Carne, C.A. (1993). Attitudes of medical students to HIV and AIDS. *Genitourinary Medicine, 69,* 377–380.

Fadiman, A. (1997). *The spirit catches you and you fall down: A Hmong child, her American doctors, and the collision of two cultures.* New York: Farrar, Strauss and Giroux.

Faith, M.S., Fontaine, K.R., Baskin, M.L., & Allison, D.B. (2007). Toward the reduction of population obesity: Macrolevel environmental approaches to the problems of food, eating, and obesity. *Psychological Bulletin, 133*(2), 205–226.

Farmer, P. (2004). An anthropology of structural violence. *Current Anthropology, 45*(3), 305–325.

Farmer, P. (2006). *AIDS and accusation: Haiti and the geography of blame.* Berkeley and Los Angeles, CA: University of California Press.

Farmer, P.E., Nizeye, B., Stulac, S., & Keshavjee (2006). Structural violence and clinical medicine. *PLoS Medicine, 3*(10), e449, 1686–1691.

Faulkner, A., & Layzell, S. (2000). *Strategies for living: A report of user-led research into people's strategies for living with mental distress.* London: Mental Health Foundation.

FEANTSA (2006). *The right to health is a human right: Ensuring access to health for people who are homeless.* Retrieved June 11, 2011, from www.feantsa.org/files/Health_Annual_Theme/Annual_theme_documents/European_report/EN_Annual_theme_report_2006_Health.pdf

Fenton, K., Johnson, A.M., & Nicoll, A. (1997). Race, ethnicity, and health: Can sexual health programmes be directed without stereotyping? *British Medical Journal, 314*(7096), 1703–1704.

Fine, C. (2010). *Delusions of gender: The real science behind sex differences.* London: Icon Books.

Finkelstein, V., & French, S. (1993). Towards a psychology of disability. In J. Swain, V. Finkelstein, S. French, & M. Oliver (Eds.), *Disabling barriers – Enabling environments* (pp. 26–33). London: Sage.

Finlay, W.M., Antaki, C., & Walton, C. (2008). Saying no to the staff: An analysis of refusals in a home for people with severe communication difficulties. *Sociology of Health & Illness, 30*(1), 55–75.

Fitzpatrick, K.M., Irwin, J., LaGory, M., & Ritchey, F. (2007). Just thinking about it: Social capital and suicide ideation among homeless persons. *Journal of Health Psychology, 12*(5), 750–760.

Fitzpatrick, R., Dawson, J., Boulton, M., McLean, J., Hart, G., & Brookes, M. (1994). Perceptions of general practice among homosexual men. *British Journal of General Practice, 44*(379), 80–82.

Fitzpatrick, S. (2005). Explaining homelessness: A critical realist perspective. *Housing, Theory and Society, 22*(1), 1–17.

Fleming, D.T., & Wasserheit, J.N. (1999). From epidemiology synergy to public health policy and practice: The contribution of other sexually transmitted diseases to sexual transmission of HIV infection. *Sexually Transmitted Infections, 75,* 3–17.

Flick, U. (2007). Homelessness and health: Challenges for health psychology. *Journal of Health Psychology, 12*(5), 691–695.

Flowers, P., Smith, J.A., Sheeran, P., & Beail, N. (1997). Health and romance: Understanding unprotected sex in relationships with gay men. *British Journal of Health Psychology, 2,* 73–86.

Fonagy, P., Gergely, G., Jurist, E., & Target, M. (2004). *Affect regulation, mentalization, and the development of the self.* London: Karnac.

Fox, D., Prilleltensky, I., & Austin, S. (Eds.) (2009). *Critical psychology: An introduction* (2nd edition). London: Sage.

Frederick, D.A., Buchanan, G.M., Sadehgi-Azar, L., Peplau, L.A., Haselton, M.G., Berezovskaya, A., & Lipinski, R.E. (2007). Desiring the muscular ideal: Men's body satisfaction in the United States, Ukraine, and Ghana. *Psychology of Men & Masculinity, 8*(2), 103–117.

Freire, P. (1972). *Pedagogy of the oppressed.* Harmondsworth: Penguin.

French, S. (1993). Disability, impairment or something in between. In J. Swain, V. Finkelstein, S. French, & M. Oliver (Eds.), *Disabling barriers – enabling environments* (pp. 17–25). London: Sage.

Freud, S. (1905). *Three essays on the theory of sexuality. The standard edition of the complete psychological works of Sigmund Freud* (J. Strachey, Trans.), Vol. 7. London: Vintage Classics.

Freud, S. (1935/1951). Letter to an American mother. *American Journal of Psychiatry, 107,* 786.

Freud, S. (2005). *The essentials of psycho-analysis.* London: Vintage Books.

Freud, S., & Breuer, J. (1895). Studies on hysteria. *The standard edition of the complete psychological works of Sigmund Freud* (J. Strachey, Trans.), Vol. 7. London: Vintage Classics.

Friedman, H.S., & Booth-Kewley, S. (1987). The 'disease-prone personality': A meta-analytic view of the construct. *American Psychologist, 42*(6), 539–555.

Frosh, S. (2006). *For and against psychoanalysis* (2nd edition). Hove: Routledge.

Fujiura, G.T., & Yamaki, K. (2000). Trends in demography of childhood poverty and disability. *Exceptional Children, 66*(2), 187–199.

Gabel, S. (2004). South Asian Indian cultural orientations toward mental retardation. *Mental Retardation, 42*(1), 12–25.

Galdas, P. (2010). The role of masculinities in white and south Asian men's help-seeking behaviour for cardiac chest pain. In B. Gough & S. Robertson (Eds.), *Men, masculinities and health: Critical perspectives* (pp. 216–231). Basingstoke: Palgrave Macmillan.

Galtung, J. (1969). Violence, peace and peace research. *Journal of Peace Research, 6,* 167–191.

Galvin, R. (2002). Disturbing notions of chronic illness and individual responsibility: Towards a genealogy of morals. *Health, 6*(2), 107–137.

Gardner, K., Samsam, S., Leavey, C., & Porcellato, L. (2010). 'The perfect size': perceptions of and influences on body image and body size in young Somali women living in Liverpool: A qualitative study. *Diversity in Health and Care, 7,* 23–34.

Garner, D.M., Garfinkel, P.E., Schwartz, D., & Thompson, M. (1980). Cultural expectations of thinness in women. *Psychological Reports, 47,* 483–491.

Gausset, Q. (2001). AIDS and cultural practices in Africa: The case of the Tonga (Zambia). *Social Science and Medicine, 52,* 509–518.

Gergen, K.J. (1985). The social constructionist movement in modern psychology. *American Psychologist, 40*(3), 266–275.

Gillespie, S.R. (Ed.) (2006). *AIDS, poverty and hunger: Challenges and responses.* Washington, DC: International Food Policy Research Institute.

Gillies, P., Tolley, K., & Wolstenholme, J. (1996). Is AIDS a disease of poverty? *AIDS Care, 8*(3), 351–363.

Glaser, B.G., & Strauss, A.L. (1967). *The discovery of grounded theory: Strategies for qualitative research.* New York: Aldine.

Gough, B. (2006). Try to be healthy, but don't forgo your masculinity: Deconstructing men's health discourse in the media. *Social Science & Medicine, 63,* 2476–2488.

Gough, B., & Edwards, G. (1998). The beer talking: Four lads, a carry out and the reproduction of masculinities. *The Sociological Review, 46*(3), 409–435.

Gough, B., & Robertson, S. (Eds.) (2010). *Men, masculinities and health: Critical perspectives.* Basingstoke: Palgrave Macmillan.

Graham, C., Sanders, S., Milhausen, R., & McBride, K. (2004). Turning on and turning off: A focus group study of the factors that affect women's sexual arousal. *Archives of Sexual Behavior, 33,* 527–538.

Gray, R.E., Fergus, K.D., & Fitch, M.I. (2005). Two black men with prostate cancer: A narrative approach. *British Journal of Health Psychology, 10,* 71–84.

Green, C.R., Anderson, K.O., Baker, T.A., Campbell, L.C., Decker, S., Fillingim, R.B., et al. (2003). The unequal burden of pain: Confronting racial and ethnic disparities in pain. *Pain Medicine, 4*(3), 277–294.

Green, C.R., Baker, T.A., Sato, Y., Washington, T.L., & Smith, E.M. (2003). Race and chronic pain: A comparative study of young black and white Americans presenting for management. *The Journal of Pain, 4*(4), 176–183.

Greene, B. (1994). Ethnic-minority lesbians and gay men: Mental health and treatment issues. *Journal of Clinical and Consulting Psychology, 62*, 243–251.

Greig, F., & Koopman, C. (2003). Multilevel analysis of women's empowerment and HIV prevention: Quantitative survey results from a preliminary study in Botswana. *AIDS and Behavior, 7*, 195–208.

Groce, N.E. (1985). *Everyone here spoke sign language: Hereditary deafness on Martha's Vinyard.* Cambridge, MA: Harvard University Press.

Groce, N.E. (2003). *Adolescents and youth with disability: Issues and challenges.* Retrieved February 24, 2006, from www.dcdd.nl/default.asp?action=article&id=2150

Groce, N.E. (2005). Immigrants, disability, and rehabilitation. In J.H. Stone (Ed.), *Culture and disability: Providing culturally competent services* (pp. 1–13). Thousand Oaks, CA: Sage.

Groce, N.E., & Zola, I.K. (1993). Multiculturalism, chronic illness, and disability. *Pediatrics, 91*(5), 1048–1055.

Grogan, S. (2000). Body image. In J. Ussher (Ed.), *Women's health: Contemporary international perspectives* (pp. 356–363). Leicester: BPS Books.

Guarnaccia, P.J., & Rogler, L.H. (1999). Research on culture-bound syndromes: New directions. *American Journal of Psychiatry, 156*, 1322–1327.

Haasen, C., Yagdiran, O., Mass, R., & Krausz, M. (2000). Potential for misdiagnosis among Turkish migrants with psychotic disorders: A clinical controlled study in Germany. *Acta Psychiatrica Scandinavica, 101*, 125–129.

Haldeman, D.C. (1994). The practice and ethics of sexual orientation conversion therapy. *Journal of Clinical and Consulting Psychology, 62*, 221–227.

Halliwell, E., & Harvey, M. (2006). Examination of a sociocultural model of disordered eating among male and female adolescents. *British Journal of Health Psychology, 11*, 235–248.

Hamilton, J.A., & Jensvold, M. (1992). Personality, psychopathology, and depressions in women. In L.S. Brown & M. Ballou (Eds.), *Personality and psychopathology: Feminist reappraisals* (pp. 116–143). New York: The Guilford Press.

Hanass-Hancock, J. (2009). Interweaving conceptualizations of gender and disability in the context of vulnerability to HIV/AIDS in KwaZulu-Natal, South Africa. *Sexuality & Disability, 27*, 35–47.

Hanlin, C.E., Bess, K., Conway, P., Evans, S.D., McCown, D., Prilleltensky, I., & Perkins, D.D. (2008). Community psychology. In C. Willig &

W. Stainton-Rogers (Eds.), *Handbook of qualitative research methods in psychology* (pp. 524–540). London: Sage.

Hanna, W.J., & Rogovsky, B. (1991). Women with disabilities: Two handicaps plus. *Disability, Handicap & Society, 6*(1), 49–63.

Hardey, M. (1998). *The social context of health.* Buckingham: Open University Press.

Hargreaves, D.A., & Tiggemann, M. (2006). 'Body image is for girls': A qualitative study of boys' body image. *Journal of Health Psychology, 11*(4), 567–576.

Harper, D. (2008). Clinical psychology. In C. Willig & W. Stainton-Rogers (Eds.), *Handbook of qualitative research methods in psychology* (pp. 430–454). London: Sage.

Harrison, J.A., Mullen, P.D., & Green, L.W. (1992). A meta-analysis of studies of the health belief model with adults. *Health Education Research, 7*(1), 107–116.

Hartung, C.M., & Widiger, T.A. (1998). Gender differences in the diagnosis of mental disorders: Conclusions and controversies of the DSM-IV. *Psychological Bulletin, 123*(3), 260–278.

Harvey, D. (2007). *A brief history of neoliberalism.* Oxford: Oxford University Press.

Hay, J.L., Ford, J.S., Klein, D., Primavera, L.H., Buckley, T.R., Stein, T.R., Shike, M., & Ostroff, J.S. (2003). Adherence to colorectal cancer screening in mammography-adherent older women. *Journal of Behavioral Medicine, 26*(6), 553–576.

Health Protection Agency (2008). *Sexually transmitted infections in black African and black Caribbean communities in the UK: 2008 report.* London: Health Protection Agency.

Health Protection Agency (2009). *HIV in the United Kingdom: 2009 report.* London: Health Protection Agency.

Heifner, C. (1997). The male experience of depression. *Perspectives in Psychiatric Care, 32*(2), 10–18.

Helman, C.G. (2007a). Anthropology and its contributions. In K. Bhui & D. Bhugra (Eds.), *Culture and mental health: A Comprehensive textbook* (pp. 11–15). London: Hodder Arnold.

Helman, C.G. (2007b). *Culture, health and illness* (5th edition). London: Hodder Arnold.

Hemingway, H., & Marmot, M. (1999). Psychosocial factors in the aetiology and prognosis of coronary heart disease: Systematic review of prospective cohort studies. *British Medical Journal, 318*, 1460–1467.

Henwood, K.L., & Pidgeon, N.F. (1992). Qualitative research and psychological theorizing. *British Journal of Psychology, 83*, 97–111.

Herman, J. (2001). *Trauma and recovery*. New York: Harper Collins.

Herman, J.L., Perry, J.C., & van der Kolk, B.A. (1989). Childhood trauma in borderline personality disorder. *American Journal of Psychiatry, 146,* 490–495.

Heyman, B., & Huckle, S. (1995). Sexuality as a perceived hazard in the lives of adults with learning difficulties. *Disability & Society, 10*(2), 139–155.

Hildebrand, H.P. (1992). A patient dying with AIDS. *The International Review of Psycho-Analysis, 19,* 457–469.

Hiles, D., & Čermák, I. (2008). Narrative psychology. In C. Willig & W. Stainton-Rogers (Eds.), *Handbook of qualitative research methods in psychology* (pp. 147–164). London: Sage.

Hinchliff, S., Gott, M., & Galena, E. (2005). 'I daresay I might find it embarrassing': General practitioners' perspectives on discussing sexual health issues with lesbian and gay patients. *Health and Social Care in the Community, 13*(4), 345–353.

Hofstede, G. (1984). *Culture's consequences: International differences in work-related values.* Newbury Park, CA: Sage.

Hollway, W., & Jefferson, T. (2000). *Doing qualitative research differently: Free association, narrative and the interview method.* London: Sage.

Hood, M.A.M., Vander Wal, J.S., & Gibbons, J.L. (2009). Culture and eating disorders. In S. Eshun & R.A.R. Gurung (Eds.), *Culture and mental health: Sociocultural influences, theory and practice* (pp. 273–295).Chichester: Wiley-Blackwell.

Howard-Barr, E.M., Rienzo, B.A., Pigg, Jr, R.M., & James, D. (2005). Teacher beliefs, professional preparation, and practices regarding exceptional students and sexuality education. *Journal of School Health, 75*(3), 99–104.

Hubbard, R. (1997). Abortion and disability: Who should and should not inhabit the world? In L. Davis (Ed.), *The disability studies reader.* London: Routledge.

Hughes, B., & Paterson, K. (1997). The social model of disability and the disappearing body: Towards a sociology of impairment. *Disability & Society, 12*(3), 325–340.

Hussain, F.A., & Cochrane, R. (2003). Living with depression: Coping strategies used by South Asian women, living in the UK, suffering from depression. *Mental Health, Religion & Culture, 6*(1), 21–44.

Iley, K., & Nazroo, J. (2007). Sociology of health and illness. In K. Bhui & D. Bhugra (Eds.), *Culture and mental health: A Comprehensive textbook* (pp. 16–23). London: Hodder Arnold.

Jacobson, J.W. (2001). Environmental postmodernism and rehabilitation of the borderline of mental retardation. *Behavioural Interventions, 16,* 209–234.

Jana, S., Basu, I., Rotheram-Borus, M.J., & Newman, P.A. (2004). The Sonagachi project: A sustainable community intervention program. *AIDS Education and Prevention, 16*(5), 405–414.

Janssen, E., McBride, K.R., Yarber, W., Hill, B.J., & Butler, S.M. (2008). Factors that influence sexual arousal in men: A focus group study. *Archives of Sexual Behavior, 37,* 252–265.

Janz, N.K., & Becker, M.H. (1984). The health belief model: A decade later. *Health Education & Behavior, 11*(1), 1–47.

Jegatheesan, B., Miller, P.J., & Fowler, S.A. (2010). Autism from a religious perspective: A study of parental beliefs in South Asian Muslim immigrant families. *Focus on Autism and Other Developmental Disabilities, 25*(2), 98–109.

Jewkes, R.K. (2009). HIV and women. In P. Rohleder, L. Swartz, S. Kalichman, & L.C. Simbayi (Eds.), *HIV/AIDS in South Africa 25 years on: Psychosocial perspectives* (pp. 27–40). New York: Springer.

Jewkes, R.K., Levin, J.B., & Penn-Kekana, L.A. (2003). Gender inequalities, intimate partner violence and HIV preventive practices: Findings of a South African cross-sectional study. *Social Science & Medicine, 56,* 125–134.

Joffe, H. (1999). *'Risk and the other'*. Cambridge: Cambridge University Press.

Johnston, K.L., & White, K.M. (2003). Binge-drinking: A test of the role of group norms in the theory of planned behaviour. *Psychology and Health, 18,* 63–77.

Johnston, M. (1996). Models of disability. *The Psychologist,* May, 205–210.

Johnston, M. (1997). Integrating models of disability: A reply to Shakespeare and Watson. *Disability & Society, 12* (2), 307–310.

Jorm, A.F., Korten, A.E., Rodgers, B., Jacomb, P.A., & Christensen, H. (2002). Sexual orientation and mental health: Results from a community survey of young and middle-aged adults. *British Journal of Psychiatry, 180,* 423–427.

Jukkala, T., Mäkinen, I.H., Kislitsyna, O., Ferlander, S., & Vågerö (2008). Economic strain, social relations, gender, and binge drinking in Moscow. *Social Science & Medicine, 66,* 663–674.

Kagan, C., Burton, M., & Siddiquee, A. (2008). Action research. In C. Willig & W. Stainton-Rogers (Eds.), *Handbook of qualitative research methods in psychology* (pp. 32–53). London: Sage.

Kai, J., Beavan, J., Faull, C., Dobson, L., Gill, P., & Beighton, A. (2007). Professional uncertainty and disempowerment responding to ethnic diversity in health care: A qualitative study. *PLoS Medicine, 4*(11), e323, doi: 10.1371/journal.pmed.0040323.

Kaminer, D., & Dixon, J. (1995). The reproduction of masculinity: A discourse analysis of men's drinking talk. *South African Journal of Psychology, 25*, 168–174.

Keel, P.K., & Klump, K.L. (2003). Are eating disorders culture-bound syndromes? Implications for conceptualizing their etiology. *Psychological Bulletin, 129*(5), 747–769.

Kiani, S. (2009). Women with disabilities in the North West province of Cameroon: Resilient and deserving of greater attention. *Disability & Society, 24*(4), 517–531.

Kienzler, H. (2008). Debating war-trauma and post-traumatic stress disorder (PTSD) in an interdisciplinary arena. *Social Science & Medicine, 67*, 218–227.

King, M. (2003). Dropping the diagnosis of homosexuality: Did it change the lot of gays and lesbians in Britain? *Australian and New Zealand Journal of Psychiatry, 37*, 684–688.

King, M., & Bartlett, A. (1999). British psychiatry and homosexuality. *British Journal of Psychiatry, 175*, 106–113.

King, M., & McKeown, E. (2003). *Mental health and social well being of gay men lesbians and bisexuals in England and Wales*. London: Mind Publications. Retrieved September 15, 2010, from: www.pcs-proud.org.uk/SummaryfindingsofLGBreport.pdf

King, M., McKeown, E., Warner, J., Ramsay, A., Johnson, K., Cort, C., Wright, L., Blizard, R., & Davidson, O. (2003). Mental health and quality of life of gay men and lesbians in England and Wales: A controlled, cross-sectional study. *British Journal of Psychiatry, 183*, 552–558.

King, M., Semlyen, J., Tai, S.S., Killaspy, H., Osborn, D., Popelyuk, D., & Nazareth, I. (2008). A systematic review of mental disorder, suicide, and deliberate self harm in lesbian, gay and bisexual people. *BMC Psychiatry, 8*(70), doi: 10.1186/1471-244X-8-70.

King, M., Smith, G., & Bartlett, A. (2004). Treatments of homosexuality in Britain since the 1950s – an oral history: The experience of professionals. *British Medical Journal*, doi: 10.1136/bmj.37984.496725.EE.

Kinsey, A.C, Pomeroy, W.B., & Martin, C.E. (1948). *Sexual behavior in the human male*. Philadelphia: W.B. Saunders Company.

Kinsey, A.C., Pomeroy, W.B., Martin, C.E., & Gebhard, P.H. (1953). *Sexual behavior in the human female*, Philadelphia: W.B. Saunders Company.

Kirmayer, L., Simpson, C., & Cargo, M. (2003). Healing traditions: Culture, community and mental health promotion with Canadian Aboriginal peoples. *Australasian Psychiatry, 11*(Suppl.), S15–S23.

Kleinman, A. (1980). *Patients and healers in the context of culture: An exploration of the borderland between anthropology, medicine, and psychiatry*. Berkeley, CA: University of California Press.

Kleinman, A. (1982). Neurasthenia and depression: A study of somatisation and culture in China. *Culture, Medicine & Psychiatry, 6*, 117–190.

Kleinman, A. (1988). *Rethinking psychiatry: From cultural category to personal experience*. New York: The Free Press.

Klotz, J. (2004). Sociocultural study of intellectual disability: Moving beyond labelling and social constructionist perspectives. *British Journal of Learning Difficulties, 32*, 93–104.

Knekt, P., Raitasalo, R., Heliövaara, M., Lehtinen, V., Pukkala, E., Teppo, L., et al. (1996). Elevated lung cancer risk among persons with depressed mood. *American Journal of Epidemiology, 144*(12), 1096–1103.

Knight, M.T.D., Wykes, T., & Hayward, P. (2003). 'People don't understand': An investigation of stigma in schizophrenia using Interpretative Phenomenological Analysis (IPA). *Journal of Mental Health, 12*(3), 209–222.

Kohli, N., & Dalal, A.K. (1998). Culture as a factor in causal understanding of illness: A study of cancer patients. *Psychology and Developing Societies, 10*(2), 115–129.

Krantz, D.S., & McCeney, M.K. (2002). Effects of psychological and social factors on organic disease: A critical assessment of research on coronary heart disease. *Annual Review of Psychology, 53*, 341–369.

Kroenke, K. (2003). Patients presenting with somatic complaints: Epidemiology, psychiatric co-morbidity and management. *International Journal of Methods in Psychiatric Research, 12*(1), 34–43.

Laing, R.D. (1990). *The divided self: An existential study in sanity and madness*. London: Penguin Books.

Langridge, D. (2007). Gay affirmative therapy: A theoretical framework and defence. *Journal of Gay & Lesbian Psychotherapy, 11*(1), 27–43.

Laumann, E.O., Paik, A., & Rosen, R. (1999). Sexual dysfunction in the United States: Prevalence and predictors. *Journal of the American Medical Association, 281*, 537–544.

Lawless, S., Kippax, S., & Crawford, J. (1996). Dirty, diseased and undeserving: The position of HIV-positive women. *Social Science & Medicine, 43*(9), 1371–1377.

Lawson, R.B., Graham, J.E., & Baker, K.M. (2007). *A history of psychology: Globalization, ideas and applications*. Upper Saddle River, NJ: Pearson Education.

LeBlanc, M., Meintel, D., & Piché, V. (1991). The African sexual system: Comment on Caldwell et al. *Population and Development Review, 17*(3), 497–505.

Lee, C., & Owens, R.G. (2002). *The psychology of men's health*. Buckingham: Open University Press.

Lee, H., Pollock, G., Lubek, I., Niemi, S., O'Brien, K., Green, M., et al. (2010). Creating new career pathways to reduce poverty, illiteracy and health risks while transforming and empowering Cambodian women's lives. *Journal of Health Psychology, 15*(7), 982–992.

Leibowitz, B., Rohleder, P., Bozalek, V., Carolissen, R., & Swartz, L. (2007). 'It doesn't matter who or what we are, we are still just people': Strategies used by university students to negotiate difference. *South African Journal of Psychology, 37*(4), 702–719.

Leit, R.A., Pope, H.G., & Gray, J.J. (2000). Cultural expectations of muscularity in men: The evolution of *Playgirl* centrefolds. *International Journal of Eating Disorders, 29*, 90–93.

Lewes, K. (1995). *Psychoanalysis and male homosexuality*. Northvale, NJ: Jason Aronson Inc.

Lewin, K. (1946). Action research and minority problems. *Journal of Social Issues, 2*, 34–46.

Lindegger, G., & Quayle, M. (2009). Masculinity and HIV/AIDS. In P. Rohleder, L. Swartz, S. Kalichman, & L.C. Simbayi (Eds.), *HIV/AIDS in South Africa 25 years on: Psychosocial perspectives* (pp. 41–54). New York: Springer.

Lipton, J.A., & Marbach, J.J. (1984). Ethnicity and the pain experience. *Social Science & Medicine, 19*(12), 1279–1298.

Lloyd, K. (2007). The history and relevance of culture-bound syndromes. In K. Bhui & D. Bhugra (Eds.), *Culture and mental health: A Comprehensive textbook* (pp. 98–105). London: Hodder Arnold.

Lloyd, M. (2001). The politics of disability and feminism: Discord or synthesis? *Sociology, 35*(3), 715–728.

Loeb, M., Eide, A.H., Jelsma, J., Toni, M., & Maart, S. (2008). Poverty and disability in Eastern and Western Cape Provinces, South Africa. *Disability & Society, 23*(4), 311–321.

Lomas, J. (1998). Social capital and health: Implications for public health and epidemiology. *Social Science & Medicine, 47*(9), 79–98.

Lopez, S., & Guarnaccia, P. (2000). Cultural psychopathology: Uncovering the social world of mental illness. *Annual Review of Psychology, 51*, 571–598.

Lorant, V., Croux, C., Weich, S., Deliège, D., Mackenbach, J., & Ansseau, M. (2007). Depression and socio-economic risk factors: 7-year longitudinal population study. *The British Journal of Psychiatry, 190*, 293–298.

Lubek, I., Wong, M.L., McCourt, M., Chew, K., Dy, B.C., Kros, S., et al. (2002). Collaboratively confronting the current Cambodian HIV/AIDS crisis in Siem Reap: A cross-disciplinary, cross-cultural 'participatory action research' project in consultative, community health change. *Asian Psychologist, 3*(1), 21–28.

Lund, C., Breen, A., Fisher, A.J., Kakuma, R., Corrigall, J., Joska, J.A., Swartz, L., & Patel, V. (2010). Poverty and common mental disorders in low and middle income countries: A systematic review. *Social Science & Medicine, 71*, 517–528.

Lund, P.M. (2001). Health and education of children with albinism in Zimbabwe. *Health Education Research: Theory & Practice, 16*(1), 1–7.

Lyons, A.C., & Chamberlain, K. (2006). *Health psychology: A critical introduction*. Cambridge: Cambridge University Press.

Lyons, A.C., & Willott, S.A. (1999). From suet pudding to superhero: Representations of men's health for women. *Health, 3*(3), 283–302.

Lyons, A.C., & Willott, S.A. (2008). Alcohol consumption, gender identities and women's changing social positions. *Sex Roles, 59*, 694–712.

MacDonald, T.H. (2005). *Third world health: Hostage to first world wealth*. Oxford: Radcliffe Publishing.

MacGregor, H. (2006). 'The grant is what I eat': The politics of social security and disability in the post-apartheid South African state. *Journal of Biosocial Science, 38*, 43–55.

MacKay, J., & Eriksen, M. (2002). *The tobacco atlas*. Geneva: World Health Organization.

MacLachlan, M. (2006a). Towards a global health contribution for critical health psychology. *Journal of Health Psychology, 11*(3), 361–365.

MacLachlan, M. (2006b). *Culture and health: A critical perspective towards global health* (2nd edition). Chichester: John Wiley & Sons.

Malanda, S., Meadows, J., & Catalan, J. (2001). Are we meeting the psychological needs of black African HIV-positive individuals in London? Controlled study of referrals to a psychological medicine unit. *AIDS Care, 13*(4), 413–419.

Malson, H. (2000). Anorexia nervosa. In J. Ussher (Ed.), *Women's health: Contemporary international perspectives* (pp. 363–372). Leicester: BPS Books.

Malson, H., Finn, D.M., Treasure, J., Clarke, S., & Anderson, G. (2004). Constructing 'the eating disordered patient': A discourse analysis of accounts of treatment experiences. *Journal of Community and Applied Social Psychology, 14*, 473–489.

Mann, J.M., Tarantola, D.J.M., & Netter, T.W. (1992). *AIDS in the world: The global AIDS policy coalition.* Cambridge, MA: Harvard University Press.

Manstead, A.S.R., Proffitt, C., & Smart, J.L. (1983). Predicting and understanding mothers' infant-feeding intentions and behavior: Testing the theory of reasoned action. *Journal of Personality and Social Psychology, 44*(4), 697–671.

Marecek, J., & Hare-Mustin, R.T. (2009). Clinical psychology: The politics of madness. In D. Fox, I. Prilleltensky, & S. Austin (Eds.), *Critical psychology: An introduction* (2nd edition) (pp. 75–92). London: Sage.

Marks, D. (1999). *Disability: Controversial debates and psychosocial issues.* London: Routledge.

Marks, D.F. (2002a). Freedom, responsibility and power: Contrasting approaches to health psychology. *Journal of Health Psychology, 7*(1), 5–19.

Marks, D.F. (Ed.) (2002b). *The health psychology reader.* London: Sage.

Marks, D.F. (2004). Rights to health, freedom from illness: A life and death matter. In M. Murray (Ed.), *Critical health psychology* (pp. 61–82). Basingstoke: Palgrave Macmillan.

Marks, D.F., Murray, M., Evans, B., & Estacio, E.V. (2011). *Health psychology: Theory, research and practice* (3rd edition). London: Sage.

Marks, D.F., & Yardley, L. (Eds.) (2004). *Research methods for clinical and health psychology.* London: Sage.

Marmot, M. (2010). *Fair society, healthy lives: The Marmot review. Strategic review of health inequalities in England post-2010.* London: University College London.

Marshall, B.L. (2002). 'Hard science': Gendered constructions of sexual dysfunction in the 'Viagra age'. *Sexualities, 5*(2), 131–158.

Marshall, H. (1994). Discourse analysis in an occupational context. In C. Cassel & G. Symon (Eds.), *Qualitative methods in organizational research* (pp. 91–106). London: Sage.

Martens, W.H.J. (2002). Homelessness and mental disorders: A comparative review of populations in various countries. *International Journal of Mental Health, 30*(4), 79–96.

Masters, W.H., & Johnson, V.E. (1966). *Human sexual response.* Boston, MA: Little Brown.

Matlin, S.L., Molock, S.D., & Tebes, J.K. (2011). Suicidality and depression among African American adolescents: The role of family and peer support and community connectedness. *American Journal of Orthopsychiatry, 81*(1), 108–117.

McCabe, M.P., Cummins, R.A., & Reid, S.B. (1994). An empirical study of the sexual abuse of people with intellectual disability. *Sexuality and Disability, 12*(4), 297–306.

McCarthy, M. (1993). Sexual experiences of women with learning difficulties in long-stay hospitals. *Sexuality and Disability, 11*(4), 277–286.

McCarthy, M. (1998). Whose body is it anyway? Pressures and control for women with learning disabilities. *Disability & Society, 13*(4), 557–574.

McCreary, D.R., Saucier, D.M., & Courtenay, W.H. (2005). The drive for muscularity and masculinity: Testing the associations among gender-role traits, behaviors, attitudes, and conflict. *Psychology of Men & Masculinity, 6*(2), 83–94.

McFarlane, E. (1997). *Diagnosis homophobic – the experiences of lesbians, gay men and bisexuals in mental health services.* London: Project for Advice Counselling and Education (PACE). Retrieved September 15, 2010, from www.pacehealth.org.uk/publications

McKeown, T. (1979). *The role of medicine: Dream, mirage or nemesis?* Oxford: Basil Blackwell.

McKinley, J. (2010). Suicides put light on pressures of gay teenagers. *New York Times*, October 3. Retrieved September 15, 2011, from www.nytimes.com/2010/10/04/us/04suicide.html

McLean, C., Campbell, C., & Cornish, F. (2003). African-Caribbean interactions with mental health services in the UK: Experiences and expectations of exclusion as (re)productive of health inequalities. *Social Science and Medicine, 56*, 657–669.

McManus, S., Meltzer, H., Brugha, T., Bebbington, P., Jenkins, R. (2009). *Adult psychiatric morbidity in England, 2007: Results of a household survey.* Leeds: NHS Information Centre for Health and Social Care. Retrieved January 14, 2011, from www.ic.nhs.uk/statistics-and-data-collections/mental-health/mental-health-surveys/adult-psychiatric-morbidity-in-england-2007-results-of-a-household-survey

McSweeney, B. (2002). Hofstede's model of national cultural differences and their consequences: A triumph of faith – a failure of analysis. *Human Relations, 55*(1), 89–118.

McVey, J., Madill, A., & Fielding, D. (2001). The relevance of lowered personal control for patients who have stoma surgery to treat cancer. *British Journal of Clinical Psychology, 40*(4), 337–360.

Meyerowitz, B.E., Richardson, J., Hudson, S., & Leedham, B. (1998). Ethnicity and cancer outcomes: Behavioral and psychosocial considerations. *Psychological Bulletin, 123*(1), 47–70.

Mgwili, V.N., & Watermeyer, B. (2006). Physically disabled women and discrimination in reproductive health care: Psychoanalytic reflections. In B. Watermeyer, L. Swartz, T. Lorenzo, M. Schneider, & M. Priestley (Eds.), *Disability and social change: A South African agenda* (pp. 261–272). Cape Town: HSRC Press.

Miles, M. (2002). Some influences of religions on attitudes towards disabilities and people with disabilities. *Journal of Religion, Disability & Health*, 6(2), 117–129.

Miller, M.N., & Pumariega, A.J. (2001). Culture and eating disorders: A historical and cross-cultural review. *Psychiatry: Interpersonal and Biological Processes*, 64(2), 93–110.

Milligan, M.S., & Neufeldt, A.H. (2001). The myth of asexuality: A survey of social and empirical evidence. *Sexuality and Disability*, 19(2), 91–109.

Miranda, J., & Patel, V. (2005). Achieving the millennium development goals: Does mental health play a role? *PLoS Medicine*, 2(10), e291, doi: 10.1371/journal.pmed.0020291.

Mitchell, A., & Purtell, R. (2009). Community approaches, social inclusion and user involvement. In H. Beinart, P. Kennedy, & S. Llewelyn (Eds.), *Clinical psychology in practice* (pp. 364–376). Chichester: BPS Blackwell.

Mokdad, A.H., Marks, J.S., Stroup, D.F., & Gerberding, J.L. (2004). Actual causes of death in the United States, 2000. *Journal of the American Medical Association*, 29(10), 1238–1245.

Moon, G., Gould, M., Brown, T., Duncan, C., Iggulden, P., Jones, K., Litva, A., Subramanian, S., & Twigg, L. (2000). *Epidemiology: An introduction*. Buckingham: Open University Press.

Morrison, V., & Bennett, P. (2009). *An introduction to health psychology* (2nd edition). Harlow: Pearson Education.

Morrow, M., Ngoc, D.H., Hoang, T.T., & Trinh, T.H. (2002). Smoking and young women in Vietnam: The influence of normative gender roles. *Social Science & Medicine*, 55, 681–690.

Moussavi, S., Chatterji, S., Verdes, E., Tandon, A., Patel, V., & Ustun, B. (2007). Depression, chronic diseases, and decrements in health: Results from the World Health Surveys. *The Lancet*, 370(9590), 851–858.

Moynihan, R. (2003). The making of a disease: Female sexual dysfunction. *British Medical Journal*, 326, 45–47.

Moynihan, R., & Henry, D. (2006). The fight against disease mongering: Generating knowledge for action. *PLoS Medicine*, 3(4), e191, 0425–0428.

Munthali, A., Mvula, P., & Ali, S. (2004). *Effective HIV/AIDS and reproductive health information to people with disabilities: A final report*. Zomba: Centre for Social Research, University of Malawi. Retrieved June 25, 2005, from www.dpi.org/en/resources/documents/FinalReportforFedomaStudyOctober2004.doc

Murali, V., & Oyebode, F. (2004). Poverty, social inequality and mental health. *Advances in Psychiatric Treatment*, 10, 216–224.

Murray, M. (Ed.) (2004). *Critical health psychology*. Basingstoke: Palgrave Macmillan.

Murray, M. (2008). Narrative psychology. In J.A. Smith (Ed.), *Qualitative psychology: A practical guide to research methods* (2nd edition) (pp. 111–132). London: Sage.

Murray, M., & Campbell, C. (2003). Living in a material world: Reflecting on some assumptions of health psychology. *Journal of Health Psychology*, 8(2), 231–236.

Murray, M., Nelson, G., Poland, B., Maticka-Tyndale, E., & Ferris, L. (2004). Assumptions and values of community health psychology. *Journal of Health Psychology*, 9(2), 323–333.

Myrtek, M. (1995). Type A behavior pattern, personality factors, disease, and physiological reactivity: A meta-analytic update. *Personality and Individual Differences*, 18(4), 491–502.

National AIDS Trust (2008). *The myth of HIV health tourism*. London: The National AIDS Trust.

Nelson, G., & Prilleltensky, I. (Eds.) (2005). *Community psychology: In pursuit of liberation and well-being*. London: Palgrave Macmillan.

Nosek, M.A., Howland, C., Rintala, D.H., Young, M.E., & Chanpong, G.F. (2001). National study of women with physical disabilities: Final report. *Sexuality and Disability*, 19(1), 5–39.

Nunkoosing, K. (2000). Constructing learning disability: Consequences for men and women with learning disabilities. *Journal of Learning Disabilities*, 4(1), 49–62.

O'Connor, R.C., & Armitage, C.J. (2003). Theory of planned behaviour and parasuicide: An exploratory study. *Current Psychology*, 22, 247–256.

Odenwald, M., van Duijl, M., & Schmitt, T. (2007). Psychopathology and culture: Disorders of possession and dissociation in intercultural clinical practice. In K. Bhui & D. Bhugra (Eds.), *Culture and mental health: A Comprehensive textbook* (pp. 87–97). London: Hodder Arnold.

Office for National Statistics (2010). *Death registrations by cause in England and Wales, 2009*. London: Office for National Statistics. Retrieved April 16, 2011, from www.statistics.gov.uk/pdfdir/dth1010.pdf

Ogden, J. (2003). Some problems with social cognition models: A pragmatic and conceptual analysis. *Health Psychology*, 22(4), 424–428.

Okello, E.S., & Ekblad, S. (2006). Lay concepts of depression among the Baganda of Uganda: A pilot study. *Transcultural Psychiatry*, 43(2), 287–313.

Oliffe, J.L., Robertson, S., Kelly, M.T., Roy, P., & Ogrodniczuk, J.S. (2010). Connecting masculinity and depression among international male university students. *Qualitative Health Research*, 20(7), 987–998.

Olivardia, R., Pope, H.G., Borowiecki, J.J., & Cohane, G.H. (2004). Biceps and body image: The relationship between muscularity and self-esteem, depression, and eating disorder symptoms. *Psychology of Men & Masculinity, 5*(2), 112–120.

Oliver, M. (1986). Social policy and disability: Some theoretical issues. *Disability, Handicap & Society, 1*(1), 5–17.

Oliver, M. (1990). *The politics of disablement.* London: Macmillan.

Oliver, M. (1993). Disability and dependency: A creation of industrial societies? In J. Swain, V. Finkelstein, S. French, & M. Oliver (Eds.), *Disabling barriers – enabling environments* (pp. 49–60). London: Sage.

Oliver, M. (1996). Defining impairment and disability: Issues at stake. In C. Barnes & G. Mercer (Eds.), *Exploring the divide: Illness and disability* (pp. 29–54). Leeds: The Disability Press. Retrieved June 25, 2005, from www.leeds.ac.uk/disability-studies/archiveuk/titles.html

Oliver, M. (2004). The social model in action: If I had a hammer. In C. Barnes & G. Mercer (Eds.), *Implementing the social model of disability: Theory and research* (pp. 18–31). Leeds: The Disability Press.

Ondeck, D.M. (2003). Impact of culture on pain. *Home Health Care Management & Practice, 15*(3), 255–257.

Oosterhoorn, R., & Kendrick, A. (2001). No sign of harm: Issues for disabled children communicating about abuse. *Child Abuse Review, 10,* 243–253.

Orbach, S. (2005). *Hungerstrike: Starving amidst plenty.* London: Karnac Books.

Orbach, S. (2009). *Bodies.* London: Profile Books.

Ouellette, J.A., & Wood, W. (1998). Habit and intention in everyday life: The multiple processes by which past behavior predicts future behavior. *Psychological Bulletin, 124*(1), 54–74.

Oyefara, J.L. (2007). Food insecurity, HIV/AIDS pandemic and sexual behaviour of female commercial sex workers in Lagos metropolis, Nigeria. *Journal of Social Aspects of HIV/AIDS, 4*(2), 626–635.

Palmer, B., Macfarlane, G., Afzal, C., Esmail, A., Silman, A., & Lunt, M. (2007). Acculturation and the prevalence of pain amongst South Asian minority ethnic groups in the UK. *Rheumatology, 46,* 1009–1014.

Pancer, M., & Foxall, K. (1998). *Our journey from better beginnings to better futures: The personal stories of community residents.* Retrieved March 27, 2011, from http://bbbf.queensu.ca/pdfs/r_story.pdf

Park, J., Turnball, A.P., & Turnbull, H.R. (2002). Impacts of poverty on quality of life in families of children with disabilities. *Exceptional Children, 68*(2), 151–170.

Parker, I. (2004). Criteria for qualitative research in psychology. *Qualitative Research in Psychology, 1,* 95–106.

Parker, I., Georgaca, E., Harper, D., McLaughlin, T., & Stowell-Smith, M. (1995). *Deconstructing psychopathology.* London: Sage.

Patel, S., Peacock, S.M., Mckinley, R.K., Clark-Carter, D., & Watson, P.J. (2008). GPs' experiences of managing chronic pain in a South Asian community: A qualitative study of the consultation process. *Family Practice, 25,* 71–77.

Patel, V. (2007). Mental health in low- and middle-income countries. *British Medical Bulletin, 81 & 82,* 81–96.

Patel, V., Abas, M., Broadhead, J., Todd, C., & Reeler, A. (2001). Depression in developing countries: Lessons from Zimbabwe. *British Medical Journal, 322,* 482–484.

Patel, V., & Kleinman, A. (2003). Poverty and common mental disorders in developing countries. *Bulletin of the World Health Organization, 81*(8), 609–615.

Payne, S. (2000). *Poverty, social exclusion and mental health: Findings from the 1999 PSE survey.* Working Paper No. 15. Retrieved November 25, 2010, from www.bris.ac.uk/poverty/pse/work_pap.htm

Peinkofer, J.R. (1994). HIV education for the deaf, a vulnerable minority. *Public Health Reports, 109*(3), 390–396.

Pennant, M.E., Bayliss, S.E., & Meads, C.A. (2009). Improving lesbian, gay and bisexual healthcare: A systematic review of qualitative literature from the UK. *Diversity in Health and Care, 6,* 193–203.

Penninx, B.W.J.H., Guralnik, J.M., Pahor, M., Ferrucci, L., Cerhan, J.R., Wallace, R.B., & Havlik, R.J. (1998). Chronically depressed mood and cancer risk in older persons. *Journal of the National Care Institute, 90*(24), 1888–1893.

Peralta, R.L. (2007). College alcohol use and the embodiment of hegemonic masculinity among European American men. *Sex Roles, 56,* 741–756.

Perkins, D.O. (2002). Predictors of non-compliance in patients with schizophrenia. *Journal of Clinical Psychiatry, 63*(12), 1121–1128.

Perry, B.M., Taylor, D., & Shaw, S.K. (2007). 'You've got to have a positive state of mind': An interpretative phenomenological analysis of hope and first episode psychosis. *Journal of Mental Health, 16*(6), 781–793.

Peters, R., Arnold, R., Petrunka, K., Angus, D., Belange, J.-M., Boyce, W., Brophy, K., Burke, S.,

Cameron, G., Craig, W., Evers, S., Herry, Y., Mamatis, D., Nelson, G., Pancer, S.M., Roberts-Fiati, G., Russell, C., & Towson, S. (2004). *Better beginnings, better futures: A comprehensive community-based project for early childhood development. Highlights of lessons learned.* Kingston, Ontario: Better Beginnings, Better Future Research Coordination Unit Technical Report. Retrieved March 27, 2011, from http://bbbf.queensu.ca/pdfs/BB-Highlights.pdf

Petros, G., Airhihenbuwa, C.O., Simbayi, L., Ramlagan, S., & Brown, B. (2006). HIV/AIDS and 'othering' in South Africa: The blame goes on. *Culture, Health and Sexuality, 8*(1), 67–77.

Philander, J.H., & Swartz, L. (2006). Needs, barriers, and concerns regarding HIV prevention among South Africans with visual impairments: A key informant study. *Journal of Visual Impairment and Blindness, 100,* 111–115.

Piccinelli, M., & Wilkinson, G. (2000). Gender differences in depression: Critical review. *British Journal of Psychiatry, 177,* 486–492.

Pilnick, A., Clegg, J., Murphy, E., & Almack, K. (2010). Questioning the answer: Questioning style, choice and self-determination in interactions with young people with intellectual disabilities. *Sociology of Health & Illness, 32*(3), 415–436.

Plant, E.A., Hyde, J.S., Keltner, D., & Devine, P.G. (2000). The gender stereotyping of emotions. *Psychology of Women Quarterly, 24*(1), 81–92.

Poku, N.K. (2005). *AIDS in Africa: How the poor are dying.* Cambridge: Polity Press.

Popay, J., Bennett, S., Thomas, C., Williams, G., Gatrell, A., & Bostock, L. (2003). Beyond 'beer, fags, egg and chips'? Exploring lay understandings of social inequalities in health. *Sociology of Health & Illness, 25*(1), 1–23.

Pope, H.G., Olivardia, R., Gruber, A., & Borowiecki, J. (1999). Evolving ideals of male body image as seen through action toys. *International Journal of Eating Disorders, 26,* 65–72.

Posel, D. (2002). 'Getting the nation talking about sex': Reflections on the politics of sexuality and 'nation-building' in post-apartheid South Africa. Paper presented at the 'On the Subject of Sex Seminar Series' at the University of the Witwatersrand, February 25, 2002. Retrieved October 31, 2006, from www.://wiserweb.wits.ac.za/events%20-%body.htm

Potter, J., & Wetherell, M. (1987). *Discourse and social psychology: Beyond attitudes and behaviour.* London: Sage.

Potter, N.N. (2009). *Mapping the edges and the in-between: A critical analysis of borderline personality disorder.* Oxford: Oxford University Press.

Power, L. (2004). HIV and sexual health in the UK: Politics and public health. *The Lancet, 364,* 108–109.

Prilleltensky, I. (2003). Poverty and power. In S.C. Carr & T.S. Sloan (Eds.), *Poverty and psychology: From global perspective to local practice* (pp. 19–44). New York: Kluwer Academic/Plenum Publishers.

Prince, M., Patel, V., Saxena, S., Maj, M., Maselko, J., Phillips, M.R., & Rahman, A. (2007). No health without mental health. *The Lancet, 370*(9590), 859–877.

Prince, R. (1985). The concept of culture-bound syndromes: Anorexia nervosa and brain-fag. *Social Science & Medicine, 21*(2), 197–203.

Putnam, R.D., Leonarchi, R., & Nanetti, R.Y. (1993). *Making democracy work: Civic traditions in modern Italy.* Princeton, NJ: Princeton University Press.

Rahav, G., Wilsnack, R., Bloomfield, K., Gmel, G., & Kuntsche, S. (2006). The influence of societal level factors on men's and women's alcohol consumption and alcohol problems. *Alcohol and Alcoholism, 41*(Suppl.), i47–i55.

Ramon, S., Castillo, H., & Morant, N. (2001). Experiencing personality disorder: A participative research project. *International Journal of Social Psychiatry, 47*(4), 1–15.

Rapley, M. (2004). *The social construction of intellectual disability.* Cambridge: Cambridge University Press.

Rapoport, R.N. (1970). Three dilemmas in action research: With special reference to the Tavistock experience. *Human Relations, 23*(6), 499–513.

Reason, P., & Bradbury, H. (2008). Introduction. In P. Reason & H. Bradbury (Eds.), *The Sage handbook of action research: Participative inquiry and practice* (pp. 1–13). London: Sage.

Reeder, L.G. (1977). Sociocultural factors in the etiology of smoking behavior: An assessment. *National Institute on Drug Abuse Research Monograph Series, 17,* 186–200.

Reid, G., & Walker, L. (2005). Editorial introduction – sex and secrecy: A focus on African sexualities. *Culture, Health and Sexuality, 7*(3), 185–194.

Renedo, A., & Jovchelovitch, S. (2007). Expert knowledge, cognitive polyphasia and health: A study on social representations of homelessness among professionals working in the voluntary sector in London. *Journal of Health Psychology, 12*(5), 779–790.

Richards, G. (1997). *'Race', racism and psychology: Towards a reflexive history.* London: Routledge.

Richards, G. (2010). *Putting psychology in its place: Critical historical perspectives* (3rd edition). London: Routledge.

Riley, J.L., Wade, J.B., Myers, C.D., Sheffield, D., Papas, R.K., & Price, D.D. (2002). Racial/ethnic differences in the experience of chronic pain. *Pain, 100*, 291–298.

Robertson, S. (2004). Men and disability. In J. Swain, S. French, C. Barnes, & C. Thomas (Eds.), *Disabling barriers – enabling environments* (2nd edition) (pp. 75–80). London: Sage.

Rogers, A., & Pilgrim, D. (2003). *Mental health and inequality*. Basingstoke: Palgrave Macmillan.

Rogers, A., & Pilgrim, D. (2005). *A sociology of mental health and illness* (3rd edition). Maidenhead: Open University Press.

Rogers, C. (2010). But it's not all about the sex: Mothering, normalisation and young learning disabled people. *Disability & Society, 25*(2), 63–74.

Rohleder, P. (2007). HIV and the 'other'. *Psychodynamic Practice, 13*(4), 401–412.

Rohleder, P. (2010). Educators' ambivalence and anxieties in providing sex education for persons with learning disabilities. *Psychodynamic Practice, 16*(2), 165–182.

Rohleder, P., Braathen, S.H., Swartz, L., & Eide, A.H. (2009). HIV/AIDS and disability in Southern Africa: A review of relevant literature. *Disability & Rehabilitation, 31*(1), 51–59.

Rohleder, P., & Swartz, L. (2009). Providing sex education to persons with learning disabilities in the era of HIV/AIDS: Tensions between discourses of human rights and restriction. *Journal of Health Psychology, 14*(4), 601–610.

Rohleder, P., Swartz, L., Schneider, M., Groce, N., & Eide, A.H. (2010). HIV/AIDS and disability organizations in South Africa. *AIDS Care, 22*(2), 221–227.

Rosenhan, D.L. (1973). On being sane in insane places. *Science, 179*, 250–258.

Rosenstock, I.M. (1974). The health belief model and preventive health behavior. *Health Education Monographs, 2*, 354–386.

Roughton, R. (2003). The International Psychoanalytic Association and homosexuality. In V. Lingiardi & J. Drescher (Eds.), *The mental health professions and homosexuality: International perspectives* (pp. 189–196). Binghamton, NY: Haworth Medical Press.

Saloojee, G., Phohole, M., Saloojee, H., & Ijsselmuiden, C. (2007). Unmet health, welfare and educational needs of disabled children in an impoverished South African peri-urban township. *Child: Care, Health & Development, 33*(3), 230–235.

Sapag, J.C., & Kawachi, I. (2010). Social capital and health in Latin America: Ecological and individual level analysis. *World Medical and Health Policy, 2*(1), 285–299.

Sarafino, E.P. (2006). *Health psychology: Biopsychosocial interactions* (5th edition). Hoboken, NJ: John Wiley & Sons.

Sarbin, T.R. (Ed.) (1986). *Narrative psychology: The storied nature of human conduct*. New York: Praeger.

Scheffler, R.M., Brown, T.T., Syme, L., Kawachi, I., Tolstykh, I., & Iribarren, C. (2008). Community-level social capital and recurrence of acute coronary syndrome. *Social Science & Medicine, 66*, 1603–1613.

Seedat, S., Scott, K.M., Angermeyer, M.C., Berglund, P., Bromet, E.J., Brugha, T.S. et al. (2009). Cross-national associations between gender and mental disorders in the WHO World Mental Health Surveys. *Archives of General Psychiatry, 66*(7), 785–795.

Sen, A. (1999). *Development as freedom*. New York: Random House.

Senior, V., Smith, J.A., Michie, S., & Marteau, T.M. (2002). Making sense of risk: An interpretative phenomenological analysis of vulnerability to heart disease. *Journal of Health Psychology, 7*(2), 157–168.

Shahid, A., Finn, L., Bessarab, D., & Thompson, S.C. (2009). Understanding, belief and perspectives of Aboriginal people in Western Australia about cancer and its impact on access to cancer services. *BMC Health Services Research, 9*, 132, doi: 10.1186/1472-6963-9-132.

Shakespeare, T. (2000). Disabled sexuality: Towards rights and recognition. *Sexuality and Disability, 18*(3), 159–166.

Shakespeare, T., Gillespie-Sells, K., & Davies, D. (1996). *The sexual politics of disability: Untold desires*. London and New York: Cassell.

Shakespeare, T., & Watson, N. (1997). Defending the social model. *Disability & Society, 12*(2), 293–300.

Sheffield, D., Biles, L.P., Orom, H., Maixner, W., David, S., & Sheps, D.S. (2000). Race and sex differences in cutaneous pain perception. *Psychosomatic Medicine, 62*(4), 517–523.

Sheldon, A. (2004). Women and disability. In J. Swain, S. French, C. Barnes, & C. Thomas (Eds.), *Disabling barriers – enabling environments* (2nd edition) (pp. 69–74). London: Sage.

Shilts, R. (1987). *And the band played on*. New York: St Martin's Press.

Shinebourne, P., & Smith, J.A. (2009). Alcohol and the self: An interpretative phenomenological analysis of the experience of addiction and its impact on the sense of self and identity. *Addiction Research and Theory, 17*(2), 152–167.

Shriver, M., Everett, C., & Morin, S. (2000). Structural interventions to encourage primary

HIV prevention among people living with HIV. *AIDS, 14*(Suppl. 1), 57–62.

Shweder, R.A. (1991). *Thinking through cultures: Expeditions in cultural psychology.* Cambridge, MA: Harvard University Press.

Silverman, D. (1998). *Harvey Sacks: Social science and conversation analysis.* Cambridge: Polity Press.

Sinason, V. (1992). *Mental handicap and the human condition: New approaches from the Tavistock.* London: Free Association Books.

Sinka, K., Mortimer, J., Evans, B., & Morgan, D. (2003). Impact of the HIV epidemic in sub-Saharan Africa on the pattern of HIV in the UK. *AIDS, 17,* 1683–1690.

Sloan, C., Gough, B., & Conner, M. (2010). Healthy masculinities? How ostensibly healthy men talk about lifestyle, health and gender. *Psychology & Health, 25*(7), 783–803

Smedley, A., & Smedley, B.D. (2005). Race as biology is fiction, racism as a social problem is real: Anthropological and historical perspectives on the social construction of race. *American Psychologist, 60*(1), 16–26.

Smetana, J.G., & Adler, N.E. (1979). Decision-making regarding abortion: A value × expectancy analysis. *Journal of Population, 2*(4), 338–357.

Smith, E., Murray, S.F., Yousafzai, A.K., & Kasonkas, L. (2004). Barriers to accessing safe motherhood and reproductive health services: The situation of women with disabilities in Lusaka, Zambia. *Disability and Rehabilitation, 26*(2), 121–127.

Smith, G., Bartlett, A., & King, M. (2004). Treatments of homosexuality in Britain since the 1950s – an oral history: The experience of patients. *British Medical Journal,* doi: 10.1136/bmj.37984.442419.EE.

Smith, J.A. (1996). Beyond the divide between cognition and discourse: Using interpretative phenomenological analysis in health psychology. *Psychology & Health, 11*(2), 261–271.

Smith, J.A. (2004). Reflecting on the development of interpretative phenomenological analysis and its contribution to qualitative research in psychology. *Qualitative Research in Psychology, 1,* 39–54.

Smith, J.A. (Ed.) (2008). *Qualitative psychology: A practical guide to research methods* (2nd edition). London: Sage.

Smith, J.A., Flowers, P., & Larkin, M. (2009). *Interpretative phenomenological analysis: Theory, method and research.* London: Sage.

Smith, J.A., & Osborn, M. (2007). Pain as an assault on the self: An interpretative phenomenological analysis of the psychological impact of chronic benign low back pain. *Psychology and Health, 22*(5), 517–534.

Smith, T.W., & Anderson, N.B. (1986). Models of personality and disease: An interactional approach to type A behavior and cardiovascular risk. *Journal of Personality and Social Psychology, 50*(6), 1166–1173.

Sobsey, D., & Doe, T. (1991). Patterns of sexual abuse and assault. *Sexuality and Disability, 9*(3), 243–259.

Sobsey, D., Randall, W., & Parrila, R.K. (1997). Gender differences in abused children with and without disabilities. *Child Abuse & Neglect, 21*(8), 707–720.

Solms, M., & Turnbull, O. (2002). *The brain and the inner world: An introduction to the neuroscience of subjective experience.* London: Karnac Books.

Sontag, S. (1991). *Illness as metaphor and AIDS and its metaphors.* London: Penguin Books.

Spitzer, R.L. (1975). On pseudoscience in science, logic in remission, and psychiatric diagnosis: A critique of Rosenhan's 'On being sane in insane places'. *Journal of Abnormal Psychology, 84*(5), 442–452.

Squire, C. (2007). *HIV in South Africa: Talking about the big thing.* London and New York: Routledge.

Stacy, A.W., Bentler, P.M., & Flay, B.R. (1994). Attitudes and health behavior in diverse populations: Drunk driving, alcohol use, binge eating, marijuana use, and cigarette use. *Health Psychology, 13*(1), 73–85.

Stainton-Rogers, W. (2009). Research methodology. In D. Fox, I. Prilleltensky, & S. Austin (Eds.), *Critical psychology: An introduction* (2nd edition) (pp. 335–354). London: Sage.

Stam, H.J. (2004). A sound mind in a sound body: A critical historical analysis of health psychology. In M. Murray (Ed.), *Critical health psychology* (pp. 15–30). Basingstoke: Palgrave Macmillan.

Steckler, A., McLeroy, K.R., Goodman, R.M., Bird, S.T., & McCormick, L. (1992). Toward integrating qualitative and quantitative methods: An introduction. *Health Education & Behaviour, 19*(1), 1–8.

Stephens, C. (2007). Community as practice: Social representations of community and their implications for health promotion. *Journal of Community & Applied Social Psychology, 17,* 103–114.

Stephens, C. (2008). *Health promotion: A psychosocial approach.* Maidenhead: Open University Press and McGraw-Hill.

Stern, S., Doolan, M., Staples, E., Szmukler, G.L., & Eisler, I. (1999). Disruption and reconstruction: Narrative insights into the experience of family members caring for a relative diagnosed with serious mental illness. *Family Process, 38*(3), 353–369.

Stillwaggon, E. (2003). Racial metaphors: Interpreting sex and AIDS in Africa. *Development and Change, 34*(5), 809–832.

Stroebe, W. (2000). *Social psychology and health* (2nd edition). Maidenhead: Open University Press.

Sukantarat, K., Greer, S., Brett, S., & Williamson, R. (2007). Physical and psychological sequelae of critical illness. *British Journal of Health Psychology, 12*(1), 65–74.

Sullivan, P.M., & Knutson, J.F. (2000). Maltreatment and disabilities: A population-based epidemiological study. *Child Abuse & Neglect, 24*(10), 1257–1273.

Suls, J., & Bunde, J. (2005). Anger, anxiety, and depression as risk factors for cardiovascular disease: The problems and implications of overlapping affective dispositions. *Psychological Bulletin, 131*(2), 260–300.

Suls, J., & Rothman, A. (2004). Evolution of the biopsychosocial model: Prospects and challenges for health psychology. *Health Psychology, 23*(2), 119–125.

Summerfield, D. (2001). The invention of post-traumatic stress disorder and the social usefulness of a psychiatric category. *British Medical Journal, 322*, 95–98.

Susser, I. (2009). *AIDS, sex and culture: Global politics and survival in southern Africa.* Chichester: Wiley-Blackwell.

Swartz, L. (1985). Anorexia nervosa as a culture-bound syndrome. *Social Science & Medicine, 20*(7), 725–730.

Swartz, L. (1986). Transcultural psychiatry in South Africa. Part I. *Transcultural Psychiatric Research Review, 23*, 273–303.

Swartz, L. (1998). *Culture and mental health: A southern African view.* Cape Town: Oxford University Press.

Swartz, L., Gibson, K., & Gelman, T. (Eds.) (2002). *Reflective practice: Psychodynamic ideas in the community.* Cape Town: HSRC Press.

Swartz, L., & Rohleder, P. (2008). Cultural psychology. In C. Willig & W. Stainton-Rogers (Eds.), *Handbook of qualitative research methods in psychology* (pp. 541–553). London: Sage.

Swartz, L., Schneider, M., & Rohleder, P. (2006). HIV/AIDS and disability: New challenges. In B. Watermeyer, L. Swartz, T. Lorenzo, M. Schneider, & M. Priestley (Eds.), *Disability and social change: A South African agenda* (pp. 108–115). Cape Town: HSRC Press.

Szasz, T.S. (1972). *The myth of mental illness: Foundations of a theory of personal conduct.* St Albans: Paladin.

The UK Collaborative Group for HIV and STI Surveillance (2007). *Testing times: HIV and other sexually transmitted infections in the United Kingdom: 2007.* London: Health Protection Agency, Centre for Infections.

Thomas, P., & Bracken, P. (2004). Critical psychiatry in practice. *Advances in Psychiatric Treatment, 10*, 361–370.

Thornton, R., & Ramphele, M. (1988). The quest for community. In E. Boonzaier & J. Sharp (Eds.), *South African keywords: The uses and abuses of political concepts* (pp. 29–39). Cape Town: David Philip Publishers.

Tiefer, L. (2006). Female sexual dysfunction: A case study of disease mongering and activist resistance. *PLoS Medicine, 3*(4), e178, 0436–0440.

Tiffin, P.A., Pearce, M.S., & Parker, L. (2005). Social mobility over the lifecourse and self reported mental health at age 50: Prospective cohort study. *Journal of Epidemiology and Community Health, 59*, 870–872.

Tiggemann, M., Martins, Y., & Churchett, L. (2008). Beyond muscles: Unexplored parts of men's body image. *Journal of Health Psychology, 13*(8), 1163–1172.

Tilley, C.M. (1998). Health care for women with physical disabilities: Literature review and theory. *Sexuality and Disability, 16*(2), 87–102.

Tomlinson, M., Rohleder, P., Swartz, L., Drimie, S., & Kagee, A. (2010). Broadening psychology's contribution to addressing issues of HIV/AIDS, poverty and nutrition: Structural issues as constraints and opportunities. *Journal of Health Psychology, 15*(7), 972–981.

Tomlinson, M., Swartz, L., Kruger, L., & Gureje, O. (2007). Manifestations of affective disturbance in sub-Saharan Africa: Key themes. *Journal of Affective Disorders, 102*, 191–198.

Treichler, P.A. (1999). *How to have theory in an epidemic: Cultural chronicles of AIDS.* Durham, NC: Duke University Press.

Tuason, M.T.G. (2008). Those who were born poor: A qualitative study of Philippine poverty. *Journal of Counseling Psychology, 55*(2), 158–171.

Twomey, D. (2003). British psychoanalytic attitudes towards homosexuality. In V. Lingiardi & J. Drescher (Eds.), *The mental health professions and homosexuality: International perspectives* (pp. 7–22). Binghamton, NY: Haworth Medical Press.

UNAIDS (2010). *Global report: UNAIDS report on the global AIDS epidemic 2010.* Geneva: Joint United Nations Programme on HIV/AIDS and World Health Organization

Ussher, J.M. (2000a). Women and mental illness. In L. Sherr & J. St Lawrence (Eds.), *Women, health and the mind* (pp. 77–90). Chichester: John Wiley & Sons.

Ussher, J.M. (Ed.) (2000b). *Women's health: Contemporary international perspectives.* Leicester: BPS Books.

Ussher, J.M. (2010). Are we medicalizing women's misery? A critical review of women's higher rates of reported depression. *Feminism & Psychology, 20*(1), 9–35.

Van de Velde, S., Bracke, P., & Levecque, K. (2010). Gender differences in depression in 23 European countries: Cross-national variation in the gender gap in depression. *Social Science & Medicine, 71,* 305–313.

Vasquez, C., & Javier, R.A. (1991). The problem with interpreters: Communicating with Spanish-speaking patients. *Hospital and Community Psychiatry, 42,* 163–165.

Voracek, M., & Fisher, M. (2002). Shapely centre-folds? Temporal change in body measures: Trend analysis. *British Medical Journal, 325,* 21–28.

Waldron, I. (1995). Contributions of changing gender differences in behaviour and social roles to changing gender differences in mortality. In D. Sabo & D.F. Gordon (Eds.), *Men's health and illness: Gender, power and the body* (pp. 22–45). Thousand Oaks, CA: Sage.

Wazakili, M., Mpofu, R., & Devlieger, P. (2006). Experiences and perceptions of sexuality and HIV/AIDS among young people with physical disabilities in a South African township: A case study. *Sexuality and Disability, 24,* 77–88.

Weems, C.F., & Overstreet, S. (2008). Child and adolescent mental health research in the context of Hurricane Katrina: An ecological needs-based perspective and introduction to the special section. *Journal of Clinical Child & Adolescent Psychology, 37*(3), 487–494.

Weems, C.F., Taylor, L.K., Cannon, M.F., Marino, R.C., Romano, D.M., Scott, B.G., Perry, A.M., & Triplett, V. (2010). Post traumatic stress, context, and the lingering effects of the Hurricane Katrina disaster among ethnic minority youth. *Journal of Abnormal Child Psychology, 38,* 49–56.

Weiser, S.D., Leiter, K., Bangsberg, D.R., Butler, M.L., Percy-de Korte, F., Hlanze, Z., Phaladze, N., Iacopino, V., & Heisler, M. (2007). Food insufficiency is associated with high-risk sexual behavior among women in Botswana and Swaziland. *PLoS Medicine, 4*(10), e260.

White, M.J., Rintala, D.H., Hart, K.A., & Fuhrer, M.J. (1993). Sexual activities, concerns and interests of men with spinal cord injury. *American Journal of Physical Medicine & Rehabilitation, 72*(6), 372–378.

White, M.J., Rintala, D.H., Hart, K.A., Young, M.E., & Fuhrer, M.J. (1992). Sexual activities, concerns and interests of men with spinal cord injury. *American Journal of Physical Medicine & Rehabilitation, 71*(4), 225–231.

Wildes, J.E., Emery, R.E., & Simons, A.D. (2001). The role of ethnicity and culture in the development of eating disturbance and body dissatisfaction: A meta-analytic review. *Clinical Psychology Review, 21*(4), 521–551.

Wilkinson, R.G. (1997). Comment: Income, inequality, and social cohesion. *American Journal of Public Health, 87*(9), 1504–1506.

Wilkinson, R.G., & Pickett, K. (2009). *The spirit level: Why more equal societies almost always do better.* London: Penguin Group.

Wilkinson, S., & Kitzinger, C. (2008). Conversation analysis. In C. Willig & W. Stainton-Rogers (Eds.), *Handbook of qualitative research methods in psychology* (pp. 54–71). London: Sage.

Willems, S., De Maesschalck, S., Deveugele, M., Derese, A., & De Maeseneer, J. (2005). Socio-economic status of the patient and doctor–patient communication: Does it make a difference? *Patient Education and Counseling, 56*(2), 139–146.

Willen, S.S., Bullon, A., & Good, M.D. (2010). Opening up a huge can of worms: Reflections on a 'cultural sensitivity' course for psychiatry residents. *Harvard Review of Psychiatry, 18,* 247–253.

Williams, D.R., Lavizzo-Mourey, R., & Warren, R.C. (1994). The concept of race and health status in America. *Public Health Reports, 109*(1), 26–41.

Williams, E.R., & Shepherd, S.M. (2000). Medical clearance of psychiatric patients. *Emergency Medicine Clinics of North America, 18*(2), 185–198.

Willig, C. (2008). *Introducing qualitative research in psychology* (2nd edition). Maidenhead: Open University Press.

Willig, C., & Stainton-Rogers, W. (Eds.) (2008). *The Sage handbook of qualitative research in psychology.* London: Sage.

Wilsnack, R.W., Vogeltanz, N.D., Wilsnack, S.C., & Harris, T.R. (2000). Gender differences in alcohol consumption and adverse drinking consequences: Cross-cultural patterns. *Addiction, 95*(2), 251–265.

Winkleby, M.A., Gardner, C.D., & Taylor, C.B. (1996). The influence of gender and socioeconomic factors on Hispanic/white differences in body mass index. *Preventive Medicine, 25,* 203–211.

Woodcock, A.J., Stenner, K., & Ingham, R. (1992). Young people talking about HIV and AIDS: Interpretations of personal risk of infection. *Health Education Research: Theory and Practice, 7*(2), 229–247.

World Health Organization (WHO) (1980). *The international classifications of impairments, disabilities, and handicaps.* Geneva: World Health Organization. Retrieved March 25, 2006, from www.alternatives.com/wow/who-old.htm

World Health Organization (WHO) (1992). *The ICD10 classification of mental and behavioural disorders.* Geneva: World Health Organization.

World Health Organization (WHO) (1998). *ICF introduction.* Geneva: World Health Organization. Retrieved June 10, 2006, from www3.who.int/icf/intros/ICF-Eng-Intro.pdf

World Health Organization (WHO) (2004). *World health report 2004 – changing history.* Geneva: World Health Organization.

World Health Organization (WHO) (2005). *WHO multi-country study on women's health and domestic violence against women: Summary report of initial results on prevalence, health outcomes and women's responses.* Geneva: World Health Organization.

World Health Organization (WHO) (2006a). *Constitution of the World Health Organization.* Geneva: World Health Organization. Retrieved October 6, 2011, from http://www.who.int/governance/eb/who_constitution_en.pdf.

World Health Organization (WHO) (2006b). *Sickle-cell anaemia: Report by the secretariat.* Geneva: World Health Organization. Retrieved April 16, 2011, from http://apps.who.int/gb/ebwha/pdf_files/WHA59/A59_9-en.pdf

World Health Organization (WHO) (2008). *The global burden of diseases: 2004 update.* Geneva: World Health Organization.

Yardley, L., & Bishop, F. (2008). Mixing qualitative and quantitative methods: A pragmatic approach. In C. Willig & W. Stainton-Rogers (Eds.), *Handbook of qualitative research methods in psychology* (pp. 352–369). London: Sage.

Yen, J., & Wilbraham, L. (2003a). Discourses of culture and illness in South African mental health care and indigenous healing, part I: Western psychiatric power. *Transcultural Psychiatry, 40*(4), 542–561.

Yen, J., & Wilbraham, L. (2003b). Discourses of culture and illness in South African mental health care and indigenous healing, part II: African mentality. *Transcultural Psychiatry, 40*(4), 562–584.

Yiengprugsawan, V., Khamma, S., Seubsman, S., Lim, L.L., & Sleigh, A.C. (2011). Social capital and health in a national cohort of 82,482 Open University adults in Thailand. *Journal of Health Psychology, 16*(4), 632–642.

Yip, W., Subramanian, S.V., Mitchell, A.D., Lee, D.T.S., Wang, J., & Kawachi, I. (2007). Does social capital enhance health and well-being? Evidence from rural China. *Social Science & Medicine, 64,* 35–49.

Young, A. (1995). *The harmony of illusions: Inventing posttraumatic stress disorder.* Princeton, NJ: Princeton University Press.

Young, R.M., & Meyer, I.H. (2005). The trouble with 'MSM' and 'WSW': Erasure of the sexual-minority person in public health discourse. *American Journal of Public Health, 95*(7): 1144–1149.

Yousafzai, A.K., Dlamini, P.J., Groce, N., & Wirz, S. (2004). Knowledge, personal risk and experiences of HIV/AIDS among people with disabilities in Swaziland. *International Journal of Rehabilitation Research, 27*(3), 247–251.

Yousafzai, A.K., & Edwards, K. (2004). *Double burden: A situation analysis of HIV/AIDS and young people with disabilities in Rwanda and Uganda.* London: Save the Children. Retrieved March 12, 2005, from www.savethechildren.org.uk/temp/scuk/cache/cmsattach/1600_Double Burden.pdf

Zola, I.K. (1966). Culture and symptoms: An analysis of patient's presenting complaints. *American Sociological Review, 31*(5), 615–630.

NDEX